# Tribal Blueprints

## Twelve Brothers and the Destiny of Israel

מגיד
MAGGID

Nechama Price

שבטי ישראל

# Tribal Blueprints

## Twelve Brothers and the Destiny of Israel

Maggid Books

*Tribal Blueprints*
*Twelve Brothers and the Destiny of Israel*
First Edition, 2020

*Maggid Books*
*An imprint of Koren Publishers Jerusalem Ltd.*

POB 8531, New Milford, CT 06776-8531, USA
& POB 4044, Jerusalem 9104001, Israel
www.maggidbooks.com



The publication of this book was made possible through the generous support of *The Jewish Book Trust*.



ISBN 978-1-59264-545-9, *hardcover*

Printed and bound in the United States

It is both an honor and a privilege to play a small role in helping to publish Nechama Price's first book, *Tribal Blueprints.*

We first met Professor Price a few years ago when she served as a Shabbat scholar-in-residence in our *shul,* the Young Israel of West Hartford, Connecticut.

We watched her inspire our entire congregation with her incredible scholarship and captivate us with her warm and open teaching style and her insightful analysis.

So began our journey with Nechama Price, a pioneer and role model for Orthodox women. As our relationship has developed we have come to appreciate even more fully the depth of her scholarship and her teaching skills. We are grateful for her leadership role at GPATS, the Graduate Program for Advanced Talmud Study for Women at Yeshiva University.

At GPATS, through her teaching and by her example she encourages and inspires young women to follow in her footsteps – to become scholars and teachers, *yoatzot halacha* and spiritual leaders. These young women represent many of the current and future leaders of the Jewish community.

We thank her for her continued tenacity in advancing women's Torah education, her role as a public educator, and her tireless service to the community as a *yoetzet halacha*. We hope this is the first of many books by Professor Price so that even a wider audience can benefit from and be inspired by her Torah knowledge and insights.

Ann and Jeremy Pava

Dedicated with love to my wonderful children

## Elisha, Nava, Ariella, and Leora

You fill every day with joy, happiness, love, and meaning.
I pray that you continue growing
in your *middot tovot* and Torah study.
In the words of Yaakov to his children:

הַמַּלְאָךְ הַגֹּאֵל אֹתִי מִכָּל-רָע יְבָרֵךְ אֶת-הַנְּעָרִים וְיִקָּרֵא בָהֶם
שְׁמִי וְשֵׁם אֲבֹתַי אַבְרָהָם וְיִצְחָק וְיִדְגּוּ לָרֹב בְּקֶרֶב הָאָרֶץ.

(Gen. 48:16)

~~~

In loving memory of my grandfathers

## Nachman Shimon ben Tuvia Moshe HaLevi
and
## Nosson ben Moshe

After surviving the Holocaust,
they proudly defined themselves by their Jewish identity.
Each one filled his life and the lives
of his children, grandchildren, and great-grandchildren
with the study and values of Torah.
~~~

# *Contents*

*Acknowledgments xi*

*Introduction xv*

*Chapter 1: Raḥel and Leah: The Mothers of the Tribes of Israel 1*

*Chapter 2: Reuven in Genesis: The Rejected Oldest Child of Yaakov 11*

*Chapter 3: Reuven in Tanakh 31*

*Chapter 4: Shimon and Levi in Genesis: The Troublesome Duo 41*

*Chapter 5: Shimon and Levi in Tanakh 61*

*Chapter 6: Yehuda in Genesis: The Natural Leader of the Family 77*

*Chapter 7: Yehuda in Tanakh 103*

*Chapter 8: Yissakhar and Zevulun in Genesis: The Youngest Sons of Leah 141*

Chapter 9: Yissakhar and Zevulun in Tanakh 149

Chapter 10: Bilha and Zilpa: The Secondary Wives of Yaakov 155

Chapter 11: Dan, Naftali, Gad, and Asher: The Children of the Maidservants 167

Chapter 12: Dan: The Oldest Son of Bilha 177

Chapter 13: Gad: The Oldest Son of Zilpa 193

Chapter 14: Naftali and Asher: The Younger Sons of Bilha and Zilpa 199

Chapter 15: Yosef in Genesis: Yaakov's Favorite Son 205

Chapter 16: Yosef in Tanakh 233

Chapter 17: Binyamin in Genesis: The Baby of the Family 255

Chapter 18: Binyamin in Tanakh 267

Conclusion 287

# *Acknowledgments*

There is no possible way to convey my feelings of *hakarat hatov*, appreciation, to everyone involved in each facet of this project. Bringing this book to publication is a momentous occasion in my life. To that end, I am grateful, not only to those who helped with this book, but also to those who invested in my journey of learning Torah.

The ideas in this book were first incubated during the two post-high school years I spent at MMY (Michlelet Mevaseret Yerushalayim). Rabbi Avishai David, Rabbi Alan Haber, Mrs. Sharon Isaacson, and Rabbi David Katz encouraged me to develop my own ideas, present them as *shiurim*, and publish articles. Each of them was beyond generous with their time and wisdom.

After returning from Israel, I was privileged to learn Torah from remarkable Torah scholars during my years as a student at Stern College for Women (SCW), followed by the Graduate Program in Advanced Talumdic Studies (GPATS), and later Nishmat's US Yoatzot Halacha Program. I thank my wonderful teachers and colleagues: Rabbi Kenneth Auman, Rabbi Assaf Bednarsh, Rabbi Gedalyah Berger, Rabbi Dr. Mordechai Cohen, Rabbanit Chana Henkin, Rabbi Moshe Kahn, Rabbanit Noa Lau, Dr. Michelle Levine, Rabbi David Nachbar, and Rabbi David Pahmer.

Certain individuals in our generation have enhanced our community's appreciation for sophisticated study of Tanakh. For me, Rabbi Menachem Leibtag, whose *parasha* sheets I read for many years, serves as one of those individuals. As the years went on, I was also influenced by the writings of Rabbi Yitzchak Etshalom, Rabbi Yoel Bin-Nun, Rabbi Yonatan Grossman, and others who publish their Torah on Yeshivat Har Etzion's Israel Koschitzky Virtual Beit Midrash (VBM).

During my years teaching at Yeshiva University, I've been blessed with exceptional mentors who have graced me with their sagacity well beyond what I deserve. They have coached me in pedagogy, school administration, public speaking, writing, and more. I am forever indebted to Deans Karen Bacon and Rabbi Dr. Ephraim Kanarfogel, who empowered me to teach Torah at SCW. This experience has been one of the great treasures of my life. Rabbi Dr. Kenneth Brander had the courage to ask me to direct GPATS even though I lacked previous administrative experience. In due time, he taught me how to dream big – both for and about myself and the Jewish people. Rabbi Dr. Jacob J. Schacter has been disarmingly gracious with his insights and counsel, while mentoring me about so many areas of Jewish leadership and education. Ann and Jeremy Pava have humbled me with their broad vision and gracious ways. This couple optimize partnership and lead by example. I am privileged and grateful for their friendship and generosity in this project and so much more.

To those directly involved with this book project, thank you. To my editors at Maggid Books: to Batya Shai, for her meticulous editing, as well as to the entire Maggid team, including Ita Olesker, Reuven Ziegler, Shira Finson, and Sara Henna Dahan. A very special thank you to Matthew Miller, publisher of Maggid Books, who approached me three years ago, saying: "I believe you have a book in you." Three incredibly special friends – Sarah Epstein, Talia Molotsky, and Lizzi Peled – who edited parts of this book and came up with the title. Ladies, thank you for your editing, and even more so for your remarkable friendship.

Much of the material found in this book comes from a course I teach at SCW. The students of SCW and GPATS have been a sounding board for many of the ideas in this book. Their sharp insights forced me to refine and review many key concepts in this book. It is an absolute pleasure to learn Torah with you.

This book – as with much of life – would not be possible without the love and support of family. My older brother, Mordy Friedman, was one of my first *ḥavrutot* in learning Tanakh, with whom I would vet new ideas and new ways to read the stories. My brothers Elli and Nachi, my in-laws René and Hilton Price, my grandmothers Liselle Schloss and Gisela Friedman, each encouraged me to follow my path. Words do not capture my appreciation for my parents, Marsha and Tom Friedman. They have always believed in me, even in a world that isn't always sure what to make of a woman who is passionate about Torah study. They supported my decision to dedicate my life to learning Torah. I thank you for allowing me to devote myself for so many years to my personal Torah study, as well as for attending my shiurim, babysitting my children so I can learn and teach, and supporting me in every way.

Thank you to my children, Elisha, Nava, Ariella, and Leora. You are my favorite *ḥavrutot*, learning partners, in the whole world! You have been especially understanding while I spent all of this time working on this book. You attend my *shiurim* and proudly identify as the children of a mom who loves to learn and teach Torah. You are my inspiration and greatest accomplishments.

It is impossible to use this platform to properly thank my husband, Jonathan. However, a small expression of my gratitude is in order. Thank you for spending *endless* hours editing this book. Every idea and every word of this volume benefits from your care and attention. This book and whatever opportunities I have to spread Torah are a tribute to your absolute belief in me. Your support, boundless love, and encouragement motivate me always. May we continue to grow together, to spread God's Torah and His values to our children, our family, students, and community.

Lastly, I thank *HaKadosh Barukh Hu* for all of His blessings, including the opportunity to be a member of the Beit Midrash, learning and teaching His Torah. I pray that I am a worthy receptacle for His bounty and that He continues to bless me with the ability and privilege to continue on this path.

# *Introduction*

When studying the narratives in the book of Genesis, some of the most captivating stories appear in conjunction with the tribes of Israel. While these brothers often act together, and collectively beget what we know today as *Benei Yisrael,* it is clear that each of our patriarch Yaakov's sons has a specific role within the family, as well as a distinct personality shaped by stories that describe his particular fears, desires, and talents.

This book focuses on each of Yaakov's sons as individuals – who they are as people and who they strive to be. Following an in-depth analysis of the stories found in the text of the Torah, we will turn to the rich rabbinic teachings about the distinctive character embodied by each son. After developing these personalities – as expressed in the proclivities, choices and experiences of each one – we will follow the lives of their descendants and the experiences of their tribes, which will enable us to identify many of the same personality patterns that were etched when the founding fathers of our nation, the people of Israel, were known simply as Yaakov's twelve sons.

Traditionally, the stories of Genesis are studied in the order presented in the Torah. Certain rabbinic sources prefer to study these stories topically (e.g., to uncover moral themes). This book is presented somewhat differently, focusing on each son's individual personality and story, according to the order of his birth. Therefore, the first chapters are focused on Reuven (and his descendants), then Shimon (and his descendants), and so on.

My preference for this style of analysis began during my post high-school years in Israel. For the first time in my life, I delved into the study of each of the tribes as separate individuals displaying distinct perspectives within the stories of the Torah and the profound lessons culled from Ḥazal, the talmudic Sages. I wondered whether it might be possible that these personalities and perspectives are reflected in their descendants. Over the past two decades, this idea evolved from a single lesson, a *shiur* I taught, to a series of three and then six *shiurim*, to a course at Stern College for Women, and now to this book.

Throughout the years, I have found myself so immersed in their stories that at times I feel as though the sons of Yaakov are people in my life, with multi-layered lessons to teach me. I hope that through this volume, you too will derive inspiration from each of Yaakov's sons as you discern their humanity and complexity of character. Perhaps each of the tribes will remind you of someone you know, or you might even find yourself identifying with a tribe or a mixture of tribes. Understanding the sons of Yaakov and their descendants in such an intimate way motivates us to appreciate the beauty of the Torah and the lessons from all its holy stories. I pray that you enjoy the journey, one that I have been on for two decades and am now privileged to share with you.

*Chapter 1*

# Raḥel and Leah: The Mothers of the Tribes of Israel

Before closely studying the sons of Yaakov and their future shared destiny as the twelve tribes of Israel, it is worthwhile to consider certain precursors to their stardom, namely the background and the environment into which they were born. A fundamental component for understanding their upbringing is an appreciation for the nature of the relationship between their parents. What are the characteristic elements and the emotional dynamic of Yaakov's relationship with each of his wives? As is true for all children, each of Yaakov's twelve sons is influenced by his parents' relationship, or more pointedly, by his father's treatment of his mother. Therefore, sensitivity to these relationships is critical for understanding the tribes of Israel. After studying the relationships between Yaakov and Raḥel, and Yaakov and Leah, respectively, it will become apparent that there is a notable correlation between how much each wife is loved and how much each son is thereby loved by Yaakov.[1]

**RAḤEL**

> Yaakov loved Raḥel. He said, "I will serve you seven years for Raḥel, your younger daughter." (Gen. 29:18)

Fact: Yaakov loves Raḥel, as the Torah describes numerous times (Gen. 29:18, 20, 30).[2] Because of this love, Yaakov acquiesces to seven years of servitude at the home of Lavan for the right to marry her. For most men, working in the field for seven years would be considered arduous, overly demanding, and time-consuming, but this is not how Yaakov feels about the experience. As a man in love, these seven years of labor fly by effortlessly: "It was in his eyes like only a few days out of love for her" (Gen. 29:20).

While the affection that he feels for Raḥel is clear, it is worthwhile to explore the nature of this love. Does the Torah offer guidance or evidence to suggest that the love that developed in the early stages of their relationship is deep and meaningful? Alternatively, might there be evidence that the love described in these early years is merely the immature passion of a first love?

**Superficial Love**

After successfully executing his mother's (Rivka's) plan for receiving the blessings of the firstborn from his father, Yitzḥak, Yaakov is urged by her to flee their home for fear of reprisal from his brother, Esav.

---

1. Yaakov's relationship with each of the maidservants, Bilha and Zilpa, will be discussed in Chapter 10.
2. It is very rare for the Torah to document the nature of the love between a husband and wife. Except for this instance, the only other occurrence is between Yitzḥak and Rivka (Gen. 24:67). Since the Torah does not convey the love between Avraham and Sarah, or Moshe and Tzippora, or other husband-wife relationships, our attention is rightfully focused on deciphering the unique meaning of the love between Yaakov and Raḥel, as it is repeatedly mentioned in Gen. 29.

Yaakov is terrified and homeless. Raḥel is the first family member whom he encounters when he follows Rivka's directive to go to her brother Lavan. She is his first reminder of home and the warm feeling of a secure environment. His anxiety overcomes him, and he becomes overwhelmed with the excitement of seeing a family member. Before even exchanging words with Raḥel, he loses his composure, kisses her, and breaks down in an emotionally charged moment.[3] At this point, Yaakov must have become aware of Raḥel's exceptional beauty (Gen. 29:17).[4] The combination of the excitement due to reconnecting with family, his renewed sense of security, and Raḥel's physical beauty evidently causes him to fall in love momentarily. However, this is a love born out of passion and the emotional high of finding a new home. He doesn't even know her yet! This love could not yet be rooted in the mature love of a couple who intimately understand and appreciate each other.[5]

If this encounter is seen as the foundation for their relationship, then over time this love may not provide the grounding that is necessary to endure the vicissitudes of life. This may provide insight into Yaakov's outburst at Raḥel many years later when he loses patience in the face of her pressing desire for children (Gen. 30:2). Certainly, it offers us a context to understand the future development of the relationship between Yaakov and Raḥel.

---

3. "Yaakov kissed Raḥel, and lifted up his voice, and wept. Yaakov told Raḥel that he was her father's brother, and that he was Rivka's son. She ran and told her father" (Gen. 29:11–12).
4. Yaakov's mother, Rivka, is also described as quite beautiful (Gen. 24:16). Raḥel's beauty might have reminded Yaakov of his mother, thus giving him a greater sense of comfort and familiarity after the stresses of escaping from Esav.
5. The Torah usually informs us about a husband's love for his wife by using the root *alef, heh, beit,* meaning love. Interestingly, many of these instances are cases of seemingly superficial affection, as found in the case of Shekhem loving Dina (Gen. 34:3), King Shlomo loving his non-Jewish wives (I Kings 11:1), and Aḥashverosh loving Esther (Esther 2:17). Even the verse using the root *aleph, heh, beit* to describe Yitzḥak's feelings towards Esav (Gen. 25:28) can be understood as superficial love, as Esav tricks Yitzḥak into thinking he was a good man (see Rashi on Gen. 25:27).

**True Love**

Conversely, the early stages of the Yaakov-Raḥel relationship may show possibilities of a rock-solid foundation for their future. If this is true, why does the Torah focus on Raḥel's beauty? Perhaps the Torah does not describe her beauty to imply superficiality, but rather to show her righteousness: her inside matches her outside. The Torah writes about the physical beauty of many righteous women – Sarah (Gen. 12:11, 14), Rivka (Gen. 24:16, 26:7), Avigail (I Sam. 25:3), Batsheva (II Sam. 11:2), and Esther (Esther 2:7). In all of these cases, their virtue is reflected by their beautiful outer appearance.[6] Thus, Raḥel's inner beauty as reflected by her external beauty is partly what attracts Yaakov to Raḥel.[7]

The bond between them continues to strengthen due to their common experiences and values. Both Yaakov and Raḥel are the younger children in their respective families, where the elder siblings (Esav and Leah, respectively) are their fathers' favorites. While it is fairly straightforward in the Torah that Yitzḥak loves and favors his elder son, Esav (see Gen. 25:28), this seems true regarding Raḥel's home, too. Recall that Raḥel's father, Lavan, tricks Yaakov into marrying his older daughter, Leah, in place of Raḥel. Why would Lavan do this, and what does it say about his concern for the implications this might have for Raḥel's future? Evidently, Lavan is concerned about his elder daughter's matrimony and wellbeing to the extent that his actions compromise Raḥel's future! Furthermore, Lavan's preference for Leah is reflected in his appointment of Raḥel to serve as the shepherd of the family sheep (Gen. 29:9),

6. Admittedly, each of these instances of beauty could be interpreted as superficial aesthetics: Avraham focuses on Sarah's beauty out of fear that it may attract the men in Egypt and Gerar. Yitzḥak is likewise afraid that Rivka's beauty may attract the men of Gerar. Naval, an evil man, marries the intelligent Avigail because of her beauty. David takes Batsheva, a married woman, because of her beauty, which he observed from his rooftop while she was bathing. Aḥashverosh marries Esther because of her superficial beauty, just as he focused on the physical beauty of Queen Vashti.

7. The root *alef, heh, beit* is also found in a number of sincere and genuinely loving relationships, including those between Yitzḥak and Rivka (Gen. 24:67) and Elkana and Ḥana (I Sam. 1:5). It is also used to describe the loving bonds between Yaakov and Yosef (Gen. 37:3), and between David and Yonatan (I Sam. 18:1).

which is the lowest position in the family.[8] Later on, in reaction to discovering some missing idols, Lavan suspects Raḥel and searches her tent more thoroughly than the others. He seems sure that Raḥel has taken his precious gods in revenge for his mistreatment of her (Gen. 31:33–35).

Yaakov and Raḥel's relationship also has the advantage of years of shared experiences. When Yaakov agrees to shepherd Lavan's sheep for seven years, he surely realizes he would either be relieving Raḥel, the family shepherd, of her lowly occupation, or working alongside her. Therefore, it is possible that for seven years they spent many hours together every day, forming the foundation of a powerful bond.

In summary, Yaakov and Raḥel share a sense of being less favored by their fathers, as well as their experience as shepherds (individually and together).[9] These experiences undoubtedly create a backdrop for a bond that could grow into a meaningful relationship. This could realistically explain why the verse tells us that the seven-year period of Yaakov's servitude passes so quickly.[10]

---

8. Gen. 29:9 states that she is "the shepherd of the family" to make clear that this is her assigned role. In fact, *Ḥizkuni* (29:9) explains that Lavan gave this job to Raḥel in order to give honor to Leah.

   This is consistent with a pattern in Tanakh of having the shepherd role assigned to the unfavored child of every family, as is the case with Yaakov, Raḥel, and David (see Chapter 7 for a fuller assessment of David). Alternatively, in cases where the job is not given to a family member, it is assigned to a "pity case," such as a runaway who receives sanctuary in exchange for performing a job, as we see with Moshe in Yitro's house and Yaakov in Lavan's house. Both men are designated as shepherds in exchange for a secure place to live (and, eventually, they both earn the right to marry "up" into the family).
9. See previous footnote with regard to Raḥel. Similarly, Yaakov is described as his family's shepherd (Gen 25:27). See Radak on Gen. 25:27, who states that this is the literal understanding of the text that Yaakov "sits in the tent." (The talmudic Sages famously add a layer of meaning to this phrase by explaining it to mean that Yaakov sat and studied Torah all day.) In addition to serving as the shepherd in Yitzḥak's home, we know that he was Lavan's shepherd for twenty years (Gen. 31:38).
10. This picture of a beautiful and strong relationship is captured in Rabbi Yaakov Medan's article "Yaakov's Love for Raḥel" (http://etzion.org.il/en/yaakov's-love-Raḥel). He supports this approach based on stories later in Genesis. Specifically, he points to at least two key plot points:

**LEAH**

The increasingly strong relationship between Yaakov and Raḥel can serve as a foil to understand Yaakov and Leah's relationship. First, the extent to which the Yaakov-Raḥel relationship is rooted in love, depth, and shared values indicates that there is little room to nurture the Yaakov-Leah relationship. As a "third wheel," the one who gets in the way of Yaakov and Raḥel's true-love relationship, Leah's position is nearly impossible to overcome. However, if Yaakov's love for Raḥel is superficial – based on the passions of its beginning – then with the passage of time we might find space for the Yaakov-Leah relationship to gain traction.

Of course, it is necessary to recognize that Yaakov does not intend to forge a relationship with Leah prior to Lavan's deceit. Lavan tricked Yaakov into marrying Leah although Raḥel was the presumptive bride. This could have caused Yaakov to struggle to love his first wife, Leah, and thereby weigh heavily on their relationship. Yaakov may not have been privy to the extent to which Leah was involved in the plan to deceive him. Was she a pawn, forced to be complicit, or did she volunteer? Even if she was not an active participant, why didn't she speak out on her wedding night and reveal her true identity? The degree of resentment and blame Yaakov harbors against Leah could also directly correlate to the extent that he loves Raḥel, the woman he was unable to marry on his wedding night because of her father's deceit.

There are three primary approaches to understanding Yaakov's relationship with Leah:

---

(1) Yaakov situates Raḥel at the back of the group in order to protect her when meeting up with Esav.

(2) Yaakov shows clear favoritism towards Raḥel's two sons (as we will discuss throughout this volume). Even the other sons acknowledge that this favoritism reflects Yaakov's love for Raḥel. This is evident in Yehuda's speech in Egypt where he states, "And he alone is left of his mother; and his father loves him" (Gen. 44:20), highlighting that the love Yaakov has for Binyamin stems from his love for Raḥel.

**Absolute Hatred**

Yaakov blames Leah for conspiring against him[11] and hates her.[12] The Torah presents his hatred towards Leah as a fact: "God saw that Leah was hated and therefore opened her womb" (Gen. 29:31). This hatred is so noticeable that Leah names her second child Shimon "because God heard that I am hated" (Gen. 29:33).

Added to this may be Yaakov's lack of attraction to his first wife. The Torah compares the physical appearance of Raḥel and Leah. Raḥel is described as beautiful, while Leah is described as having "*einayim rakot*," "tender eyes" (Gen. 29:17). The commentaries discuss what this means: it could mean that her eyes are beautiful,[13] possibly implying that every feature other than her eyes is unattractive,[14] or it could imply that her eyes are sensitive to the outside world and that she is sickly (or suffers from allergies).[15] Alternatively, it could imply that she cries all the time, which causes her eyes to be red, puffy, and unattractive.[16] Common to each explanation is that Yaakov may not have been attracted to Leah in the way that he was to Raḥel, the striking beauty.

**Inferior Love**

There is a second perspective, based on the verse "And Yaakov loved Raḥel *also* from Leah" (Gen. 29:30), implying that Yaakov *does* love

11. See Genesis Rabba 70:19, which explains that when Yaakov realizes in the morning that he married the wrong sister, he yells at Leah, asking her why she didn't reveal her identity to him that night and let him know that she was an imposter. She answers him that she learned this trait of trickery from him. He was her teacher! He pretended to be his brother and stated to his father: "I am Esav, your eldest son" (Gen. 27:19). So too, she pretended to be her sister, and responded to his calling her sister's name. It is understandable that reminding Yaakov of the lowest moment of his life, which caused him to run away from home and never return, could truly cause him to hate her.
12. This view is found in the Abarbanel on Gen 29:31, which states that Yaakov hates her so much that his hatred is obvious to all in the way he treats her and in how he speaks to her.
13. Rav Saadia Gaon on Gen. 20:17.
14. Rabbi S. R. Hirsch on Gen. 29:17.
15. *Ḥizkuni* on Gen. 29:9.
16. Rashi on Gen. 29:17 writes that she cries all the time because she believes that she is destined to marry Yitzḥak's oldest son Esav, while Raḥel is to marry the younger son, Yaakov.

Leah. Radak explains that Yaakov's love for Leah is overshadowed by the incredible and overwhelming love that he has for Raḥel. Since his love for Leah is so inferior, she *feels* hated. Therefore God opens her womb because she *feels* hated and not because she truly is hated.

It is also possible that Yaakov does not blame Leah for the trickery, since Yaakov yells only at Lavan after the wedding and not at his new bride, Leah (Gen. 29:25). He was familiar with the cultural norm of his time: If a father tells a daughter to marry someone, she has no choice in the matter. Therefore, he could not earnestly blame her for following the command of her father.

### "I Love Her, I Love Her Not," or: Utter Confusion

But there is a third perspective, found in Ramban on Gen. 29:30, that Yaakov feels *both* emotions towards her, simply because he is confused about how he feels. Sometimes he feels love towards Leah as his first wife, but at the same time he also feels hatred towards her for her actions of trickery and for her intrusion into his life with Raḥel.

Yaakov and Leah also have some things in common. Both disguise themselves as their siblings to get what they want, as directed by their parent.[17] Similarly, both take advantage of the emotional vulnerability of their sibling and offer an unfair deal in exchange for something they desire. Yaakov takes the birthright from Esav and in exchange gives him a bowl of soup; Leah gets a night with Yaakov in exchange for giving Raḥel a bunch of flowers (this incident will be discussed further in Chapter 2). These similarities could either kindle a bond or, conversely, deepen the hatred. Seeing one's own flaws in someone else might evoke negative feelings and could further explain Yaakov's hatred of Leah. He sees in her everything he dislikes about himself.

---

17. Yaakov disguises himself as Esav in order to receive the blessing from his father, as instructed by his mother, Rivka. Leah pretends to be Raḥel on her wedding night, in order to marry Yaakov, as ordered by her father, Lavan. According to the Talmud in Bava Batra 123b, she acts based on the instructions of her sister, who sought to save her from humiliation on her wedding night.

## CONCLUSION

This discussion is only about Yaakov's original relationship with his wives after their weddings. Upon analysis of each of the brothers and their individual roles within the family, it will become evident how Yaakov's relationship with his wives continually evolves and how it affects each of the children differently. Every emotion that a person feels, be it love or hatred, evolves over time. Feelings can change, as other emotions and life challenges interweave with the original feelings and blur the lines of love or hatred. Eventually, Raḥel and Leah identify less as Yaakov's wives and more as the mothers of his children and the mothers of the Jewish nation.[18] All of these developments create a more nuanced picture that will be further developed throughout this book.

---

18. The poetic ending of this love triangle is the location where each person in it is buried. Raḥel is buried far away from Yaakov, in Raḥel's tomb, located near Efrat. Leah is buried in the Cave of Makhpela in Hebron, right next to her husband Yaakov, who actually requests to be buried next to her (Gen. 49:31). Leah, who struggled her entire life for Yaakov's attention and love, lies next to him permanently in death. On the other hand, Raḥel, who grappled with her desire for children and with her infertility, is in a location that would allow her to act as the mother of the entire Jewish people and plead on their behalf on their way into the diaspora.

    In the book of Jeremiah, we are told about Raḥel's bravery and love for her children: "Thus says God: A voice is heard in Ramah, lamentation, and bitter weeping, Raḥel weeping for her children; she refuses to be comforted for her children, because they are no more. Thus says God: Refrain your voice from weeping, and your eyes from tears; for your work shall be rewarded, says God; and they shall come again from the land of the enemy" (Jer. 31:14–15). *Metzudat David* on Jer. 31:15 relates this story to our story of Raḥel in Genesis as quoted in the *Midrash Aggada* (30:15): Raḥel turns to God and asks him to forgive the Jewish people in the merit of her giving over the signs to her sister, to teach her how to pretend to be Raḥel on the night of her wedding to Yaakov. Raḥel sacrifices her hopes and dreams to allow her sister to avoid mortifying embarrassment. In this merit, God promises to save the Jewish people from the exile following the destruction of the holy Temple, and to return them to Israel.

    In the end, both women are rewarded with everything that they most desired. Leah's permanent residence is next to the husband she always wanted to love her back, and Raḥel's permanent residence allows her the ability to mother the entire Jewish nation. Foremost, however, all of their children join together to form the chosen nation of Israel. Everyone is chosen; no one is rejected!

*Chapter 2*

# Reuven in Genesis: The Rejected Oldest Child of Yaakov

Reuven is the first child of Yaakov, born to his first wife, Leah. During the biblical period, it was assumed that the firstborn, the eldest son, would become the next leader of his family, the heir to his father's position or throne.[1] Therefore, the eldest is pledged

1. This observation may offer context to many details in the Torah. As illustration, consider these four examples:
   (1) Esav: Yaakov intended to bless Esav, "his oldest son" (Gen. 27:1).
   (2) Menashe and Ephraim: Yosef appears upset with his father, Yaakov, for switching his hands and not putting his right hand on the oldest grandson, Menashe, when he was blessing him and his brother (Gen. 48:17–18).
   (3) Elazar: Aharon's oldest son after the deaths of the two who preceded him (Nadav and Avihu) is selected as the high priest (Num. 20:26).
   (4) Shlomo: King David felt compelled to announce that his successor for the monarchy was Shlomo, as he was not the eldest child and therefore was not the obvious choice (I Kings 1:33).

material possession in keeping with his position, in the form of an enhanced portion of his father's estate.[2] Despite the presumption of the oldest son's leadership, however, we often encounter a contrary situation in the Torah. In fact, many of our greatest leaders are *not* the eldest of their families, as in the cases of Shet,[3] Yitzḥak,[4] Yaakov,[5] Yehuda,[6] Moshe,[7] Otniel,[8] Gidon,[9] David,[10] and Shlomo.[11] With this background, we question the role and eventual destiny of Reuven, the firstborn of the tribes of Israel.[12]

Is Reuven destined for greatness as a function of his birth order? Will it automatically make him the accepted leader of his family? Or is he doomed to fail like so many other eldest children in the Torah? What is the role of Reuven in his family and throughout Jewish history?

---

2. Deut. 21:15–17. Even if the oldest son is born to the hated wife, he is assured his right to the birthright and receipt of the double portion.
3. Shet is Adam's third son, born after Kayin and Hevel (Gen. 5:3).
4. Yitzḥak is Avraham's second son, born after Yishmael (Gen. 21:2).
5. Yaakov is Yitzḥak's second son, born after his twin, Esav (Gen. 25:26).
6. Yehuda is Yaakov's fourth son, born after Reuven, Shimon, and Levi (Gen. 29:35).
7. Moshe is Amram's third child, born after Miriam and Aharon (Ex. 2:2).
8. It is stated twice that he is Kalev's *younger* brother (Judges 1:13, 3:9).
9. Gidon tells the angel that he is the *youngest* in his family (Judges 6:15).
10. David is Yishai's eighth son; seven older brothers are presented to Shmuel before him (I Sam. 16:10–11).
11. Shlomo is born to David after his half-brothers, Amnon, Kilav/Daniel, Avshalom, Adoniyahu, Shefatya, and Yitre'am (II Sam. 3:2–4). His birth is recorded after the birth of these six sons of David (II Sam. 12:24).
12. Interestingly, the birth-order status of many of our other leaders is ambiguous. As illustration, consider these two examples:
    (1) Shem is listed first on numerous occasions (Gen. 5:32, 6:10, 7:13, 9:18). Possibly, this is due to age order. Alternatively, it is due to his greater status. In fact, the text is ambiguous regarding who is oldest – Shem or Yafet – as seen in the phrase, "*aḥi Yafet hagadol*," (Gen. 10:21), which can be translated as "the elder brother of Yafet" or "the older brother Yafet." This might imply either that Shem is the older brother of Yafet, or that Yafet is the older brother of Shem.
    (2) Avraham: The text is unclear about whether Avraham was listed first amongst his brothers because he is oldest or because of his unique role (Gen. 11:26). See this debated in Sanhedrin 69b.

## BIRTH OF REUVEN

> And Leah conceived and bore a son, and she named him Reuven, for she said, "Because God has seen my affliction. Perhaps now my husband will love me." (Gen. 29:32)

Parents invest considerable time and forethought in selecting names for their children. Names have significance! This is a universal truth that is reflected in the Torah, where a given name carries special meaning for the parent or for the child, and often highlights his or her unique role.[13] Accordingly, all of the twelve tribes are a reflection of their names and are affected by the circumstances that led to their naming. Each name given by their mothers[14] foreshadows the pathway and destiny of that child, starting with the status of the relationship of his parents at the time of the naming.

Reuven's name is a combination of two Hebrew words, *reu* and *ben*, and literally means, "See, a son!" Leah is declaring to Yaakov, "We have a child together! Our rocky relationship can now improve." However, it is God, not Yaakov, who sees and recognizes her affliction. "Perhaps my husband will love me" reveals her apparent longing for Yaakov's love. Reuven's name gives us a window into understanding his parents' complicated relationship. The loneliness and sadness that his mother feels becomes an important part of Reuven's personality and his life's mission. As Leah's oldest son, Reuven feels a strong sense of responsibility to improve her situation. In fact, each of the stories in the Torah about Reuven reflects his unique place in the family, his desire to fix his mother's predicament, and his yearning for both of them to have the love and stature that he perceives as their right.

---

13. Consider these examples. Ḥava: "Mother of all living creatures" (Gen. 3:20); Kayin: "I acquired a person from God" (4:1); Menashe: "God let me forget all of my toil" (41:51); Ephraim: "God caused me to be fruitful" (41:52); Moshe: "From the water, I drew you out" (Ex. 2:10), and many others.
14. Exceptions: According to Radak on Gen. 29:34, Levi is given his name by both his mother and his father. Binyamin is named Ben Oni by his mother, Raḥel, but his father subsequently changes his name to Binyamin (Gen. 35:18).

## STORY OF THE MANDRAKES

> Reuven went in the days of the wheat harvest, and found mandrakes in the field, and brought them to his mother, Leah. Then Raḥel said to Leah, "Please give me some of your son's mandrakes." She said to her, "Is it a small matter that you have taken away my husband? Would you take away my son's mandrakes, also?" Raḥel said, "Therefore he will lie with you tonight for your son's mandrakes." Yaakov came from the field in the evening, and Leah went out to meet him, and said, "You must come with me; for I have surely traded for you with my son's mandrakes." And he slept with her that night. (Gen. 30:14–16)

By the time we are introduced to the first narrative including Reuven, Yaakov's family has grown; Leah has four sons: Reuven, Shimon, Levi, and Yehuda. Raḥel is barren, so she gives over her maidservant, Bilha, to marry Yaakov and have children on her behalf. Soon after, Bilha has two sons, Dan and Naftali. Now, Leah finds herself in a quandary, as she is unable to have any more children and fears that Raḥel's maid may continue to reproduce (Gen. 29:35, 30:9). Leah copies her sister by giving her maidservant, Zilpa, to Yaakov as a wife, and she bears him two children, Gad and Asher. This situates our first story with Reuven soon after the birth of Yaakov's eighth son.

Young Reuven goes to the field to pick flowers and proudly presents them to his mother, Leah. Raḥel desires the flowers and requests them from her sister. Leah agrees to transfer them to Raḥel only in return for one of Raḥel's nights with Yaakov.

What a bizarre story! So many details are difficult to comprehend. Why did Raḥel want the flowers? What could be so special about these flowers that they are worth trading a night with Yaakov? And finally, what makes this story important enough to be included in the text of the Torah?

Broadly, there are two ways to understand this story, each of which will impact our analysis of Reuven.

### Token of Love

This story could be the pure and innocent depiction of a sensitive young boy who recognizes his mother's sadness and tries to cheer her up with a bouquet of flowers. These flowers are a token of his love to make up for the lack of love and gestures of affection that she should receive from her husband. Moreover, Reuven may be aware of his parents' strained relationship, either because Leah talks to her eldest son about her predicament or just because it is something that he observes in their home. He watches Yaakov's treatment of her during the day and sees her crying at night. As her oldest son, Reuven may be the shoulder that Leah cries on. So too, he may know the significance behind his own name, his mother's desperate plea for love, and he wants to help her fill that void.

According to this line of thinking, Raḥel trades a night with Yaakov for these flowers because they embody a child's love for his mother. She is desperate to feel the tangible love of a child. Raḥel's anguish is passionately expressed only a few verses earlier, when she lashes out at Yaakov saying, "Give me children or else I will die" (Gen. 30:1). Clearly, to Raḥel, these flowers embody what she covets most in the world – the love of a child for his mother; she believes that acquiring them is worth relinquishing a night with Yaakov. The significance of this story is to display the level of extreme desperation that both Raḥel and Leah feel, and what they are willing to sacrifice.

### Fertility Flowers

Alternatively, a second possibility is that this story is about the physical struggle of infertility. Many commentators, including Ibn Ezra and Sforno on Gen. 30:14, posit that the mandrakes enabled conception, either through their impact on the male's ability to procreate or by providing an environment that enhances intimacy. If this is so, it explains why Raḥel, who struggles mightily with infertility, would trade a night with Yaakov to acquire them. Only with this understanding of the mandrakes does the trade seem fair to both women. Accordingly, this story fits into the context of the broader narrative, i.e., the race to have children who will become the tribes of Israel.[15]

15. There are many commentators, including Ramban and Radak on Gen. 30:14, who reject this possibility. They argue that viewing these flowers as a fertility aid is implausible, as they have never heard of any flowers with this power. Furthermore, post facto, the woman who receives the flowers, Raḥel, is not the one who gets pregnant. Even Ibn Ezra – who quotes the view that the flowers help with fertility – questions the validity of this approach at the end of his commentary.

Consistent with these two interpretations for the role of the mandrakes, two fundamentally divergent paths to understanding Reuven's role in the story emerge.

If the mandrakes are to promote fertility, then everything Reuven does is for the sake of his mother. He is acutely aware of her desire for more children.[16] He realizes that his father's love for his mother is based on her ability to have children, and he involves himself in his parents' personal matters. Our story reveals a young Reuven overstepping his boundaries by invading his parents' private affairs for his mother's sake.

However, if the mandrakes are a token of love, then the emergent picture is rather different. Even as a youngster, Reuven recognizes his mother's sadness. He gives her flowers as a token of *his* love. Perhaps, as she is occupied with trying to have more children and gaining her husband's love, she is not giving proper attention to her eldest son. Reuven feels left out and craves his mother's attention, hoping that she might find satisfaction in the love of her children. How tragically disappointing it must have been for him to come home and discover his flowers in his aunt's tent. His mother discarded this token of his love for her just to spend more time with his father.

## MEETING WITH ESAV

> Then the handmaids came near with their children, and they bowed down. Leah also and her children came near and bowed down. After them, Yosef came near with Raḥel, and they bowed down. (Gen. 33:6–7)

The first time we see any hint to Yaakov's lack of acknowledgement of Reuven's elevated firstborn status by not treating him as the most valued child is in the context of the reunion between Yaakov and his brother Esav. Years earlier, Yaakov ran away from his father's home to escape from Esav, who swore to exact revenge on him for receiving the blessing of the

---

16. Sforno on Gen. 30:14 states outright that Reuven recognizes her suffering associated with the cessation of her childbearing.

firstborn from their father by pretending to be Esav (according to their mother's plan). Now, on his journey back to his father's home, Yaakov must face his brother. Terrified, Yaakov tries numerous plans to appease Esav's wrath, beginning with sending messengers to his brother. Next, he separates his family into two groups to travel separately, in order to ensure that at least half of the family will survive the encounter. He then sends presents to his brother as a bribe. In a last-minute desperate act intended to save the entire family, Yaakov tries to separate himself from the rest of them by running away, as Esav would not know that that they belonged to him if he was not with them.[17] However, all of his plans fail when Yaakov is delayed by an unnamed "*ish*," "man," an anonymous individual who struggles with him and holds him back until morning. Under pressure, Yaakov devises his final plan and places his family in a specific order, putting the most treasured ones in the back for greater protection. In this setup, Yaakov clearly demonstrates to every member of his family who is the most precious to him: Yaakov places Yosef, the eldest son of Raḥel, at the very back, the most protected position, thereby demonstrating that Yosef is more valuable to him than Reuven, the eldest of Leah and the firstborn of Yaakov's progeny.

It should not be surprising that these two stories in Reuven's life lead us to the third story, the rebellion of Reuven against his father.

## REUVEN AND BILHA

> It happened, while Yisrael lived in that land, that Reuven went and lay with Bilha, his father's concubine, and Yisrael heard of it. Now the sons of Yaakov were twelve. (Gen. 35:22)

This episode presents a shocking scenario: Reuven lies with Bilha, his father's third wife. What could have motivated Reuven to do this? What might he have intended to accomplish? This turn of events is baffling.

17. See Rashbam on Gen. 32:25 for an explanation as to why "Yaakov was left alone" (Gen. 32:25). God sends the "*ish*" to fight with Yaakov to stop him from abandoning his family, thus forcing him to face his brother and come up with a new plan.

There are two distinct interpretive approaches to Reuven's behavior, captured in the Talmud[18] and in the commentaries.[19] While one approach recognizes that the words of this verse – that Reuven engaged in sexual activity with his father's wife, Bilha – should be understood literally, there is an alternate view that interprets this verse non-literally, alluding to a different act of rebellion.

**Literal Understanding**

> "*Vayishkav et Bilha.*" (Gen. 35:22)

Throughout the Torah, the root *shin, kaf, bet,* which means "to lie," is utilized to depict sexual relations between a man and woman. The literal explanation of the word *shakhav* is to lie with a woman.[20] Typically the phrase *shakhav et* is used to describe a situation of a man forcing himself on a woman,[21] which suggests that these words are telling us Reuven had sexual relations with his father's wife Bilha. The difficulty of this approach is in understanding his motive. How could Reuven think that this act might improve his relationship with his father?

In order to comprehend this episode, let us consider three similar stories in Tanakh where a man lies with his father's or leader's wife or concubine.

---

18. The Talmud in Shabbat 55b quotes the opinion of R. Yonatan that if anyone says Reuven sinned, they are mistaken. However, R. Yehoshua says that Reuven "trampled on the law and sinned and acted lewdly," implying that he believes that Reuven did lie with Bilha.
19. Rashi, Ibn Ezra, Ramban, Abarbanel, and *Ḥizkuni* all interpret this verse non-literally. In contrast, Rashbam, Radak, and Sforno believe that the verse should be read literally and that Reuven did lie with Bilha.
20. This same root – *shin, kaf, beit* – is used to describe the sexual relations of Lot and his daughters (Gen. 19:32–35), Yaakov and Leah before the birth of Yissakhar (Gen. 30:16), Shekhem with Dina (Gen. 34:2), Potiphar's wife's intentions with Yosef (Gen. 39:7), and Amnon with Tamar (II Sam. 13:14).
21. This combination of words is used in two rape stories: Shekhem with Dina (Gen. 34:2) and Amnon with Tamar (II Sam. 13:14). It is also used to describe consensual relations (Lev. 15:24) and forbidden sexual relationships (Lev. 20:11, 12, 13, 18, 20, and Num. 5:13).

## Avner and Ritzpa

The first story occurs in II Samuel (3:7–11), immediately following the death of King Shaul. Shaul's son Ishboshet inherits the throne, thus leading the ten tribes of Israel, while David becomes king of the other two tribes. Due to Ishboshet's youth and inexperience, Avner, Shaul's military general and close relative,[22] manipulates him. One day, Ishboshet confronts Avner, accusing him of having sexual relations with Ritzpa, the concubine of the prior king, Shaul. Avner responds by abandoning Ishboshet for David, bringing with him the ten tribes. Ultimately, this helps unite the twelve tribes under David's rule. At first glance, it seems that Avner overreacts to the accusation. Why such a strident response? Simply because having relations with the concubine of a leader is much more significant than the act itself, due to the symbolism and message it sends, i.e., that this person is entitled to the rights of the king! Specifically, it proclaims that he is an heir to the throne. Ishboshet is actually accusing Avner of trying to usurp his rulership, an act of treason. His true intentions exposed, Avner has no choice but to abandon Ishboshet and flee to David's army.

## Avshalom and David's Concubines

The second story occurs later in II Samuel (16:21–22). David's son Avshalom rebels against his father and succeeds in overthrowing David from his palace.[23] To assert his newfound power, Avshalom ascends to the roof of David's palace and rapes ten of David's concubines.[24] This is not only a sexual act, but it also represents Avshalom's undeniable message to his father: that he deserves to be the king of the Jewish people.

---

22. I Sam. 14:51.
23. Avshalom was removed from David's home after killing his older brother Amnon for raping his sister, Tamar. Years later, David permitted his return, but by then it was clear that Avshalom would not inherit the throne.
24. Ironically, this is the same location where David stood when he saw Batsheva bathing and sent his soldiers to bring her to him (II Sam. 11:2). This focus on the "*gag*," "roof," of the palace leads us to assert that the action of Avshalom was an act of punishment to David for lying with Batsheva, the wife of Uriah the Ḥittite.

### Adoniyahu and Avishag

The third story occurs in I Kings chapter 2, when David is old and nearing death. Adoniyahu, a younger son of David, anoints himself as king. After David announces that the next king to inherit his throne will be his son Shlomo, Adoniyahu is forced to step down. As part of his desperate attempt to retain the throne, Adoniyahu beseeches Batsheva to request her son Shlomo's permission for Adoniyahu to marry David's concubine, Avishag.[25] Shlomo immediately detects his brother's true intentions – to usurp the kingdom – and sentences him to death for treason.[26]

Each of these episodes depicts a close relative – a son, brother, or uncle – staking a claim as heir to the throne. Each one attempts to assert his authority by having relations with the wife or concubine of the king. With this as background, Reuven's motivation becomes clear. Reuven is conveying to his father, the leader of the family, that he expects to inherit the leadership position. He is trying to show Yaakov that his first choice for this position, Yosef, was a mistaken decision, as was his favoritism of what is in his opinion the wrong wife, Raḥel. Reuven is standing up to his father, protesting his own mistreatment as well as that of his mother and all of the disregarded children of Leah.[27]

### Non-Literal Approach

The primary evidence, supplied by the Talmud and commentators, for why the verse is not intended to be understood literally is based on the last few words of our verse: "and the sons of Yaakov were twelve." It is hard to believe – according to this interpretation – that Reuven would remain counted among the tribes of Israel after doing as reprehensible

---

25. Avishag was the beautiful woman chosen to keep David warm during his older years. He laid next to her for warmth, but never had sexual relations with her (I Kings 1:3–4).
26. Shlomo compares Adoniyahu's request to a coup attempt: "Why do you request Avishag the Shunammite for Adoniyahu? Request for him the kingdom" (I Kings 2:22). Adoniyahu reveals his true intentions when he says to Batsheva as a preface to his request, "You know that the kingdom was mine, and that all Israel set their faces on me, that I should reign: however, the kingdom is turned about, and become my brother's…" (I Kings 2:15).
27. See Rabbi Yaakov Medan, "Anyone Who Says Reuven Sinned…," http://etzion.org.il/en/anyone-who-says-reuven-sinned; and Rabbi Alex Israel, "Reuven: Cover Up or Peshat?" http://etzion.org.il/en/reuven-cover-or-peshat.

an act as having relations with his father's maidservant.[28] Additionally, the words "and Yisrael heard" imply that he did not actively respond to his son's action. Yaakov's passive reaction would be extremely challenging to understand if Reuven had truly slept with his wife.[29]

Interestingly, even though Yaakov does not respond to Reuven immediately when the story is told in Genesis 35, he does react at the end of his life. Yaakov states that Reuven loses his status as firstborn "because you went up to your father's bed, then defiled it. He went up to my couch" (Gen. 49:4). These words show that Yaakov was profoundly disturbed by Reuven's desecration of his bed. However, neither our verse nor Yaakov's deathbed statement provide much clarity as to the exact nature of Reuven's actual transgression. Commentators speculate about what the specific transgression was. Did he move his father's bed into a different tent? Perhaps he removed his father's bed from the tent of Raḥel's maid after her death, and placed it in its rightful space, in his mother's tent?[30] Alternatively, maybe Reuven did something to Bilha or to her bed to prevent his father from having relations with her or bearing more children on behalf of Raḥel?[31] There does seem to be a

28. It is also difficult to fathom that one of the tribes of Israel would commit such a heinous act against his father.

29. Admittedly, it is possible that the lack of reaction by Yaakov is just a function of Yaakov's character. Other instances of Yaakov's muted reaction include the following:
    (1) In response to Shekhem's rape of his daughter Dina, the verse states "*veheḥerish* Yaakov," "and Yaakov was quiet" (Gen. 34:5)
    (2) In response to Shimon and Levi's justification for murdering the inhabitants of the city of Shekhem, when they say that they couldn't allow Shekhem to treat their sister as a prostitute, Yaakov is silent (Gen. 34:31).
    (3) When he senses the jealousy of the brothers towards Yosef, the verse says: "*ve'aviv shamar et hadavar*," "and their father observed the matter" (Gen.37:11), but did nothing about it.

30. Shabbat 55b; Rashi on Gen. 35:22.

31. *Midrash Tanhuma* (*Vayeḥi* 11) records that Reuven lay in Bilha's bed at the moment Yaakov was about to come lie with her, to force Yaakov to leave Bilha's tent and go to Leah's bed instead.

    Ramban on 35:22 writes that Reuven's intention was to prevent Bilha from having additional children who might take away from his portion of inheritance. As the eldest child, Reuven was destined to receive a double portion, and had the most to lose if Yaakov had more children, each of whom would also receive a portion of the inheritance.

common denominator among these suggestions: Reuven is doing this act to help his mother by removing the competition, Bilha, and at the same time he is helping himself by negating the possibility of future competition, in the form of siblings, challenging his own leadership and right to inheritance.

According to the non-literal approach, Reuven's behavior is not primarily about his own status in the family, but rather about defending the honor of his mother. Just as he did in his younger years when he brought her flowers, now as an adult he looks out for his mother. Reuven intends to communicate to his father the injustice of his mother's treatment after the death of Raḥel. Yaakov's elevation of Bilha's status over his mother is insulting, wrong, and hurtful. Reuven again inserts himself

---

Rabbi Yaakov Tzvi Mecklenberg in his Torah commentary *Haketav Vehakabbala* on 35:22 writes that the intention of Reuven's act was to publicly declare that Bilha was not a true wife of Yaakov, but rather was only a concubine. He explains that we are to read the verse "and Reuven defiled Bilha with his words and his father heard his words," with emphasis on "words." By publicly calling her a concubine, a lower level wife, he embarrassed her and Yaakov and caused Yaakov to never have relations with her again. Rabbi Mecklenberg supports this approach by observing that this is the only time in the text that Bilha (or Zilpa) is referred to as a concubine instead of a full wife.

Rabbi S. R. Hirsch on Gen. 35:21–22 actually attempts to interpret Reuven's behavior in a positive light. After the death of Raḥel, Yaakov had separated himself from all of his remaining wives, pitching his tent a distance away from the rest of the family. By lying in Bilha's bed, Reuven was trying to show his father that his separation from his wives was hurting the family. He was hoping his father would realize his mistake and come back to all of his wives, including Leah. Unfortunately, Yaakov does not heed the message and remains separate, leading to the reality that "and the children of Yisrael were twelve": i.e., he had no more children.

Rabbi Yaakov Medan in "Anyone Who Says Reuven Sinned…" presents both sides, and posits that Reuven might have tied up Bilha, removed her from Yaakov's tent, and replaced her with his own mother. Yaakov again slept with Leah, while believing he was with a different wife. Yosef saw Reuven tie up Bilha and drag her away. He reported to his father that he believed Reuven did this in order to rape her. Rabbi Medan finds support for this narrative in the verse, "Reuven lay with Bilha… and his father heard." Yaakov heard, i.e., was told by Yosef, that this is what Reuven did. However, Rabbi Medan recognizes that Reuven would never have actually had relations with Bilha; he hated her and everything she represented to him and his mother.

into his parents' complicated relationship, overstepping a line, but possibly with good intentions.

This story offers us insight into the bigger picture of Reuven's personality that will continue to be revealed in the rest of his stories. He struggles with his position within the family, as he believes that he, the oldest, should lead. But his growing resentment of his father's treatment of him and his mother causes him to act hastily. Thus, the reaction caused by his behavior with Bilha does not end where he intends. He wants to be recognized as the leader of the family, but after his stunt with Bilha, his father disregards him completely.[32] Reuven never considers the implications of his actions; thus, inevitably, they don't succeed as he would like.

However, Reuven never forsakes his dream to become the leader of the family. In future stories, Reuven will try to prove to his family that he is deserving of the role. Unfortunately, he will fail in every attempt.

## REUVEN – THE FAILED LEADER OF THE BROTHERS

The tragedy of Reuven is the disconnect between his belief in his capabilities and the impact of his actions. He genuinely believes that he can resolve every problem in the family. Regrettably, whenever an opportunity arises for Reuven to prove himself, his solutions are inappropriate, ignored, or rejected. We see this pattern emerge in the final three stories recorded about his life.

### Sale of Yosef

> Reuven heard it, and delivered him out of their hand, and said, "Let's not take his life." Reuven said to them, "Shed no blood. Throw him into this pit that is in the wilderness, but lay no hand on him" – that he might deliver him out of their hand, to restore him to his father. (Gen. 37:21–22)

32. In fact, this may explain why Yaakov is silent in reaction to Reuven's action. This is the ultimate punishment for Reuven. Yaakov purposely ignores the son who desperately seeks his father's attention and approval.

Beginning in Genesis 37, Yaakov expresses a clear preference for Raḥel's oldest son, Yosef. He presents Yosef with a distinctive coat to wear in his brothers' view, thus signifying his unique love for him and Yosef's elevated status. Concurrently, Yosef has visions of leadership that he divulges to his brothers, arousing their jealousy about his special treatment and their animosity due to his dreams.[33] These emotions reach a tipping point when Yaakov sends Yosef to check on his brothers while they are shepherding his sheep. As he approaches them, the brothers plot his murder. It is at this moment that Reuven steps up to lead.

Reuven instructs his brothers not to murder Yosef; rather, he suggests, they should throw him into a pit and leave him at the mercy of nature. While we, the readers, know that Reuven plans to save Yosef, the brothers are unaware of that stage of his plan. He feels forced to hide his desire to save his brother, perhaps because he is afraid the other brothers will thwart his plan or because he fears they will ignore him and shatter his belief that he is the leader. It seems Reuven has good intentions that are not realized because of his flaws and insecurities.

In fact, on inspection, there are numerous elements of this plan that seem lacking. First, how could Reuven have not been aware of other things in the pit that could endanger Yosef's life?[34] Second, how was Reuven comfortable leaving the scene instead of remaining near the pit to keep watch? How could he be so sure that Yosef would still be there when he returned? Why did he leave? Lastly, how does Reuven intend to explain to the brothers that Yosef is still alive?

It seems that because Reuven believes he is the leader of the family, he assumes that his brothers would not swerve from his plans, and that even if he leaves the scene, Yosef would still be there when

33. These feelings of hatred and jealousy of the brothers are described in the text of the Torah after specific events: "And they hated him" (Gen. 37:4) after seeing the special coat; "And they continued to hate him" (Gen. 37:5) after hearing the first dream; "And they were jealous" (Gen. 37:11) after their father doesn't get angry about Yosef's second dream wherein the entire family, including Yaakov, bow to him.

34. The Talmud in Shabbat 22a posits that the verse writes "And the pit was empty, it had no water," using repetitive language, to emphasize that the pit was only empty of water but did have snakes and scorpions inside.

he returns. He probably does not anticipate having to explain Yosef's survival to the brothers because he expects they would respect his decision to save him.

Of course, Reuven's blind spot is that his brothers do not consider him as their leader; therefore, they do not feel compelled to listen to him. Consequently, immediately after he leaves, Yehuda suggests a new plan: Sell Yosef! All the brothers listen to him, in spite of Reuven's plan.[35] It is unclear what transpired after this point in the story. Either the brothers sell Yosef to the Yishmaelites, or alternatively, Midianite merchants discover him in the pit and sell him.[36] Whichever story is correct, Reuven's plan has failed. Therefore, when Reuven returns to the scene, he is shocked that Yosef is no longer inside the pit!

We are plagued by the following question: Why did Reuven want to save Yosef, his biggest rival for the attention of his father? Why did he not step aside and allow his brothers to murder Yosef? What were his true intentions in this story?

One approach: Reuven's intentions to save Yosef were pure. In his mind, as the leader of the family, it was his responsibility to save Yosef. Said another way, while he may have wanted to help his mother

35. Many commentators attempt to explain where Reuven went after Yosef was thrown in the pit. Rashi and Radak on 37:29 write that he went home to help his father. In their understanding, the brothers shared responsibility in caring for Yaakov, and that day's duty was Reuven's. Otherwise, it is possible that Yosef, the "*ben zekunim*," i.e., a child born in his parents' later years, had the responsibility to take care of their father at all times. However, now that Yosef was in the pit and not able to tend to their father, Reuven felt a need to go home and check on him. This reinforces the message that Reuven's primary concern is his father's approval. Rashi posits an alternative explanation: Reuven was fasting and repenting for his actions with Bilha. After throwing Yosef into a pit, the brothers all left to eat. Reuven, who was fasting, separated himself from his brothers. (This explanation allows Rashi to connect this story with the prior one.) Radak also offers a second explanation: Reuven simply went off to shepherd sheep. Not all the brothers could sit down to eat at the same time, as they had to take turns watching the sheep. Rabbi Avraham ben HaRambam on 37:29 writes that Reuven intentionally slipped away from his brothers to prepare his plan for rescuing Yosef.

36. See Rashbam, *Ḥizkuni,* and Bekhor Shor on Gen. 37:28.

and himself gain favor with Yaakov, he would never resort to murder. For once, his actions are completely selfless.

An alternative approach: His behavior is another example of his selfish motives. He strategizes that being Yosef's savior by bringing him home to Yaakov will create hero-status for himself. By saving the favorite son, he might gain his father's recognition as leader of the family. Therefore, while he felt no urgency to stop the brothers out of a sense of sincere altruism, he utilized their motivation to harm Yosef as an opportunity to differentiate himself. An alternate possibility is that his motivation to save Yosef merely stems from his fear of being the target of his father's blame, which he assumes will be directed at him because he is the oldest child.[37] This fear is evident in Reuven's own words when he comes to the empty pit: "The boy is missing, what will be of me!" (Gen. 37:30).[38]

The common theme that runs through these various explanations for his behavior is clear: Reuven perceives that he is the family leader and is thus expected to be responsible for his brothers, both Yosef and the others, but he fails to protect Yosef, who is sold to Egypt. He proves to be unable to manage his brothers and continues to disappoint his father.

**Blaming his Brothers**

> Reuven answered them, saying, "Didn't I speak to you, saying, 'Don't sin against the child,' and you wouldn't listen? Therefore also, behold, his blood is required." (Gen. 42:22)

Nine years after the sale of Yosef, a famine forces the brothers to descend to Egypt in search of food. There, unbeknownst to them, they are face to face with their brother Yosef. During these intervening

37. *Ḥizkuni* on Gen. 37:30 adds that especially because his father knows that Reuven is upset about Yosef's elevated status in the family, Yaakov would certainly blame Reuven for Yosef's disappearance.
38. These words could also be support for the first way of explaining Reuven's reasoning according to the non-altruistic approach, i.e., that Reuven believed that saving Yosef was his opportunity to improve the way his father viewed him, but once his plans went wrong and Yosef has disappeared and therefore Reuven is not the hero, he now worries, "What will be of me!"

years, Yosef has grown into the second most important member of the Egyptian government. He recognizes his brothers but they do not recognize him. Yosef puts them through a series of trials: he accuses them of spying, jails them for three days, keeps Shimon in jail, and then releases the rest to return home, but only after he instructs them not to return for more food without their youngest brother, their father's new favorite son. The brothers recognize the cosmic connection between these events and their treatment of Yosef – God must be punishing them.

At this point, Reuven again attempts to lead the brothers. The role of a leader during a crisis is to keep his constituents calm and to fashion a plan to help them prevail. However, Reuven does the opposite. Instead of taking any responsibility for the events that have befallen them, he pointedly blames them for their current predicament. Reuven directly accuses them of being at fault for what they did to Yosef and for disregarding his words to leave Yosef alone.

Of course, Reuven's reaction is bizarre and seemingly out of place. First, it seems that Reuven is not even telling the truth, as he never said outright not to hurt Yosef.[39] During that prior episode, Reuven did suggest that instead of actively murdering Yosef, the brothers should abandon him in a pit. How can he now claim that he said to leave Yosef alone? Second, and more importantly, even if he did make those comments earlier, mentioning it at this point is extremely inappropriate. Why point fingers about a prior event when the group is now in trouble? That is not effective leadership; a leader should accept responsibility and plan

39. There is a hint in the words of the Torah that Reuven did tell his brothers not to touch Yosef. Verse 21 states that Reuven said, "*vayomer... lo nakenu nafesh*," "and he said...let us not take his life." But in verse 22, there is a second "*vayomer*," "and he said," implying a second speech. In this verse, Reuven provides his idea to throw Yosef in the pit. The repetition of "*vayomer*" could imply that there is a pause between his two speeches. This would mean that his first statement to his brothers was simply "Don't hurt Yosef," thus matching what he is claiming he said in chapter 42. Only after they did not listen did he speak up a second time, suggesting they throw Yosef in the pit (Malbim on Gen. 37:21). For a further analysis of instances of "*vayomer*" repetition in the Torah see Rabbi Elchanan Samet, "Reuven's Attempt to Save Yosef," http://etzion.org.il/en/reuvens-attempt-save-yosef.

the next move. This story clearly depicts Reuven's continued inability to serve as a suitable leader for his brothers.

**Protector of Binyamin**

> Reuven spoke to his father, saying, "Kill my two sons if I don't bring him back to you. Deliver him into my hand, and I will bring him to you again." (Gen. 42:37)

The brothers return home from their trip to Egypt without Shimon and tell their father that the leader of Egypt refused to allow them to return for more food without their youngest brother, Binyamin, the remaining child of Raḥel.

Reuven tries again to prove himself to his father by instantly volunteering to be the protector of Binyamin. However, in his swiftness to speak, he doesn't fully consider the implications of his offer. He proposes to his father that if he is not able to safely restore Binyamin to Yaakov, Yaakov can kill both of his (Reuven's) sons. The idea that a grandfather would want to kill his grandchildren in revenge for losing a son is ludicrous.[40] His words display a lack of forethought and help explain why Yaakov would obviously refuse his proposal.

Ramban on 42:37, however, presents a different approach. He writes that Reuven's offer wasn't outrageous at all but should be understood as Reuven's inarticulate way of saying that he would take responsibility if anything happens to Binyamin. But, Ramban writes, Yaakov simply didn't trust Reuven. Yaakov knows from past experience that Reuven is not trustworthy or responsible, and therefore he would never

---

40. Rashi on Gen. 42:38 labels Reuven as "a stupid firstborn" for proposing this deal. Other commentators find it impossible to conclude that Reuven could have meant what he said literally. Sforno on 42:37 says that Reuven only meant that if he loses Binyamin his sons would be cursed, but not that Yaakov would murder them. Rabbi Yaakov Tzvi Mecklenberg, in his commentary *Haketav Vehakabbala* on 42:37, writes that Reuven's intention was that his children would not inherit land if he was unsuccessful in his mission. Of course, no matter the exact details of his proposal, Reuven is willing to negotiate a plan that could have very negative effects on his own children if he fails to protect Binyamin.

entrust his favorite child into his hands, regardless of the offer. In this incident, Yaakov rejects his eldest son once again.

Considering the landscape of Reuven's life, one observes the tragedy of a man who never aligns his vision with reality. He spends his life chasing an impossible dream. Reuven would never be the head of his family, not because he is a son of Leah, the non-favored wife, but because he lacks the traits that are imperative for leadership. Reuven lacks dependability, persistence, patience, and control, and therefore does not command respect. He is too quick to blame others for his mistakes and desperately wants his father's approval.

## THE BLESSING OF YAAKOV

> "Reuven, you are my firstborn, my might, and the beginning of my strength, the pre-eminence of dignity, and the pre-eminence of power. Unstable as water, you shall not have the pre-eminence, because you went up to your father's bed and defiled it. He went up to my couch." (Gen. 49:3–4)

Reuven's lack of leadership qualities is captured in Yaakov's deathbed message to his oldest son. Yaakov's message to Reuven is concise and to the point. He tells his son that he had all the potential in the world but squandered it.[41] Yaakov's meaning is clear: Reuven's fall is not because of his mother's status as the unfavored wife; rather, it is because of his own failure to lead and his recklessness in his action of defiling his father's bed. Yaakov declares outright: "You do not deserve the honor of the firstborn!"

Reuven will of course always be the oldest of Yaakov's sons, and will continue to hold the title of firstborn, as the eldest tribe of the Jewish people. Because of this, he receives certain honors: he is given a blessing first by his father in Gen. 49, and is listed first many times in the Torah, each time identified as the firstborn,[42] but he loses his right

41. Rashi on 49:3 points out that Reuven should have received the priesthood and kingship.
42. Gen. 35:23, 46:8, 49:3, Ex. 6:14, Num. 26:5, I Chr. 5:1.

to the double inheritance. The double portion is given to Yosef, who has both his sons, Ephraim and Menashe, inherit separate pieces of land in Israel (Gen. 48:22, Josh. ch. 16 and 17).[43] Reuven loses his leadership role in the family during his life and then throughout history to his younger brothers, Yehuda and Yosef. The book of Chronicles states:

> The sons of Reuven the firstborn of Yisrael, for he was the firstborn; but because he defiled his father's couch, his birthright was given to the sons of Yosef the son of Yisrael; and the genealogy is not to be reckoned after the birthright. For Yehuda prevailed above his brothers, and of him came the prince; but the birthright was Yosef's. (I Chr. 5:1–2)

43. Rabbenu Baḥya on Gen. 36:23 observes an obvious point: It is impossible to change the birth order or biological status of being the oldest child. It is a fact; either you are born first or you are not. However, that does not protect the honors that come along with that biological status. Reuven loses all of those honors. Sforno on Num. 1:20 maintains that even being called firstborn is part of the honor and that Reuven is only called the firstborn because he repented and therefore deserved to keep his title.

*Chapter 3*

# Reuven in Tanakh

From the analysis presented in the previous chapter about Reuven, it is clear that his ambitions do not match reality. As the oldest child of Yaakov, Reuven dreams of leading the family and being the chosen one to head the Jewish nation. Unfortunately, his lack of leadership skills, charisma, and forethought, as well as his failure to command the respected trust of others, create a contradiction between his self-assessment and the way he is perceived by those around him. The conflict between his aspirations and reality continues to plague his descendants. This will be evident for the tribe as a whole, as well as for individuals from the tribe of Reuven who attempt to lead.

## THE TRIBE OF REUVEN

The paradox of Reuven's status of firstborn on the one hand, and his being the rejected son on the other, is alluded to in many stories in the books of Numbers and Deuteronomy. For example, in the beginning and at the end of the book of Numbers, Moshe counts the Jewish people. In both lists, Reuven as the oldest child is given the honor of being counted first and of being called the "the firstborn of Yisrael" (Num. 1:20, 26:5). However, in the next chapter (Num. 2), when Moshe arranges the order of travel for the Jewish people in the desert, Reuven is not put in front. The responsibility of leading the Jewish people in their forty-year journey is given to the tribe of Yehuda, Reuven's younger brother. However, Reuven is not completely overlooked. His tribe is allotted the honor of being at the forefront of one of the encampments on the south side, leading two of his brothers, Shimon and Gad. Our picture of Reuven is consistent and clear: He is deserving of some honor as the eldest, but because of his lack of leadership qualities he cannot be the leader of the nation. Therefore, Reuven is designated to lead an encampment which includes the tribes of two other brothers, while at the same time his tribe follows behind Yehuda, who leads the entire nation.

The positioning of the tribes in Deuteronomy situates Reuven in a similar fashion. When Moshe describes the Jewish people's future while gathering them on the mountains of Gerizim and Ebal to read the blessings and curses, Reuven is placed on the mountain of curses, along with the maidservants' children (Gad, Asher, Dan, and Naftali), as well as Zevulun, the youngest child of Leah (Deut. 27:13). He is banned from the mountain of blessings, unable to stand with Raḥel's children and Leah's older children (Shimon, Levi, Yehuda, Yissakhar, Yosef, and Binyamin). This exclusion disgraces and humiliates the tribe of Reuven, especially when the following curse is read: "Cursed be he who lies with his father's wife, because he has uncovered his father's skirt. All the people shall say, amen" (Deut. 27:20). These words echo in our minds, reminding us of Reuven's action with his father's wife Bilha.

The slighting of the tribe of Reuven continues in Moshe's final messages to each tribe at the end of his life. Although Moshe blesses the tribe of Reuven first, his final words to Reuven are empty and appear almost meaningless: "Let Reuven live, and not die; nor let his men be few" (Deut. 33:6). There is nothing in this statement that is negative or insulting, but it is also neither complimentary nor admiring. It lacks any perceptible sentiment. Moshe's concluding message for the tribe of Reuven is that the group, as a whole, lacks individuality and accomplishment.

### INDIVIDUALS FROM THE TRIBE OF REUVEN

Reuven's propensity for failed leadership not only plagues his tribe throughout their history, but it afflicts individual members of the tribe as well. Every story that is recorded in Torah about Reuven's descendants reflects the struggles, desires, and disappointments that are representative of the original Reuven and of his tribe as a unit.[1]

### Datan and Aviram

> Now Koraḥ, the son of Yitzhar, the son of Kehat, the son of Levi, with Datan and Aviram, the sons of Eliav, and On, the son of Pelet, sons of Reuven, took men: They rose up before Moshe, with certain of the children of Israel, two hundred fifty princes of the congregation, called to the assembly, men of renown. They assembled themselves together against Moshe and against Aharon, and said to them, "You take too much on you, seeing all the congregation is holy, every one of them, and God is among them: why then lift yourselves up above the assembly of God?" (Num. 16:1–3)

The first significant offspring from the tribe of Reuven – Datan and Aviram – appear as leaders in the Koraḥ rebellion.[2] Koraḥ, from the tribe

---

1. There is one exception: The only positive figure that comes from Reuven is the prophet Hoshea, the first of the twelve Minor Prophets. Rabbinic tradition assumes that Hoshea is from the tribe of Reuven because we are told that his father's name is Be'eri (Hosh. 1:1), and a man by the name of Be'era is the priest of the tribe of Reuven during that time (I Chr. 5:6). Hoshea metaphorically compares worship of other gods to that of an unfaithful wife. Hoshea is told to marry a woman named Gomer who is unfaithful after having three children with him, somewhat reminding us of the episode between Reuven and Bilha. Hoshea also beseeches the Jewish people to repent for their evil ways: "Return, children of Israel" (Hosh. 14:2). The talmudic Sages use this emphasis on *teshuva* in Hoshea as evidence that Reuven must have repented for his sin with Bilha and therefore merited to have his future descendant cry out to the Jewish people to repent. This is one of the reasons that the Sages assume Reuven leaves the pit to go cry and mourn about his earlier deeds (Genesis Rabba 84:19). This technique of the Sages – assuming that each tribe has its own personality and inherent coherence – underlies the methodological basis for this book. In this instance, the Sages assume that Reuven must have repented because a future descendant is a role model for repentance.
2. There is a third man from Reuven listed in the verses above, On son of Pelet, whose name is never mentioned again in the rest of the Koraḥ incident, nor in the rest of Tanakh. The Talmud in Sanhedrin 109b–110a explains that On intended to join the rebellion but, unbeknownst to him, was saved by his wife. After she purposely intoxicated him, he fell asleep and slept through the rebellion. When his associates

of Levi, is the mastermind behind an uprising against the leadership of Moshe and Aharon. This occurs during their second year in the desert, in the wake of the news that the Jewish people will not be traveling directly into Israel. Koraḥ amasses two hundred and fifty men, many from the tribe of Reuven, to confront Moshe with their complaints.[3] However, Datan and Aviram are completely different. While it is true that they are listed in the first verse, thus labeling them as leaders of the rebellion, as the story unfolds it becomes clear that they are not even present at the uprising itself. Amazingly, on two occasions Moshe must look for them because they are missing from the scene. First, Moshe is forced to send a message to invite them to deliberate with him, but they refuse to come (Num. 16:12). Later, when their absence is obvious, Moshe goes to their homes because they are not among the two hundred and fifty men in the field (16:25). Therefore, it appears that Datan and Aviram are not really leading this rebellion.

Furthermore, Datan and Aviram do not seem to be complaining about the same issues as Koraḥ and his followers, who are bothered by nepotism – that Moshe appointed his brother Aharon as high priest. The dramatic display of Koraḥ and his followers, each of them bringing an incense offering, a sacrifice typically given by the high priest (Ex. 30:7), illuminates their central critique about Aharon. Datan and Aviram, on the other hand, protest against the particular leadership of Moshe. They accuse him of being unable to lead the Jewish people into the land of Israel (Num. 16:13–14). Datan and Aviram never mention Aharon or his role as high priest.

---

arrived at his home to get him, she scared them away by sitting in front of her home with her hair uncovered. Ironically, this story illustrates a typical characteristic of a member of the tribe of Reuven: He intends to lead, but is outflanked by someone else. Just as Reuven was missing at the key event, i.e., the sale of Yosef, so too was On absent at his moment of possible leadership, i.e., the Koraḥ rebellion.

3. Many commentators, including Abarbanel on Num. 26:1 and *Toledot Yitzḥak* on Num. 17:1, conclude that the majority of those who joined this rebellion were from the tribe of Reuven. The members of this tribe were angered by their loss of leadership, since their ancestor was the oldest child of Yaakov. Evidence is found in the numbers of men in the tribe. Specifically, their numbers decrease from the first years to the last years in the desert. In the second year there are 46,500 men in the tribe of Reuven above the age of twenty (Num. 1:21). In the fortieth year the people are recounted. This time, Reuven has 43,730 males above the age of twenty (Num. 26:7). Many commentators ascribe this population decrease to plagues and rebellions.

Evidently, Datan and Aviram are engaging in their own private rebellion against the role of Moshe himself, but not leading or controlling anyone. They alone are attacking the leadership of Moshe, blaming him for the problems besetting the Jewish people (Num. 16:14). Instead of recognizing that the delay in entering the land is a direct result of the sin of the ten spies, including a representative from the tribe of Reuven, they point a finger at Moshe.

This behavior resembles that of the progenitor of the tribe of Reuven in Genesis in a number of important ways. Recall that Reuven was a loner who lacked the support of his brothers, none of whom followed him in any endeavor. Reuven never directly confronted his father Yaakov about his concerns; rather, he alluded to them indirectly by rebelling against him in the episode with Bilha. Similarly, Datan and Aviram do not approach Moshe to challenge him; instead, they wait for Moshe to confront them, via messages and by approaching their tents. Similarly, in Egypt, Reuven focused his energy on blaming his brothers rather than on offering actionable solutions; correspondingly, Datan and Aviram blame Moshe for the failings of the Jewish people instead of accepting responsibility or suggesting the next step.

Datan and Aviram, like Reuven himself, revolt against leadership and blame others for their mistakes, but they do not know how to stand up as leaders. Therefore, just as Reuven's attempts at leadership are unsuccessful and precipitate his downfall, Datan and Aviram are literally swallowed up into the ground. Their private rebellion accomplishes nothing and leads nowhere.

The Sages take the role of Datan and Aviram one significant step further. According to them, Datan and Aviram are the duo who plagues Moshe's entire leadership, from his early days in Egypt until the second year in the desert, regularly questioning his right to lead.[4] Whether it truly

4. Even though the Koraḥ story is the only instance where their names are explicitly noted in Torah, the Sages attribute the following earlier stories to Datan and Aviram:
   (1) They are the "*shenei anashim ivrim nitzim*" (Ex. 2:13), i.e., the two Jewish men whom Moshe encounters fighting with each other, and they angrily rebuff his efforts to stop them: "Who made you our leader? Will you kill us as you did the Egyptian?"
   (2) They reveal to Pharaoh that Moshe was the individual who killed an Egyptian, thus forcing him to flee to Midian (Rashi on Ex. 2:12–15). God alludes to them

was Datan and Aviram in all of these stories or not, the Sages evidently view these two men as personifying an anti-establishment stance while simultaneously craving to become the establishment themselves even though they lack the requisite qualities. This is the persona of Reuven!

## Reuven and Gad

A second story about the descendants of Reuven occurs at the end of the book of Numbers. The tribes of Reuven and Gad approach Moshe for permission to remain on the eastern bank of the Jordan River. Although

---

in conversation with Moshe, telling Moshe before he returns to Egypt, "The men who want to kill you are dead" (Rashi on Gen. 4:19). Evidently, Moshe is anxious about facing these two troublemakers who previously had tried to undermine him. Rashi explains that they were not truly dead (clearly, they are alive later in the Torah); rather, says Rashi, they were so poor that he could consider them dead as they would no longer have any influence.

(3) They are also the men who confront Moshe ("*nitzavim likratam,*" "standing before them"; Ex. 5:20) after his first unsuccessful attempt to convince Pharaoh to release the Jewish people (Rashi on Ex. 5:20).

(4) They are the men who revolt at the Red Sea, trying to influence the Jews to return to Egypt (Ex. 14:11).

(5) Additionally, they are the ones who leave over their manna, disobeying Moshe's explicit command (Rashi on Ex. 16:20).

(6) They react to the spies' report by saying, "Let us return to Egypt" (Numbers 14:4), causing the nation to become despondent, eventually leading to the nation's forty years in the desert (Exodus Rabba 1:29).

Also, each of these stories contains language similar to the story of Datan and Aviram in the book of Numbers: a word with the same root as the word *nitzim* from Ex. 2:13 also appears in Num. 26:9: "Datan and Aviram... who incited (*hitzu*) against Moses"; the word *nitzavim* from Ex. 5:20 also appears in Num. 16:27: "Datan and Aviram went out standing (*nitzavim*)"; and the word *anashim* from Ex. 2:13 also appears in Num. 16:26: "these wicked men (*ha'anashim*)."

In summary, the Sages believe that every rebellion against the leadership of Moshe where individuals claim that Moshe is not able to fulfill his promise to take the Jewish people into Israel necessarily involves Datan and Aviram.

Methodologically, ascribing all of these episodes to these two individuals reflects a trend in midrashic writing known as the "conservation of personalities." This trend is broadly defined by the Sages' connecting lesser-known or anonymous figures with better-known individuals. Two examples in midrashic literature are the claims that Ketura is Hagar (Rashi on Gen. 25:1) and that Shifra and Puah are Yokheved and Miriam (Rashi on Ex. 1:15).

the Torah bases their request on their large quantities of cattle and consequent need for more farmland (Num. 32:1), that is clearly not their sole motivation. Moshe's immediate reaction – anger and suspicion – proves that he believes that their intentions are impure. He worries that Reuven and Gad will eventually fully separate themselves from the Jewish people. Consider this perspective: Reuven, always angered by the loss of leadership, attempts to find a new land to control that is distanced from the leadership of others.[5]

Yet even in this potential rebellion, Reuven is not the instigator or leader. After the initial verse in Numbers 32 where this story begins, the tribe of Gad is recorded before the elder tribe of Reuven. This is contrary to the usual pattern in the Torah wherein the elder or the more important person or tribe is listed first.[6] Therefore, the fact that Gad and Reuven are listed out of order must highlight something important. Ramban on Num. 32:1 writes that Gad is listed first to indicate the tribe's central role in this story. It is Gad's idea to live on the other side of the Jordan River, and it is Gad who leads the negotiations with

---

There are two approaches to interpreting the Sages' words in these statements: One approach suggests understanding the Sages' linkage of names literally. Accordingly, they are actually identifying the historical characters in these stories. For example, Datan and Aviram are guilty of rebelling against Moshe. Alternatively, the Sages' statements are not intended to be taken literally; rather, the significance of these midrashim is to associate Datan and Aviram thematically with the individuals that rebel against Moshe. Either way, Datan and Aviram represent the men who plague Moshe's entire leadership. With that in mind, it is easy to understand why Moshe mentions their downfall in his final speech before his death. In the same breath, he thanks God for his victory against the Egyptians and acknowledges his triumph against his lifelong adversaries Datan and Aviram: "And what he did to Datan and Aviram, the sons of Eliav, the son of Reuven; how the earth opened its mouth, and swallowed them up, and their households, and their tents, and every living thing that followed them, in the midst of all Israel" (Deut.11:6). Egypt represents Moshe's enemy from outside the nation, and Datan and Aviram represent Moshe's adversaries from within the nation of Israel.

5. See Chapter 13 to understand Gad's role.
6. See Sanhedrin 69b, which considers the placement of Avraham's name amongst his brothers'. The Talmud assumes that Avraham's name is listed first either because he is the oldest child of Teraḥ, or because he is most important, superior in wisdom to his brothers, Naḥor and Haran. See further in Chapter 4, note 21 below.

Moshe.[7] Once again, the tribe of Reuven appears to want to lead but instead takes the position of a follower.

Abarbanel[8] insightfully adds that Reuven and Gad join in this quest because of their shared sense of injustice. Both tribes are overlooked eldest children. (Gad is the eldest child of Zilpa, Leah's maidservant.) They find commonality in their plight and join together to request land where they can be independent and rule themselves, separate from the rest of the Jewish people.[9]

Moshe's reaction to their request confirms his fear that Reuven and Gad could eventually abandon the Jewish people to start their own nation. A generation later in the book of Joshua (chapter 22), after a series of battles to conquer the land of Israel, Yehoshua sends Reuven and Gad back to their land on the other side of the Jordan River. Unfortunately, news spreads quickly that upon their return home they have built an altar of their own. Yehoshua imagines that his fears – and those of his master, Moshe – are materializing; Reuven and Gad are separating from the Jewish people and building a new place of worship in their own land outside of Israel. The Jewish people gather an army to wipe out the rebellious tribes. However, before battle, Yehoshua sends Pinḥas, grandson of Aharon, to ask Reuven and Gad about their intentions. They explain that the altar is a symbol for future generations to show that even if they live outside of Israel, they are truly part of the Jewish people. It is not a replacement for the Tabernacle. Even though the story ends peacefully, with war avoided, we can discern Yehoshua's instinctive reaction – his

7. This is one of many cases in the Torah where we see that names are out of order to teach us that the one listed first is the instigator. This is evident when Miriam's name is listed before Aharon's in the story of them speaking negatively about Moshe. Rashi notes that the reason for the order of names is to clarify that she is the instigator and that she speaks up before Aharon, thus explaining why only she is punished with *tzaraat* (Num. 12:1). Similarly, when Shem and Yafet cover their drunken father Noaḥ, Shem's name is listed first. Rashi there points out that this is meant to teach us that Shem was the instigator in saving their father from embarrassment and therefore deserved the greater blessing (Gen. 9:23).
8. See Abarbanel on Num. 32, in his answer to question one.
9. Rabbi S. R. Hirsch on Num. 32:1 explains their incentive to live outside of Israel was simply that "settling by themselves within special boundaries outside those of the general nation appealed to them."

concern that the tribe of Reuven's intention to live on the other side of the Jordan River was driven by a long-term goal to eventually start its own nation and be free from the rule of the younger tribes.

In fact, Reuven's isolation from the rest of the Jewish people has catastrophic implications for the tribe throughout the book of Judges. Each time an enemy attacks the territories on the eastern bank of the Jordan River, including the land of the tribe of Reuven, none of the other tribes come to defend them.[10] Until each enemy enters the land of Israel, there is ambivalence toward the plight of Reuven and Gad. Their separation from the rest of the nation ultimately precipitates the ruin of the tribe of Reuven when the tribe finally leads the Jewish people for the first time, but into exile. Reuven and Gad are the first tribes to be exiled during the time of Pul and Tilgat-Pilneser, the Kings of Assyria (I Chr. 5:26).

The tribe of Reuven has a tragic trajectory. It chases a dream of leadership, a false dream that can never be a reality. Reuven – the person and the tribe – lack the skills to lead but suffer from the ambition of leadership. As foretold by Yaakov on his deathbed, Reuven has lost all forms of leadership, and this will be the tribe's principal struggle throughout history.

---

10. During the period of Ehud, Moab passes through and conquers the land of Reuven on its path into the land of Binyamin (Judges ch. 3). During the period of Gidon, Midian certainly tramples through the land of Reuven on its way into the land of Menashe (Judges ch. 6). So too, in the period of Yiftaḥ, Amon demolishes the land of Reuven on its way up to the land of Menashe (Judges ch. 10).

*Chapter 4*

# Shimon and Levi in Genesis: The Troublesome Duo

> She conceived again, and bore a son, and said, "Because God has heard that I am hated, He has therefore also given me this son." She named him Shimon. She conceived again, and bore a son, and said, "Now this time will my husband be joined to me, because I have borne him three sons." Therefore, his name was called Levi. (Gen. 29:33–34)

The naming of each child born to Leah and Yaakov offers us a unique perspective into their relationship, mainly reflecting Leah's key emotions at the time of that birth. Reuven's name, as previously discussed, reveals his mother's hope that her husband might finally love her. She is naively optimistic in thinking that his birth would repair her domestic situation. By the time Shimon is born, it seems that all her hope is gone. Leah asserts that she is loathed and names her son accordingly. Shimon's name is therefore an expression of Leah's absolute despair. Even with two babies, she thinks that Yaakov hates her, and doesn't have any aspiration of improvement for the future.

Soon afterwards, however, the birth of Levi introduces a change in Leah's emotions since his name reflects her feelings of hope. After bearing a third son for Yaakov, she expects that her husband will begin to treat her differently. Perhaps her feelings are guided by anticipation for an intimacy born from pragmatism – she only has two hands but three sons.[1] Alternatively, she believes that Yaakov may actually start to love her now that she has proven her fertility and parenting ability. Leah supposes that if she can manage to rear three of Yaakov's sons, he will love her when she gives birth to even more children.[2] Maybe Yaakov has already changed his attitude and is now showing her and their new son more attention, as the naming of Levi is in masculine form, implying Yaakov's involvement.[3]

At the outset, let us posit two truths about Shimon and Levi, reflected in their names, which are manifest throughout their lives and continue well beyond their deaths.

First, the difficult relationship between Yaakov and Leah is evident to Shimon and Levi, as their names so obviously reflect the situation at home. Both brothers' lives are cast in the shadow of the sadness and antipathy that surrounds their mother. It causes them to grow up with strong feelings of anger against injustice, as they perceive the unfairness in the way their mother is treated. Thus they want to protect other members of the family of Leah, signaling their view that Yaakov deserves blame for discriminating against them and her.

Second, because Shimon and Levi are close in age and share the same mother and related life situations, they develop a particular bond. They become a duo that is uniquely described by their father on his deathbed as a brotherhood: "Shimon and Levi are brothers" (Gen. 49:5). Obviously, all of the tribes share a biological connection, but Yaakov specifically notes the camaraderie of these two, blessing them together.

In spite of their closeness and shared experiences, we will consider whether Shimon and Levi's primary early attributes are identical.

1. *Ḥizkuni* on Gen. 19:34.
2. Sforno on Gen. 29:34.
3. Radak on Gen. 29:34.

Does one of them instigate while the other follows, or are they equal partners in their endeavors? With regard to the selection of their names, how much relevance should be ascribed to Shimon's name, which represents Leah's anger and despair about her feeling of being hated by Yaakov, versus Levi's slightly more optimistic name?

Let us contemplate some of the key episodes of their lives. In this chapter, we will study the unique role played by Shimon and Levi in the episode with Shekhem and Dina. Subsequently, we will focus on Shimon's imprisonment in Egypt at the hands of Yosef. Finally, we will analyze the significance of Shimon's marriage to a Canaanite woman.

## SHEKHEM AND DINA

> It happened on the third day, when they were sore,[4] that two of Yaakov's sons, Shimon and Levi, Dina's brothers, each took his sword, came upon the unsuspecting city, and killed all the males. They killed Ḥamor and Shekhem, his son, with the edge of the sword, and took Dina out of Shekhem's house, and left. (Gen. 34:25–26)

Dina, the daughter of Leah, was kidnapped and raped by Shekhem. In reaction, Shimon and Levi swiftly and harshly decide to solve the injustice done to their sister: they kill the males of Shekhem's city and rescue their sister because they believe it is their responsibility to protect her from harm. Therefore, they consider their actions to be justifiable. They later defend themselves by saying, "Should he deal with our sister as with a prostitute?" (Gen. 34:31). They feel strongly that family members must stand up for each other! Shimon and Levi go to great lengths – even murder – to protect the safety and reputation of their family.

Is their behavior indeed justified? Specifically, were they allowed to murder Shekhem and Ḥamor in order to save their sister? Was it appropriate for them to kill all the men of the city? Did they go too far

4. This is referring to the men of Shekhem who underwent a circumcision, as part of the agreement between the brothers of Dina and the prince of Shekhem. The agreement was that the brothers would allow their sister to marry Shekhem if he had all the men of his city circumcised.

in their fit of revenge? To address these questions, let us begin by distinguishing between the reactions of Shimon and Levi as compared to Yaakov and as compared to the other brothers.

**Yaakov**

A palpable omission in this story is Yaakov's reaction to the sexual assault of his daughter. After raping Dina, Shekhem decides he wants to marry her and sends Ḥamor, his father, to negotiate an arrangement with Yaakov, her father. When Yaakov hears from Ḥamor about the travesty done to his daughter, he is silent (Gen. 34:5). His lack of response – saying and doing nothing, patiently waiting for his sons to come home – is shocking! It sits in stark contrast to the reaction of his sons. They lead the negotiations and design a plan, without any obvious consultation with their father.[5]

Instead of focusing his anger on the rape of his daughter, Yaakov only expresses anger in his censure of Shimon and Levi for murdering the people of the city. He blames them for ruining the family's reputation and causing the family to be in a situation where they fear retribution from the surrounding inhabitants.[6] He seems to have no words of rebuke or anger towards the rapist of his own daughter, but only for his sons who act in his stead.

Yaakov's passivity might have been the catalyst for Shimon and Levi's harsh reaction. They give vent to their anger on the city of Shekhem: their actions reflect their fury against its prince, Ḥamor, for raping their sister, as well as their resentment towards their father for his apparent lack of appropriate concern for the family of Leah.[7]

5. Verse 11 describes Shekhem talking with Yaakov and his sons. Two verses later it is only "the sons of Yaakov" (v. 13) who respond to Shekhem. Yaakov is no longer a visible participant in the conversation.
6. Yaakov's reaction is even more astonishing when we consider that this is the first time he rebukes his children. Yaakov was silent about the episode between Reuven and Bilha and was silent when his daughter was raped. As discussed in Chapter 2, one explanation for his silence after Reuven's action is his awareness that the harshest punishment for Reuven is precisely the lack of attention from his father.
7. This perspective is signaled by the language that the text uses to document Dina's genealogy. Initially, she is referred to as "daughter of Leah" (Gen. 34:1), thus reminding us that she is not Raḥel's daughter. Later she is referred to as a "daughter

**The Brothers**

In what ways do Shimon and Levi behave differently from the other brothers? Initially, all of the brothers react to Ḥamor's offer by negotiating the terms allowing the family to join together with Shekhem: he is to marry Dina and all the males of the city are to be circumcised.

> The sons of Yaakov answered Shekhem and Ḥamor his father with deceit, and spoke, because he had defiled Dina their sister. (Gen. 34:13)

All of the brothers, not just Shimon and Levi, were involved in this deceitful plan. Why, then, does Yaakov assign blame just to Shimon and Levi after the incident? Why are they alone held responsible?

The simplest response is that they were the only ones to commit the act of murdering the men of Shekhem. The individuals who actualize the plot deserve more blame than those whose role is limited to discussions and plans.[8]

Alternatively, perhaps Shimon and Levi modified the family's plan, thus doing more than the brothers agreed to. For example, the brothers' plan may have been to murder only Shekhem and Ḥamor, but Shimon and Levi decided to murder all of the city's men.[9]

A third explanation is that perhaps the brothers did not expect that the plan would come to fruition. They had no intention to murder anyone at all! Their plan was simply to offer a deal they thought was so ridiculous that there was no way Shekhem or Ḥamor would accept

---

of Yaakov" (Gen. 34:3), thereby explaining why Ḥamor comes to negotiate with Yaakov. She is then referred to as "sister of Shimon and Levi" and "their sister" (Gen. 34:13, 25, 27, 31). Substituting "daughter of Yaakov" with "sister of Shimon and Levi" highlights the discrepancy between her brothers' concern for her and her father's passive reaction. This point is a vital piece of information that explains the actions of Shimon and Levi. For further analysis of this language, see Rabbi Tamir Granot, "Power of Judgment, Shimon and Levi in Shekhem," https://www.etzion.org.il/en/power-judgment-shimon-and-levi-shekhem.

8. See Radak on Gen. 34:25 and Abarbanel at the end of his commentary on chapter 34.
9. Rabbi S. R. Hirsch on Gen. 34:25 writes that had Shimon and Levi killed only Shekhem and Ḥamor, their father wouldn't have said a word. It was only their action of killing the men of the city that deserved his rebuke.

it. Who would think that the males of the city would agree to be circumcised? They expected their proposal to be rejected and their sister returned.[10] And what would they do if the men of Shekhem did agree to circumcise themselves? On the third day following their circumcisions, when the pain would render them relatively powerless, the brothers would presumably enter the palace to rescue Dina. While rescuing Dina, it is Shimon and Levi alone who decide, unbeknownst to the rest of the brothers, to murder Shekhem, Ḥamor, and all the men of the city.[11]

If Shimon and Levi acted alone, then we truly see the solidarity between them and see them as a separate unit from the rest of the brothers. They view themselves as a unit acting together against the world of injustice and act without the permission of their father or even the approval of their brothers.

We are left with the question of whether their actions against the city of Shekhem are justifiable. Although revenge against the people who abused their sister is their rationalization for murdering of Shekhem and Ḥamor (Shekhem's father, who condones his actions and tries to justify them), how do we understand Shimon and Levi's reasoning for murdering all the males of the city?

### Murder of Shekhem and Ḥamor

The murder of Shekhem, and possibly that of his father, who justifies Shekhem's actions and tries to negotiate a deal on behalf of his son, is justified in rabbinic tradition. The transgressions of theft and of engaging in forbidden sexual relationships are both Noahide laws that even non-Jews such as Shekhem and Ḥamor would have been obligated to keep, and those that violate them are deserving of death.[12] Therefore, Shimon and Levi felt justified in killing them.[13]

---

10. This is exactly what is implied by their words "But if you do not listen to us, to be circumcised, then we will take our sister, and we will be gone" (Gen. 34:17). They appear to assume that their offer will be rejected.
11. See Ramban on Gen. 34:13, Bekhor Shor on 34:25, and *Shadal* on 34:13.
12. The seven Noahide Laws are referred to many times in the Talmud and listed in a baraita in Sanhedrin 56a–56b.
13. Most commentators, including Ramban (cf. above), critique Shimon and Levi only for murdering the men of the city but not for murdering Shekhem and Ḥamor.

**Murdering the Men of Shekhem**

While the killing of Shekhem and Ḥamor might be justifiable, what might justify slaying the other men of the city?[14]

Superficially, the simplest explanation is collective punishment. According to this explanation, the men of the city are culpable for not stopping Shekhem or holding him accountable for his treatment of Dina. They should have employed a system to judge him for his crime. For their lack of involvement, Shimon and Levi hold them

---

There are other explanations – motivated by linguistic and narrative considerations – for the justification of the murder of these two individuals. The sons of Yaakov describe the actions of Shekhem with the language "*nevala asa beYisrael*," "an outrage was done to Yisrael" (Gen. 34:7). This phrase is used again in two other places. In Deut. 22:21, when describing the act of rape, the verse says "*asta nevala beYisrael*," "for an outrage was done to Yisrael". This phrase also appears in a third story, found in the book of Joshua. After the destruction of Jericho, Yehoshua commands the Jewish people not to take any spoils of the land. Akhan disregards the command, steals some of the spoils, and hides them under his tent. His actions are described in the verse using the same words (Josh. 7:15). As a result, he is stoned to death by the Jewish people as commanded by God. Although the specific acts differ, his punishment is very similar to Shekhem's. The choice of this language shows that the appropriate reaction to this type of action is death. Furthermore, Shekhem's behavior has parallels to an equally heinous incident of rape during the reign of King David, when Prince Amnon, King David's oldest son, sexually assaults his half-sister Tamar. Amnon feigns illness and tricks his good-hearted, physically attractive half-sister, who innocently intends to nurse him back to health, into being alone with him, and then brutally rapes her. As in the story of Dina's rape, here too, there is no reaction by her father nor any consequences or demotion given to Amnon, the heir to the throne, for his evil deeds. It is Tamar's full brother, Avshalom, who avenges the crime by murdering Amnon. As the story continues, it is clear that Avshalom's anger is not limited to his brother Amnon, but is also directed at his father, David. Like Yaakov before him, David expresses anger at the avenger, Avshalom, but is silent about the criminal, Amnon, who committed a crime against a member of his family. Years later, Avshalom rapes ten of David's concubines and leads a rebellion against his father. Avshalom's general behavior seems eerily parallel to Shimon and Levi's reaction to the heinous crime and their father's inaction.

14. In fact, Ramban on Gen. 34:13 points out that Shekhem deserved death, but the rest of the city did not. His evidence: If they all deserved death, then Yaakov would have killed them.

liable.[15] They are so infuriated by the mistreatment of their sister that they blame every person who had any knowledge of the kidnapping.

Alternatively, Shimon and Levi may have felt a need to punish the entire city in order to send a clear message to all the surrounding nations: Do not mess with our sister! Shimon and Levi wanted to set a strong precedent that the women of the family of Yaakov are not to be harmed. Their family may be small, but that does not mean they can be pushed around.

A third possibility is that the reason has little to do with Yaakov's family, but rather with the implication of killing a king and a prince. Had they left survivors in Shekhem, Yaakov's family would have had to fear retribution or incrimination. Shimon and Levi avoided all of these concerns by killing all those who witnessed their crime.

However, if this is their reason for murdering the males of the city, then we are left baffled by their father's reaction to their conduct. When we analyze Yaakov's rebuke of Shimon and Levi, we learn that he may not have felt they were unjustified for this behavior! When Yaakov breaks his silence to reprimand his sons, we presume that he was displeased with their behavior. But the details of his rebuke don't exactly show that he is upset about the crime itself; rather, he seems to only care about the potential fallout. He says, "You have spoiled my reputation among those who live in the land. We are few in number and they will gather and destroy me and my home" (Gen. 34:30).

Yaakov never says that their actions were corrupt or immoral! His reprimand only expresses concern for how other clans may react to this episode and what impact it might have on the family's safety. If they did something wrong, he should have said that outright!

Ironically, Yaakov's fears prove unfounded, as the Torah reveals in the next chapter: "They traveled: and a terror of God was on the cities that were around them, and they didn't pursue the sons of Yaakov" (Gen. 35:5). The reaction of the other nations seems to

15. Rambam, quoted in Ramban on Gen. 34:13. See the list of Noahide laws in Sanhedrin 56a, where the mitzva of setting up courts is the first law.

legitimize the perspective of Shimon and Levi.[16] They demonstrated to the world not to trifle with their family, and that the daughters of Yaakov are off-limits.[17]

Another justification for their behavior might stem from Yaakov's reaction to their final defense of their actions: When they said, "Should he deal with our sister as with a prostitute?" (Gen. 34:31), Yaakov was silent and didn't respond. His sons interpret that silence as a form of agreement.[18] It is possible that Yaakov is convinced by their argument, so he stops his critique and walks away.[19] In summary, they felt justified in their attack of the city's inhabitants, and perhaps Yaakov agreed.

In addition to contrasting Shimon and Levi's actions to those of the other brothers and their father, a third vantage point might be helpful to consider regarding Shimon and Levi's behavior. What role did Ḥamor intend to play in this story? Recall that he was both the father of the attacker, Shekhem, as well as the king of the land. Under what pretenses did Ḥamor approach Yaakov to make a deal?

Amazingly, each time Ḥamor speaks, he adds a new angle to his perspective. At first, when Ḥamor negotiates with Yaakov and his

16. Admittedly, the other nations choosing to stay away from the family of Yaakov may not be *because* of the actions of Shimon and Levi, but *despite* them. After the family repents in Gen. 35, God may have repaired the harm caused by Shimon and Levi and ensured that no one would harm the family. This reading can be easily seen in the words "a terror of God was on the cities" (Gen. 35:5).
17. Rabbi S. R. Hirsch on 34:25 writes that "there are times when the family of Yaakov too must grasp the sword to protect the purity and honor of their women. They had no desire to act prudently. They wanted to make themselves feared so that nobody would attempt anything similar. The daughters of Yaakov were not to be considered as being at anybody's disposal."
18. In fact, there is a concept in Jewish law that when one is quiet it is considered as if he agrees. See, for example, Yevamot 87b–88a and Bava Metzia 37b.
19. Alternatively, it could be that when Yaakov walks away from them he is reflecting his disagreement with their plan. His rebuke of their behavior is deferred until right before he dies, when he reveals his feelings of disgust towards them, cursing their anger and actions.

    In many respects, Yaakov's reaction here resembles his reaction to Reuven's encounter with Bilha. Yaakov walks away silently without agreeing or disagreeing with his son. However, he reflects about the encounter on his deathbed.

family, he seems to present a reasonable offer to the sons of Yaakov: "Make marriages with us. Give your daughters to us, and take our daughters for yourselves. You shall dwell with us: and the land will be before you. Live and trade in it, and acquire possessions in it" (Gen. 34:9–10). His offer allows the sons of Yaakov to flourish in his land. It is to this deal that the brothers agree, with the condition that the men of Shekhem become circumcised. The brothers respond: "Then will we give our daughters to you, and we will take your daughters to us, and we will dwell with you, and we will become one people." (Gen. 34:16)

However, when Ḥamor repeats the deal to his people, he appears motivated by the opportunity to acquire Yaakov's wealth: "Won't their cattle and their substance and all their animals be ours? Only let us give our consent to them, and they will dwell with us" (Gen. 34:23). In fact, this verse reveals the real motivation behind the consent of all the men of Shekhem. The only reason they would agree to mutilate their bodies is to gain access to all of the possessions of the family of Yaakov.

If so, it seems reasonable that Shimon and Levi could have uncovered this conspiracy against their family, and therefore felt the entire city was worthy of punishment.[20] Furthermore, Malbim on Gen. 34:25–26 proposes that the entire city of Shekhem had already gathered around the palace, ready to wage war against the family of Yaakov if they tried to steal Dina away from Prince Shekhem. Later, they remained at their posts, ready to fight, in order to punish the family for making them endure the pain of circumcision. Shimon and Levi were not only murdering people that intended to steal all their money, but people that were already gathered with the intention of murdering their family. The only way to get into the castle to rescue

---

20. See Abarbanel at the end of his commentary on chapter 34, where he writes that the true intention of the men of Shekhem was to take all of Yaakov's possessions! From Abarbanel's words, we can understand that this is the reason the brothers were allowed to loot the city and take their things. Shimon and Levi were justified in murdering them because they were at fault for not preventing their leader from being involved in the major crimes of forbidden relations and thievery, and for not holding him responsible for his crimes, as well as for their desire to steal the wealth of Yaakov.

their sister was to kill all the men of the city who were standing guard around the palace walls.

Each of these approaches suggests the same strong characteristics of anger and zealotry in Shimon's and Levi's personalities. Their anger is clear: They are incensed by the abuse of their sister, as well as their father's lack of apparent concern, and both reasons lead to their revenge. Their zealousness is manifest in the drastic methods with which they engage with the enemy as they murder an entire city in reaction to a crime against their sister.

Through these actions, they demonstrate their strong connection to family and their sense of responsibility to protect its members. They feel they have no choice other than to fight the injustice done to their sister, especially since their father is virtually absent.

As noted earlier, it is unclear whether these behavioral attributes are equally applicable to the two brothers, or if one brother leads and the other follows. What evidence for either claim might we glean from this episode?

Throughout the story, Shimon's name precedes Levi's name. This could simply reflect birth order; however, it may be hinting to Shimon's enhanced role.[21] In either case, this naming order makes it unlikely that Levi is the leader and Shimon the follower.[22]

Irrespective of whether we find evidence in this story to differentiate Shimon from Levi, there are other episodes to consider. In fact, there are two important narratives in Genesis where Shimon is referenced without Levi. These stories may offer us insight into how to Shimon and Levi diverge.

---

21. A similar discussion is found in Sanhedrin 69b regarding the order of names in the story of Avraham, who is listed before his brothers in the Torah (Gen. 11:26–27). The Talmud presents two approaches: the order of the names is based on either chronology or importance. Similarly, one can use either approach to explain why Miriam is listed before Aharon in Numbers 12:1. It is either because she is older, or because she instigated the slander against Moshe. Rashi takes the second approach and states that the order of their names indicates that she spoke first and Aharon listened, further evidenced by the verb being written in the singular feminine form, "*vatedaber*," "and she spoke."
22. See Chapter 3 for a discussion regarding the order of Reuven's and Gad's names as provided in Numbers 32.

## JAILED BY YOSEF

Let's fast forward to Genesis 42. The ten oldest sons of Yaakov descend to Egypt to collect food during the famine. Yosef has become the viceroy of Egypt and is in charge of rationing the food that was stored during the seven years of plenty.

How traumatic it must have been for Yosef when the brothers, who had thrown him in a pit and sold him as a slave, come begging for food. Yosef immediately recognizes his brothers, but they do not realize who he is. In his role as Egyptian viceroy, he accuses them of spying and throws them all in jail for three days. After releasing them, he provides them with food to take home, along with a command to return with their youngest brother, Binyamin. As they are about to leave, Yosef does one final act: he sends Shimon to jail, thus preventing him from returning home to Yaakov with his brothers (Gen. 42:24).

Why does Yosef select Shimon for this treatment? It is very unlikely that the selection is random, since everything Yosef does in this story seems intentional. Presumably, there must be an explanation behind Yosef's selection of Shimon.

At first glance, Yosef chooses Shimon because he fears him. The episode with Shekhem likely convinced Yosef that he is better off locking up Shimon, thus avoiding the physical threat he presents. Why does he not also jail Levi? Perhaps he is not as violent as Shimon, at least when left unprovoked by Shimon. Alternatively, maybe he has decided that he should jail one of them, but the selection of Shimon over Levi is random.[23]

Yosef's motivation to imprison Shimon may not just be to protect himself; it might have additional significance. Shimon is thrown into jail immediately after the brothers admit their guilt about the episode that occurred years earlier, when they had heard Yosef scream, pleading for his life, but they ignored him (Gen. 42:21). The language describing the brothers speaking to one another in Egypt is "*vayomeru ish el aḥiv,*" "and one man said to his brother." This is the exact same phrase that was used on the day that Yosef was sold to Egypt. Back then, when Yosef came to check on his brothers, the verse begins with the exact same words:

23. This is the second view quoted in Rashi on Gen. 42:24. Yosef is scared that if left together, Shimon and Levi might murder him, so he separates them.

"*Vayomeru ish el aḥiv.*" The brothers continue, "Here comes the dreamer! Let us kill him and throw his body into one of the pits and claim that a wild animal ate him" (Gen. 37:19–20). The linguistic parallel might be a way of connecting our story in Egypt, where a brother is thrown in jail, to this earlier event. Yosef singles out and incarcerates the brother who suggested Yosef's murder, a plan that included throwing his dead body into a pit.[24] So Yosef reacts against Shimon, who had earlier plotted his murder in reaction to a perceived injustice by their father against the family of Leah.

On the other hand, even if Yosef had not overheard the brothers' conversation regarding killing him, it might have been Shimon who orchestrated the actual physical acts against Yosef, i.e., lifting him up, restraining him, and throwing him into the pit, thus causing Yosef to believe that it was Shimon's idea all along. Now, years later, it is only logical that he restrains the same brother who threw him into the pit.[25] Shimon's willingness to throw his brother into a pit to die highlights again that Shimon's anger is even stronger than that of the rest of the brothers.

But there is a second layer to understanding this story, beyond Yosef's reaction to Shimon. How does the rest of the family perceive him, and what attempt do they make to redeem him? When the brothers return from Egypt without Shimon, Yaakov immediately discounts any possibility of saving him. Yaakov nonchalantly states that Shimon is gone and there is no hope for his return: "You have bereaved me of my children! Yosef is no more, Shimon is no more, and you want to take

24. This is Rashi's first explanation of this episode, found in his commentary on Gen. 42:24. Later, commenting on Gen. 49:25, Rashi provides further support for this view by systematically rejecting the possibility that any of the other brothers was part of this conversation. He says that it couldn't have been Reuven who suggested the plan because he is the one who tells the brothers not to kill Yosef. It couldn't have been Yehuda because he later suggests selling Yosef. It couldn't have been the maidservants' children because they didn't hate Yosef. It couldn't have been Yissakhar and Zevulun because they would never speak up in the presence of their older brothers. So the brothers referred to by "*ish el aḥiv*," "one man to his brother," must be Shimon and Levi, which resembles Yaakov's recognition of them as "*aḥim*," "brothers," on his deathbed (Gen. 49:5).
25. This is especially fitting because the word "*bor*," "pit," is used in the text to describe both jail and the pit (Gen. 37:24, 40:15).

Binyamin away. All these things are against me" (Gen 42:36). There is no discussion of sending the brothers on a rescue mission to save Shimon! Even when the brothers propose a plan to their father that would allow them to bring Binyamin to Egypt, there is no urgency to liberate Shimon. It seems clear that Yaakov would never be willing to risk the life of his then-favorite son, Binyamin, on Shimon's behalf.

Only when Yehuda finally convinces his father to let him be accountable for Binyamin and return to Egypt with him does Yaakov voice any optimism about Shimon's return. He states: "May God Almighty give you mercy before the man, that he may release to you your other brother and Binyamin. If I am bereaved of my children, I am bereaved" (Gen. 43:14). However, he does not utter Shimon's name, but rather refers to him as "your other brother." Ramban on 43:14 writes that there are three distinct readings of this verse.[26] First, Yaakov is referring to Shimon, but because of his aversion to him and his actions with Shekhem, he can't bring himself to state his name. Second, he quotes Rashi, who writes that the word "brother" refers to Yosef, and "other" refers to Shimon. Shimon is described as nothing more than an unnamed "other!" Last, he quotes another view found in the Sages that completely excludes Shimon. "*Aḥikhem*," "your brothers," refers to the all of the brothers going down to Egypt. "*Aḥer ve'et Binyamin*," "the other and Binyamin," emphasizes Yaakov's hope for particular assistance from God to protect Yehuda, who is accompanying Binyamin down to Egypt. If so, there is no mention of Shimon at all. Accordingly, Yaakov appears to harbor no real consideration for Shimon to ever return home.[27] What is he hopeful for? One can posit that he is hoping that Yosef – the son he believes to be dead – will be found alive, or that he is hoping that Binyamin will come home safely with the other brothers, but he does not have any thoughts about Shimon here.

Collectively, these perspectives shine a light on Yaakov's perception of his second son. He seems, at best, indifferent to Shimon, and he is possibly even angry or antagonistic.

---

26. These readings are based on the many views found in the Sages, quoted in Genesis Rabba 92:3.
27. See Rashi on Gen. 43:14.

Since this story of Yosef jailing one brother focuses exclusively on Shimon and not at all on Levi, it might suggest something unique about Shimon. As we will see, the fact that only Shimon is jailed is not the only factor that distinguishes Shimon from Levi.

### MARRYING A CANAANITE

Genesis 46 presents the names of all the members of Yaakov's household who accompany him to Egypt. The Torah notes a child of Shimon who is a son of a Canaanite woman. The patriarchs of Israel do not marry women from Canaan. Avraham sends his servant to Aram, his hometown, to find Yitzḥak a wife, instructing him that under no circumstances may Yitzḥak marry a Canaanite woman. Yitzḥak continues this tradition by commanding his son Yaakov not to take a wife from the daughters of Canaan (Gen. 24:3, 37, 28:1). Even Esav knows that "the women of Canaan were bad in the eyes of Yitzḥak his father" (Gen. 28:8). So too, in Deuteronomy, God charges the Jewish people not to marry into the nations of Canaan when they enter into Israel (Deut. 7:3). Therefore, at least superficially, when Shimon marries a woman from Canaan, he is rejecting his family's values. This behavior might make sense for a son who is angry with his father for the mistreatment to his mother and who feels abandoned during his period in jail. Marrying a woman from Canaan strikes a blow against his father.[28]

However, it may not be fair to censure Shimon for having married a Canaanite woman. It actually might be true that all of the sons of Yaakov married women from Canaan. While their father, grandfather, and great-grandfather were not allowed to marry Canaanite women, we hear of no warning to Yaakov's sons not to marry Canaanite women. Perhaps the prohibition did not apply to them.[29] Why this distinction?

28. Ibn Ezra on Gen. 46:10 writes that in this list of Yaakov's grandchildren, the only one listed as born to a Canaanite woman is a child of Shimon's, proving that he did something wrong when he married her.
29. This is debated in Genesis Rabba 84:19, where R. Yehuda asserts that the sons of Yaakov were not allowed to marry women from Canaan, and therefore each married their half-sisters. R. Neḥemia says they married local women from Canaan. Ramban on 38:2 quotes this midrash and attempts to limit R. Neḥemia's assertion,

The patriarchs were individuals who lived on their own, away from a family support system. If they had married local women, they might have been susceptible to being influenced by those women's families and their values. Once the family of Yaakov was established, a wife of one of his sons would be influenced by her husband's family and imbibe their values.[30] If this is true, then Shimon did nothing wrong – or even unusual – when he married a Canaanite woman.

A third possibility shared by the Sages offers a different perspective on Shimon and his Canaanite wife. The Sages suggest that perhaps this Canaanite woman is actually his sister Dina, who had a son after she was impregnated by Shekhem, a Canaanite. The child noted in the list of Yaakov's family is Dina and Shekhem's son.[31] Shimon adopted his sister's son as his own. This suggestion reveals a protective, brotherly aspect of Shimon's personality.

There is one last possibility for how identifying this wife and son affects our understanding of Shimon's personality. Rather than defining the Hebrew "*ben haKenaanit*" as "child of a Canaanite woman," it can be translated more loosely. Numbers Rabba 21 writes that the title is descriptive of a certain model of behavior. This explanation posits that Shimon's son from the Canaanite woman, Shaul, is a sinner, who acts like a Canaanite.[32] Potentially, this might reflect a relationship between

---

claiming that they did marry local women but only those who originated from other countries, such as Amon and Moab. If so, even R. Neḥemia agrees that the tribes were forbidden from marrying Canaanite women.

30. See Rabbi Elchanan Samet, "Yehuda and Tamar – A Story Within a Story?" at http://etzion.org.il/en/yehuda-and-tamar-story-within-story.

31. Rashi on 46:10 writes that Dina agreed to leave Ḥamor's palace only if Shimon would marry her; effectively, Dina and Shekhem's son becomes Shimon's stepson.

32. In Gen. 38, Yehuda marries a daughter of a man from Canaan as well, who is referred to as a "Canaanite" in I Chr. 2:3. Pesaḥim 50a translates this word as "merchant," refusing to translate it literally. It is inconceivable that Yehuda would marry a woman from Canaan, knowing that the patriarchs were forbidden from doing so. Interestingly, there is no similar statement in the Talmud about Shimon, nor do the commentators translate "*haKenaanit*" as merchant in the verse about Shimon. Clearly, that Shimon would rebel against his family values is not a surprise or impossibility, and therefore it does not require reinterpretation.

Shimon and his son: the father who misbehaves creates a son who follows in his footsteps.[33]

To summarize, the fact that Shimon has a son who is titled "the son of a Canaanite woman" calls into question whether this is a further act of rebellion against his father. This explanation asserts that in harboring so much anger against his father for the mistreatment of his mother, sister, and brothers, Shimon rejects his father by marrying a woman who would be the subject of his father's disapproval.[34]

## BLESSING OF YAAKOV

> "Shimon and Levi are brothers; weapons of violence are their swords. My soul, don't come into their council; my glory, don't be united to their assembly; for in their anger they killed a man, in their self-will they hamstrung an ox. Cursed be their anger, for it was fierce, and their wrath, for it was cruel. I will divide them in Yaakov, scatter them in Israel." (Gen. 49:5–7)

As the final words on his deathbed, Yaakov blesses each of his sons with a unique message. However, he speaks to Shimon and Levi together as a unit, giving one message to both. In it, he reprimands their actions and reproaches them for their anger. His words are so harsh that they sound more like a curse than a blessing.[35] Commentators debate if these words are referring only to the murder of Shekhem, or if Yaakov

33. The Talmud in Sanhedrin 82b states that Shaul, the son of the Canaanite woman, is really Zimri, who is intimate with a Midianite woman, thereby acting like the Canaanites.

34. This might remind the reader of the reaction of Yitzḥak when Esav marries a Canaanite woman: "When Esav was forty years old, he took as wife Yehudit, the daughter of Be'eri the Hittite, and Bassemat, the daughter of Eilon the Hittite. They were a grief of mind for Yitzḥak and Rivka" (Gen. 26:34–35). Even Esav recognized this as an act of rebellion towards his father's values: "Esav saw that the daughters of Canaan didn't please Yitzḥak, his father," (Gen. 28:8), which motivated him to marry another wife from the family of Yishmael.

35. Sforno on 49:5 writes that within these words, Yaakov is expressing a punishment: As a result of their actions, they will also be passed over for kingship, like their older brother Reuven. The monarchy will be given to the next son in line, Yehuda.

is also blaming them for hurting Yosef as well.[36] It seems that Yaakov observes the potential for future negative repercussions as a result of their actions in Genesis.

Yaakov concludes his remarks with a punishment: "They will be divided among Yaakov and scattered in Israel." At first glance, it seems he punishes both brothers equally. Rashbam on 49:7 writes that the goal is to keep Shimon and Levi apart throughout history, to avoid the dangerous dynamic caused by their partnership. Yaakov is cursing the actions of these two brothers when they act as a unit. Apart, they are not as dangerous, and therefore the conclusion is to separate them.

However, there is an additional way to understand these words of Yaakov, which highlights another difference between Shimon and Levi.[37] Even though they are equally reprimanded, the follow-through of the punishment differs vastly. After the Jewish people enter Israel and Yehoshua divides up the land, the tribe of Shimon is given a portion of land that is located inside of the property of Yehuda (Josh. 19:9). Shimon is intentionally placed on the southern border of Israel, fully surrounded by an appointed watchman, as it were, in the form of Yehuda, to ensure that he conducts himself appropriately.[38] In contrast, Levi's tribe is scattered throughout the land, living in Levite cities inside other tribes' territories (Josh. 21:3–7). The tribe of Levi lives among the Jewish people because, as history will prove, Levi can be a positive influence in a contained environment. The benefit of his tribe being present all through the land is its ability to thereby teach and influence everyone.[39]

---

36. Rashi on 49:5 writes that the first part ("*hargu ish*," "they killed a man") is referring to Shekhem, and the second ("*ikru shor*," "they hamstrung an ox") is referring to Yosef. But Ramban, Ibn Ezra, and Radak all agree that the entire curse is referring to Shekhem. "*Shor*," "ox," which is a very large animal, could be referring to Shekhem, the prince of the land, or more literally to the animals they killed.
37. Radak on 49:7 writes that the words of Yaakov are the reason for the future inheritance and exact locations of the land given to the tribes of Shimon and Levi.
38. This explains why Yehuda joins with Shimon to fight for their territory in Israel in Judges ch. 1, as Shimon's land is located inside the territory of Yehuda.
39. Being the teachers of the Jewish people is the role given to the tribe of Levi in Deuteronomy 17:9–10: "And you shall come to the priests, the Levites, and to the judge who shall be in those days: and you shall inquire; and they shall show you

However, to avoid the pitfalls of his aggression, Yaakov's blessing foretells that they are to be scattered.

### SHIMON VERSUS LEVI

Shimon and Levi play similar roles in the stories of Genesis. They both display traits of extreme anger and hatred of injustice. They tend to overreact, and therefore both tribes need to be scattered later in history. Nevertheless, there are many reasons to think that Shimon was the real aggressor in their partnership.

The characteristics of Shimon and Levi – such as their zealous protection of family – are not necessarily negative. In fact, in the right context, each of their behaviors can be constructive and valuable. In the next chapter we will see how Levi's descendants are able to use these qualities for either good or evil, but Shimon's offspring utilize the traits only for evil. In that case we must ask why Yaakov would curse the brothers equally. Why not speak to each separately, cursing the one who deserves the curse and blessing the one who deserves to be blessed?

We can simply answer that he was cursing only those who would use these traits for evil in the future, whether they were from the tribe of Shimon or Levi. However, the *Toldot Yitzḥak* on Gen. 49:5–7 paints a slightly different picture. He observes that Yaakov envisioned both virtue and challenge in their futures, but lacked the clarity to know who would produce worthy descendants and who would have evil children. Thus, Yaakov had a dilemma. How could he curse someone who would later generate Moshe, the leader of the Jewish people? But at the same time, how could he bless someone who would have sinful descendants, like Zimri? Therefore, Yaakov doesn't curse Shimon and Levi! Instead, he curses their actions and their anger. Yaakov wasn't sure which tribe would redeem itself in history, and consequently left his message intentionally vague. Unfortunately, Shimon's descendants manifest all of these attributes in a negative way. In contrast, many of Levi's descendants become the greatest leaders in history. While we

---

the sentence of judgment. You shall do according to the tenor of the sentence they shall show you from that place which God shall choose; and you shall observe to do according to all that they shall teach you."

are left questioning the exact roles played by Shimon and Levi in the stories in Genesis, there is no question that their descendants develop into clear personality and moral types.

*Chapter 5*

# Shimon and Levi in Tanakh

As we saw in the previous chapter, Shimon and Levi grow up in a challenging family situation. They are born to an unloved mother, their father seemingly ignores the rape of their sister, and their younger half-brother is the primary recipient of their father's affection. Their lives exhibit moments of acting out based on anger and zealotry, which they demonstrate when they murder an entire city to avenge their sister's mistreatment. Lastly, we noticed that there may be differences between the experiences of Shimon and those of Levi, as Shimon seems to misbehave on his own, not just in coordination with Levi. Let's consider how these factors are reflected in the lives of their descendants.

## SHIMON IN TANAKH

Unfortunately, Shimon's anger and fanaticism will plague his descendants throughout history. He will have children who revolt against authority and protest injustices. This behavior will limit their ability to attain any meaningful leadership positions. In fact, their role among the Jewish people will be constrained in an attempt to avoid the potential anger and fanaticism, which includes living in a secluded location, away from their partner, the tribe of Levi.

**Zimri – Prince of the Tribe of Shimon**

Numbers 25 introduces Zimri, the prince and leader of the tribe of Shimon, when he is steering a group of demonstrators against Moshe at the rebellion of Baal Peor. This is the only story about an individual from the tribe of Shimon in the Torah. As part of Midian's endeavor to destroy the Jewish people, after Bilam's failed attempt to curse the Jewish nation, the women of Midian and Moab enter the Jewish camp to seduce the men and sway them to serve idols. Moshe sends the leaders of the tribes to slay those who are sinning in order to prevent the spread of their influence. Zimri, the tribal leader of Shimon, explicitly contradicts Moshe's command. Instead of fighting those who are sinning, he joins them. He has sexual relations with a Midianite woman "in front of the eyes of Moshe and the eyes of entire Jewish people" (Num. 25:6). From the emphasis on the public nature of his action, clearly this is not an act focused on personal enjoyment; rather, it is a public display of rebellion against the authority of Moshe. He does not secretly sin; he shamelessly violates the command of the leader openly, trying to incite those around him to do the same.

The Sages[1] focus on Shimon's rebellion against the perceived injustice of this situation. Zimri and the tribe of Shimon are personally attacking Moshe's family life. The backstory begins in Exodus 2, when Moshe flees from Pharaoh after killing an Egyptian. He settles in Midian and marries Tzippora, the daughter of Yitro, priest of Midian. Zimri is questioning Moshe's right to marry outside of the Jewish people. He is highlighting a contradiction between the leader's actions and his rhetoric: He says not to marry them, but he himself is married to one. Moshe just commanded all the leaders to kill all the men who are engaging in relations with women who come from the same place as his own wife! To revolt against this inconsistency, Zimri publicly takes a Midianite woman and has carnal relations with her as an open challenge to Moshe. In this midrash, it is not only Zimri who is attacking Moshe,

1. See Sanhedrin 82a.

but it is the entire tribe who is questioning Moshe's actions. They are all bothered by the injustice of this apparent moral inconsistency, and therefore they follow Zimri's lead in publicly questioning Moshe.[2]

There is one more layer of meaning offered by the Sages.[3] The Talmud writes that Kozbi, the Midianite woman taken by Zimri, is really a Midianite princess. Part of the textual evidence for this is the focus on her name, which is mentioned in Num. 25:8. Tangential characters' names are not usually recorded in the text of the Torah because their identities are not significant. At first blush, it would seem sufficient to refer to her as an anonymous Midianite woman. From the inclusion of her name in the text we can learn that her identity is evidently vital to our understanding of the story. Zimri's act of rebellion is so much worse because he doesn't just have relations with a random Midianite woman, but with the princess herself! Of course, this further attacks the seeming hypocrisy of Moshe, who had married the daughter of the priest of Midian so many years earlier.

The *Midrash Aggada* on Num. 25:2 writes that she is actually the daughter of King Balak, the man who wanted to murder the entire Jewish people. Zimri would thus have been considered as siding with the enemy, effectively acting as a traitor.

The Talmud[4] takes this line of thinking a step further. When Zimri engages Kozbi, she tells him that she will only consent to the greatest man of the Jewish people. Zimri replies that he is a prince, the prince of the tribe of Shimon. He argues that he is greater than Moshe because he is a descendant of Shimon, Yaakov's second-born, while Moshe is from Levi, Yaakov's third-born. According to this story, Zimri is having relations with the woman who was sent to seduce Moshe himself! He

---

2. Rashi on Num. 25:6 quotes the Talmud from Sanhedrin 82b which describes how the entire tribe of Shimon, with Zimri their leader and the Midianite woman, question Moshe, saying, "Is she allowed or forbidden? If you say forbidden, what gives you the right to marry the daughter of Yitro?" Rashi on Gen. 49:6 states that this future act of the whole tribe against Moshe is one of the reasons that Yaakov curses Shimon on his deathbed with the words "amongst them my soul should not come."
3. See Sanhedrin 82a, where she is described as a princess. On the next page, she is identified as Shevilnai, the daughter of Tzur. She is called Kozbi, a name derived from the Hebrew root *kaf, zayin, bet,* meaning to deceive, because she didn't listen to her father, who had told her to seduce the leader of the Jewish people.
4. See Sanhedrin 82a.

tricks her by claiming that he is superior to Moshe, thereby directly contesting Moshe's leadership.

### The Role of the Tribe of Shimon

> There is no tribe of all of the tribes that did not have one judge [i.e., leader] come from them. (Sukkah 27b)

The Talmud posits that every tribe had at least one opportunity for an individual from their tribe to have a leadership position among the Jewish people.[5] *Yalkut Shimoni* I:247 adds that this is true for all tribes except the tribe of Shimon, because of the act of Zimri. The tribe of Shimon is rejected from leadership as punishment for Zimri's rebellion. The midrash concludes that in addition to there being no individuals from Shimon who lead, the tribe of Shimon lacks collective leadership. The tribe's placement is in the encampment of Reuven, so during the forty years in the desert, Shimon is led by his older brother. Once they enter Israel, he is given land inside the territory of Yehuda and follows Yehuda's lead in conquering the land (Judges 1:3).[6] Shimon is even left out of Moshe's final blessings to the Jewish people.[7] Shimon is the forgotten tribe in our history. No leaders, no role at all.

5. This idea is based on the verse in II Sam. 7:7, where God states, "In all the places where I have walked with all the children of Israel, I have said one thing to all the tribes of Israel whom I commanded to shepherd my nation Israel." God speaks to leaders of the Jewish people from all the children, from all of the tribes. That there are other tribes without a national leader will be addressed in subsequent chapters of this volume.
6. The language used to describe Shimon's role under Yehuda's leadership, "*vayelekh ito Shimon*," "and Shimon went with him" (Judges 1:3), parallels the language of Lot following Avraham to Israel, "*Vayelekh ito Lot*," "and Lot went with him" (Gen. 12:4). Both are blindly following their leader, as they have no other choice.
7. Rashi on Deut. 33:7 writes that it is possible that Moshe hinted to the tribe of Shimon in his blessing to Yehuda, when he says "*Shema Hashem kol Yehuda*," "God should listen to voice of Yehuda" (Deuteronomy 33:7). This hints to Shimon, who is located within the territory of Yehuda. Ibn Ezra on 33:6 writes that Moshe leaves Shimon out because most of the sinners of Baal Peor who are seduced by Midianite women, as well as their leader, are from the tribe of Shimon. Ralbag on Num. 26:10 adds that Shimon was involved in *most* of the complaints and sins in the desert.

**LEVI IN TANAKH**

As we established from the stories in Genesis, Levi shares much of Shimon's anger and passion in the face of injustice. He, too, murders all the males of Shekhem in order to punish them for the atrocity done to his sister. These exact qualities will repeat themselves in the stories and personalities of Levi's descendants. In contrast to Shimon, many of Levi's offspring will utilize these traits productively, to wipe out evil and to lead the Jewish people, but unfortunately, there will remain some negative manifestations of these attributes in the tribe of Levi as well.

Before we study Levi's descendants to determine how much they reflect his key attributes, it will be helpful to consider why the basic traits found in some of our villains from Shimon's and Levi's families are instrumental to some of our leaders. What is it about these attributes – i.e., anger and zealotry – that motivates heroic leadership?

There is actually a fairly straightforward explanation. The leadership that is manifest in Levi and his progeny is infused with passion. Leaders from this tribe are less focused on the various styles of intellectual or calculated leadership that are more commonly found in descendants of Yosef or Yehuda. Passion reveals itself in numerous ways, two of which are anger and zealotry. What Levi learns to do, and Shimon does not, is to channel his passion productively. His children learn how to use their passion to remedy the ills of society and to fight for meaningful causes.

---

He infers this from the change in population during the period in the desert. Specifically, the numbers of eligible male soldiers from the tribe of Shimon decreases from 59,300 to 22,200. Ralbag concludes that this significant decrease must be the result of a punishment due to Shimon's involvement in many sins, rebellions, and complaints. Similarly, he suggests this is also the reason that Moshe does not bless their tribe, and that Yaakov's blessing is really a curse. Ramban on Deut. 33:6 asserts that sinning alone is not the reason they are excluded from the blessings, as the rest of the Jewish people sinned with the golden calf and the spies but they were forgiven and blessed. Rather, there must be a different reason for Shimon's exclusion from the blessings. We should note that the Jewish people are always counted (or listed or blessed) as a unit comprising twelve tribes. Since Yosef's two sons are each counted as separate tribes at this point, there would be thirteen; therefore, Moshe removed Shimon from the counting for three reasons: his was not a big tribe, he was not blessed by Yaakov on his deathbed, and he doesn't have his own inheritance of land.

Ultimately, the evidence that anger and zealotry can be positive attributes can be seen in God Himself. The Torah often describes God as being angry (see Ex. 4:14, 32:10 and Num. 11:1, 10, 12:9, 22:22, 25:3, 32:10, 13). Similarly, God is described as "a zealous God" (see Ex. 20:4, 34:14 and Deut. 4:24, 5:8, 6:15). Given that these traits are descriptions of God, we should expect them to be part of the personality of our greatest leaders.

**Anger**

Moshe, the ultimate leader from the tribe of Levi, sometimes expresses anger. Often, this anger is a reflection of his frustration with the behavior and attitude of the people, especially those who saw and directly experienced God's miracles. Each time members of the Jewish nation do not listen to the words of God, he becomes enraged. For instance, he is infuriated by a group of Jews who save manna until the next day instead of believing that God would provide more (Ex. 16:20).[8] Moshe is visibly irate when the people sin via the golden calf (Ex. 32:19), leading him to break the precious holy tablets.[9] He becomes irritated when people complain about the manna and request meat (Num. 11:10).[10] And he is incensed at Datan and Aviram when they accuse him of not taking the Jewish people into the land of Israel (Num. 16:15).[11] Moshe is so exasperated by the Jewish people's request for water that he accuses them of being rebellious people, and he hits the rock twice (Num. 20:10–11). As we noted above, he flares up when they don't kill all the women in the war against Midian (Num. 31:14).[12] To summarize, Moshe clearly shows his anger at the Jewish people, but only when they undermine God's command or show incomplete faith.

Displaying anger is not limited to Moshe. This trait is also found in other famous descendants of Levi. Many generations after the death of Moshe, Eli the high priest becomes very angry and accuses Ḥana, who is silently praying to God, of drunkenness in the Tabernacle (I Sam. 1:14).

---

8. The verse says "*Vayiktzof aleihem Moshe,*" "And Moshe was angry at them."
9. The verse says "*Vayiḥar af Moshe,*" "And Moshe was angry."
10. The verse says "*Uve'einei Moshe ra,*" "And it was bad in Moshe's eyes."
11. The verse says "*Vayiḥar leMoshe meod,*" "And Moshe was very angry."
12. The verse says "*Vayiktzof Moshe,*" "And Moshe was angry."

Similarly, Shmuel the prophet becomes so upset at the Jewish people when they ask for a king that he admonishes them three times for their request (I Sam. chs. 8, 10, 12). He even asks God to shower them with miraculous rain to prove that they were wrong.

The trait of anger is found in numerous descendants of Levi. Often, the anger is directed toward those who are sinning against God. However, at times, their anger is wrongfully directed at someone undeserving of their wrath. It is not a surprise that Moshe's inability to control his temper when the Jewish people ask for water is the sin that prevents him from entering Israel. [13]

**Fighting Against Injustice**

As noted earlier, another of Levi's defining attributes is the desire to right a wrong and fight against wrongdoers if necessary. This trait is repeatedly displayed by his descendants.

The Torah's introduction of Moshe in Exodus chapter 2 focuses on his struggle against injustice. At the outset, he kills an Egyptian to prevent the brutal beating of an elderly Jewish slave. Soon afterward, he attempts to prevent one Jewish man from hitting another. After running away from Egypt and entering Midian, his first act is to chase away shepherds who are preventing Tzippora and her sisters from drawing water from a well. Moshe's sense of justice is not limited to protecting Jews. Any person who is being abused is the beneficiary of his help, which he feels compelled to offer as a result of his aversion to injustice. In fact, Ibn Ezra on Gen. 2:3 writes that it is this particular pattern of conduct – fighting wrong and immoral behavior – that earns Moshe the role of

13. There is a disagreement among the commentators as to the sin of Moshe at Mei Meriva. However, most mention the issue of Moshe losing his temper at the Jewish people. Rashi on Num. 20:10 claims his sin was hitting the rock instead of speaking to it. Ramban on 20:8 states that the problem was hitting the rock twice instead of once. Rambam (quoted in Ramban on 20:8) writes that his sin was losing his temper and calling the Jewish people "rebellious people." *Ha'amek Davar* on 20:8–11 writes that because Moshe was angry, he forgot to lead the people in prayer. All of these commentaries have in common that Moshe lost his temper and therefore acted inappropriately. Moshe's reaction directly contrasts that of God, who shows no anger at their request for water.

leader of the Jewish people. Only an individual who spends his life battling injustice is worthy to lead the fight against as great a wrong as the slavery of the Jewish people in Egypt.

There are, however, times that this trait may be overextended by other descendants of Levi:

### Miriam and Aharon

> Miriam and Aharon spoke against Moshe because of the Cushite woman whom he had married; for he had married a Cushite woman. They said, "Has God indeed spoken only with Moshe? Hasn't he spoken also with us?" God heard it. (Num. 12:1–2)

Aharon and Miriam, Moshe's siblings, speak amongst themselves to report an injustice. They believe that Moshe's treatment of his wife Tzippora is unjust. Even if the person to blame is their own brother, whom they have supported throughout his leadership, Aharon and Miriam prove that Levites will always rise up if they think an injustice is committed.

There are numerous explanations regarding the content of this verse; specifically, who is the "Cushite woman"? She may be a woman from the land of Cush (i.e., someone other than Tzippora, who is from Midian). If so, then what was their complaint? Perhaps their murmuring is about a previous marriage to a woman from Cush.[14] Alternatively, they may be alluding to Tzippora. Why then use the description of "Cushite"? They may be describing her complexion,[15] or her appearance (either ugly[16] or beautiful[17]). Otherwise, the complaint – similar to Zimri's critique, but in private – is about Moshe's and Tzippora's marriage. The Sages[18] focus the complaint on Moshe's and Tzippora's recent physical separation, positing that his relationship with God necessitated exclusivity in order for

14. See Rashbam and *Ḥizkuni* on Num. 12:1.
15. See Ibn Ezra on Num. 12:1.
16. Rabbenu Baḥya on Num. 12:1 writes that Miriam was accusing Moshe of leaving Tzippora because she is ugly (based on his understanding of the translation of "*kushit*").
17. See Rashi on Num. 12:1.
18. See Yevamot 61b–62a.

him to be available for prophecy at all times.[19] No matter how one may understand this story, Moshe's siblings felt he was acting unfairly towards his wife, or improperly in his role as leader.[20]

**Koraḥ**

> Now Koraḥ, the son of Yitzhar, the son of Kehat, the son of Levi, with Datan and Aviram, the sons of Eliav, and On, the son of Pelet, sons of Reuven, took men: and they rose up before Moshe, with certain of the children of Israel, two hundred fifty princes of the congregation, called to the assembly, men of renown. And they assembled themselves together against Moshe and against Aharon, and said to them, "You take too much on you, seeing all the congregation are holy, every one of them, and God is among them: why then lift yourselves up above the assembly of God?" (Num. 16:1–3)

Koraḥ accuses Moshe of nepotism: Is it not enough that Moshe is the leader; does he need to also pick his brother as the high priest?[21]

---

19. There are numerous ways to understand this view of the Sages concerning what Miriam and Aharon were upset about, and what the injustice was that they were expressing. Rashi on Num. 12:1 writes that Miriam was upset on behalf of Tzippora, who had confided in her that Moshe had physically separated from her. Miriam didn't understand why Moshe felt a need to leave his wife. She assumed that if she and Aharon were also prophets and they didn't have to separate from their spouses, then Moshe should behave similarly. *Panim Yafot* on Num. 12:1 says that Miriam was angry that Moshe was leaving Tzippora because she wasn't Jewish and therefore her sons would not be able to become leaders. He intended to remarry and have children who could inherit his leadership position.
20. An entirely different view of this story is presented by Rabbi Amnon Bazak in his article "The Episode of the Cushite Woman" at http://etzion.org.il/en/episode-cushite-woman. Rabbi Bazak cites *Midrash Tadshe* (*Baraita de-Rabbi Pinḥas ben Yair*), who writes: "We find that there are three sins that cause a blight [*tzaraat*] to adhere to people: one is for senseless jealousy, as was the case with Miriam." Rabbi Bazak explains that Miriam and Aharon were protesting Moshe's allowance of seventy other men to prophesy and lead the Jewish people. Later, Yehoshua also protests Eldad and Meidad's (two of the seventy men) role in prophesying. In that context, Moshe says, "*Hamekaneh ata li*," "Are you jealous for my sake?" (Num. 11:29). In both stories, the protest against others standing up to lead is highlighted by the trait of zealotry.
21. Rashi on Num. 16:3 understands that what Koraḥ meant by "*Rav lakhem*," "You take too much upon you," is "You took too much greatness for yourself. You are not the

Ramban writes[22] that this was a broader rebellion against Moshe's leadership, consisting of members of the tribes of Levi and Reuven and eldest children from other tribes. The objectors from the tribe of Levi are upset that only Aharon's sons were chosen to be priests. The men from Reuven are distressed that national leadership was taken away from their tribe. The firstborn children are disturbed that their status was transferred to Levi. Koraḥ, himself an oldest child from the tribe of Levi, was offended that the leadership was not given to him.[23]

These stories illustrate the complexity of this trait: Fighting perceived injustices can prove highly ennobling, but may also be the way that some individuals make self-benefiting claims against other people. When Moshe kills the Egyptian, or saves Tzippora and her sisters, it is clearly virtuous. On the other hand, when Aharon and Miriam quietly state a perceived injustice, they are directly rebuked by God. And when Koraḥ leads a rebellion against Moshe's right to leadership, he is swallowed up by the ground.

## Zealotry and Excessive Reactions

Responding with gusto – perhaps even overreacting – is a pattern found in the tribe of Levi. These actions are normally on behalf of God – a result of zealousness for God.

Let's begin with Moshe's sense of zealotry, which can be intense when it is in reaction to misdeeds or complaints against God. In response to an Egyptian injuring a Jew, he kills the Egyptian.[24] This was a risky thing to do; after his act, he needed to escape and leave behind everything and everyone familiar and dear to him. Later, when Moshe sees the Jewish people worshipping the golden calf, he throws the precious

only people who heard God at Sinai; all the Jewish people heard His voice, so if you took leadership you should not have given your brother the priesthood."

22. This is his way of explaining Ibn Ezra's remark about the Jews not knowing that the Levites were chosen to replace the tribe of Reuven.

23. In Exodus chapter 6, we are told the lineage of the tribe of Levi. Levi's son Kehat had four sons: Amram, Yitzhar, Ḥevron, and Uziel. Koraḥ is the oldest son of Yitzhar and Aharon is the second child of Amram (Ex. 6:16–21).

24. While, theoretically, the death of the Egyptian could have been unintentional, this is not the view of the Sages. Rashi on Ex. 2:12 quotes Exodus Rabba 1:29 where it is written that Moshe saw that in the future no convert would come from this Egyptian, and then he killed him. That is, Moshe's behavior was intentional.

tablets that God Himself had given him to the ground and destroys them (Ex. 32:19).[25] Ibn Ezra on 32:19 writes "from much zealousness Moshe broke the tablets."[26] He then destroys the idol, grinds it up, puts it in the water, and makes the worshippers of the golden calf drink the mixture.[27] Next, he gathers an army consisting of members of the tribe of Levi, who slay all the sinners with swords. What an overwhelming response to their sin!

We see a similar type of reaction to sin by Moshe's great-nephew Pinḥas. In Numbers chapter 25, Pinḥas murders Zimri and Kozbi by piercing them with a spear while they are publicly engaged in carnal relations. Without hesitating or asking for Moshe's permission, he executes the offenders. Pinḥas acts instantly and aggressively to assassinate the sinners and stop the plague. God praises Pinḥas for his attribute of zealousness

---

25. Ex. 32:19 states, "It happened, as soon as he came near to the camp, that he saw the calf and the dancing: and Moshe's anger grew hot, and he threw the tablets out of his hands, and broke them beneath the mountain." Perhaps he didn't throw them; perhaps he dropped them accidentally. In fact, Rashbam on 32:19 writes that the tablets became very heavy in his arms so he started to drop them. To avoid hurting his feet, he threw them a bit away from himself. In contrast, Rashi on 32:19 recognizes that Moshe couldn't give the tablets with God's law on it to a nation who sinned this way. That certainly sounds like Rashi assumes intentionality on Moshe's part. This reading is consistent with the way that the root *shin, lamed, khaf* is used in the rest of Torah. It is an active word, meaning "to throw," not "to drop." There are many instances of this language in Torah. Examples include the following:
   (1) "*Vayashlekh*," "And he threw": Aharon threw his stick on the floor and it turned into a snake (Ex. 7:10). Moshe threw a piece of a tree into the bitter water to sweeten it (Ex. 15:25). They purposely threw, as commanded by God (i.e., it was not accidental at all).
   (2) "*Va'ashlikhehu*," "And I threw it": Similarly, Aharon later threw all the gold into the fire, during the episode with the golden calf (Ex. 32:24). He didn't drop the gold into the fire, but intentionally threw it inside.

   However, the most compelling proof that Moshe intentionally threw the tablets is what he himself says in Deuteronomy 9:17, "I took hold of the two tables, and cast them out of my two hands, and broke them before your eyes."
26. Ibn Ezra provides various explanations for how Moshe justified throwing the tablets which had the holy words of God on them. Two possibilities are: (1) the words disappeared from the tablets, or (2) God commanded him to drop them. However, Ibn Ezra concludes that Moshe threw them because "he was zealous for God and out of anger he broke them."
27. Ex. 32:20 states that, "He took the calf which they had made, burnt it with fire, ground it to powder, scattered it on the water, and made the children of Israel drink of it."

in the face of injustice. He states that the motivation of Pinḥas is "*bekano et kinati betokham*," "that he was zealous with My zealotry among them" (Numbers 25:11). God admits that Pinḥas's actions prevented God from "consuming the children of Israel in my jealousy." Pinḥas acted fanatically as the agent of God to prevent a more severe punishment to the Jewish nation.

This description of Pinḥas reminds us of a future personality, Eliyahu the prophet. Eliyahu describes himself as a zealot for God, using parallel language to God's description of Pinḥas, "*kano kineiti laHashem*," "I am zealous for God" (I Kings 19:4). In fact, the similarities are so strong that the Sages assert that Pinḥas is Eliyahu![28] If this statement is taken literally, then Eliyahu is from the tribe of Levi as well, reflecting so much of the personality that is discernible in the tribe's leaders.[29]

Therefore, it comes as little surprise that we find many parallels between the experiences of Eliyahu and Moshe. Eliyahu gathers the Jewish people at Mount Carmel ***where*** God reveals Himself to them (I Kings 19). Before him, Moshe has an awesome revelation of God on the mountain of Sinai (Ex. 20). Immediately after these two events, the Jewish people sin. For Eliyahu, the sin is the people's return to serving idols; for Moshe, it is their worship of the golden calf (Ex. 32). What was Eliyahu's reaction to the idol worship? He runs away and begs God to kill him, as he is overly zealous and frustrated for God. This story reminds us of a similar one later in Moshe's life, when the Jewish people grumble for meat, rejecting the food that falls from the sky, and Moshe gives up

---

28. *Yalkut Shimoni* 761. This is part of a larger trend in Ḥazal to conserve names in Tanakh. See Chapter 3, note 4 for an introduction to the Sages' approach to this method, sometimes called "conservation of personalities." Rabbenu Baḥya on 25:12 explains that Pinḥas is rewarded with the gift of "My covenant of peace" (Numbers 25:12). What is the content of this gift? The simple explanation is that he will be protected from his brother Zimri. However, based on the midrashic understanding that Pinḥas is Eliyahu, these words might refer to the gift that he will live forever. *Meshekh Ḥokhma* provides further evidence of this view from the following verse in I Chronicles 9:20, describing the time period of the kings: "Pinḥas the son of Elazar was ruler over them in time past, and God was with him." This would also explain the peculiarity that Pinḥas was alive at the end of the book of Joshua (22:13) as well as at the end of the book of Judges: "And Pinḥas the son of Elazar the son of Aharon stood before them in those days" (Judges 20:28).
29. See Rabbenu Baḥya on Ex. 18:27.

and asks to die (Num. 11:14–15). Both leaders react dramatically, willing to die rather than continue dealing with an erring nation.

These traits of the tribe of Levi – anger, zealotry, and hatred of injustice – are defining characteristics of powerful leaders throughout our history: Moshe, Aharon, and Miriam lead us in the desert. Eli judges the Jewish people for forty years at the end of the period of Judges. Elkana, father of Shmuel, leads his family and others on a journey to Shiloh each year to worship God. Shmuel, the prophet and judge, leads the Jewish people for most of his life, and anoints Shaul and David as monarchs. Eliyahu, Yirmiyahu,[30] and Yeḥezkel[31] prophesy for numerous kings in order to advise them during their rules, as they do for Yehoshua, son of the high priest Yehotzadak, who works together with the leader Zerubavel.[32]

Beyond the individuals from the tribe of Levi who serve as leaders, the entire tribe is selected for collective leadership, and is singled out from among the other tribes numerous times in the Torah. In the book of Numbers, chapter 1 describes the military count of the entire Jewish people except for Levi, who is counted separately in chapter 3. "*Vehayu li haLevi'im, Ani Hashem*," They will be for me the Levites, for I am God (Num. 3:45). They are set aside to be the "army of God," working in the house of worship, and not out on the battlefield against the enemy.

In the layout of the encampment in the desert, Levi is separated once again (Num. 2). This tribe is not in any of the other tribes' camps; rather, all three of Levi's sons' families are placed in the center of the camp and have the honor of carrying the Tabernacle and all its utensils (Num. ch. 4). Again, in Numbers 8, God separates this tribe with a special role. "Take the Levites from among the children of Israel, and cleanse them" (Num. 8:5). They service the Tent of Meeting as representatives of the nation. God states, "Thus you shall separate the Levites from among the children of Israel, and the Levites shall be mine" (Num. 8:14).

In return for the tribe's service, the Jewish people must provide them with provisions. Numbers 18 introduces a differentiated guide for these provisions. Aharon and his descendants, the priests, receive the

30. Jer. 1:1 states that Yirmiyahu is from a group of priests who live in Anatot.
31. In Ezek. 1:3 Yeḥezkel is called a priest.
32. Zerubavel's experiences are found in the books of Haggai and Zechariah.

portion known as *teruma* while the rest of the tribe receives *maaser* (tithes). God recognizes that the tribe of Levi needs to be rewarded and supported by the rest of the Jewish people for their service to the nation and to God.

Conversely, because of its unique role on behalf of the whole nation, the tribe of Levi does not receive a distinct portion of land in Israel. God says, "You shall have no inheritance in their land, neither shall you have any portion among them: I am your portion and your inheritance among the children of Israel" (Num. 18:20). They must receive tithes from the Jewish people because they have no inheritance on which to grow food. They are restricted and must live scattered throughout the land, with no territory of their own.

The lack of apportionment seems to indicate the unique nature of this tribe: spread among the Jewish people, they live all over the land in order to influence the entire nation. However, given our understanding of Levi and his progeny, spreading out the tribe might simply be a necessity to prevent an overconcentration of power in one location, where their strong personalities could be dangerous if unrestrained.

In fact, there is evidence of leaders from this tribe whose power is taken too far. The book of Judges shares the story of an anonymous member of the tribe of Levi who pretends to be a priest for all who come to worship in the house of Micha (Judges 18:9–11). His behavior is motivated by the promise of large sums of money from Micha in return for his services. Even worse, another nameless Levite instigates a war against a different tribe of Israel. After his concubine is raped, he cuts up her body and sends each piece to a different tribe of Israel, rousing them to fight and almost wipe out the tribe of Binyamin (Judges 19–20). Both of these narratives present a Levite man who oversteps the lines of his leadership and acts in a grossly inappropriate fashion.

The tribe of Levi mindfully balances this tension. It is geographically disjointed to mitigate the extremism, but at the same time, it provides the nation with its teachers and leaders. The Levites serve as the protectors of the House of God. The entire tribe represents the Jewish people before God, bringing their sacrifices, caring for the Tent of Meeting, singing prayers, and teaching Torah to the Jewish people. In Deuteronomy, Moshe tells the people that if they need help in deciphering a halakhic question or if there is a fight among them about what to do, they should go to the priest, Levite, or judge to find out the answer. He warns them that if one disobeys the words of the priest or judge, he will be put to death (Deut. 17:8–12).

How did this tribe merit to be selected for these unique leadership roles? According to the Sages, they consciously evaded Pharaoh's outreach to help build his pyramids, thus keeping themselves separated from the Egyptians and avoiding slavery.[33] They join Moshe in punishing those who worshipped the golden calf. They answer to the call of, "whoever is for God, come to me" (Ex. 32:26). As a reward and a consequence, God chooses them to be His, saying, "Thus you shall separate the Levites from among the children of Israel, and the Levites shall be mine" (Num. 18:14).

## HOW SHIMON AND LEVI DIFFER

Shimon and Levi are partners in the book of Genesis. They are more closely connected than the other brothers and share similar personalities. However, in the rest of Torah and beyond, their destinies diverge. In fact, Shimon and Levi become enemies.

As noted earlier, the tribe of Shimon, led by the tribal prince Zimri, rebels against Moshe, who is from the tribe of Levi. Pinḥas, Aharon's grandson and Moshe's great-nephew, and therefore also a Levite, pierces a spear through Zimri's and Kozbi's bodies. Thus, in this incident a member of the tribe of Levi expresses his zealotry by killing a member of the tribe of Shimon! *Toldot Yitzḥak* on Numbers 25:11 writes that this action destroyed the brotherhood between Shimon and Levi. At this

33. This is the opinion of R. Yehoshua ben Levi in Exodus Rabba 5:16. Rashi on Exodus 5:4 adds a proof that the tribe of Levi was never enslaved, as Moshe and Aharon could come and go as they pleased with no consequences. *Ḥizkuni* on 5:4 adds that Levites never volunteered to work for Pharaoh because they wanted to keep themselves separate, as they knew that in the future they would have a special job of serving in the house of God. Rabbenu Baḥya writes that even Pharaoh understood the tribe of Levi's special job to safeguard the traditions and laws. Cognizant of the fact that each nation has a group of wise men who are the teachers of the nation, Pharaoh allowed Levi to continue to study in lieu of joining the other tribes in their work. Rambam writes that Yaakov predestined Levi to sit and learn Torah, and this knowledge was passed down from father to son in the tribe. Consequently, Levi was the only tribe to never worship foreign deities in Egypt, and they never intermingled with Egyptian society (Rambam, *Hilkhot Avoda Zara* 1:3).

moment, they turned from brothers to enemies. From then on, in the words of *Toldot Yitzḥak*, there is "a great war" between the two tribes.

However, there is possible evidence documented by other commentaries that the tension between these two tribes precedes this event. Malbim on Numbers 1:20 writes that the majority of the sinners in the episode of the golden calf were from the tribe of Shimon. When Moshe calls out to the Jewish people: "Whoever is for God, come to me," the tribe of Levi joins Moshe to wipe out the sinners (Ex. 32:26). In this story too, the tribe of Levi murders members of the sinning tribe of Shimon. The verse says: "Each man should kill his brother (*ish et aḥiv*), his friend" (Ex. 32:27). This language of "*ish et aḥiv*" reminds us of the language of Yaakov, who calls Shimon and Levi "*aḥim*," brothers. In the events leading up to the selling of Yosef, we may also recall the Sages' attribution of the phrase "and they said one man to his brother," "*vayomeru ish el aḥiv*" (Gen. 37:19), to Shimon and Levi.

In Genesis, Shimon and Levi work together and both are cursed by their father, Yaakov. In later years, however, Shimon continues to rebel and Levi fights against him. Abarbanel on Deuteronomy 33 writes that this is the reason that Moshe blesses Levi but Shimon is left out completely. He writes "even though both drink from the same cup," meaning they share a propensity for outrage, Levi's later ability to channel this personality trait for good purposes counters its negative origins in Genesis. Unfortunately, Shimon never redeems himself by using his traits for anything positive, and he is therefore held accountable for his earlier misdeeds in Genesis. Because his tribe continues down the road of sin and evil, it is removed from Moshe's blessing of the twelve tribes.

## CONCLUSION

The histories of Shimon and Levi diverge in significant ways. Shimon lacks a national presence and never learns how to channel his anger for positive purposes. Levi reflects more of a balance. His tribe's anger is a good trait when used to stand up for God or to correct societal ills. The tribe of Levi's zealotry is epitomized by Pinḥas's heroic act at the exact moment in time that leadership was required. Moreover, Levi teaches the lesson of channeling our most intense personality traits to serve God, the Jewish people, and humanity.

*Chapter 6*

# Yehuda in Genesis: The Natural Leader of the Family

Beginning with his birth, Yehuda is different from his older brothers. Throughout his life, he manifests all of the leadership qualities that are absent in Reuven. He lacks the anger and resentment of Shimon and Levi. Yehuda, the fourth son of Yaakov, is the first child with the temperament and life experiences to make him suitable to lead the family.

## NAMING OF YEHUDA

> She conceived again, and bore a son. She said, "This time I will praise God." Therefore, she named him Yehuda. Then she stopped bearing. (Gen. 29:35)

The name given to Yehuda reflects a radical improvement in the home environment. As discussed previously, with Reuven's name,

Leah expresses hope that Yaakov will begin to love her, Shimon's name exposes her feelings of being unloved, and Levi's name reignites a sense of optimism. With the birth of Yehuda, we see that finally, a son's birth elicits feelings of happiness and praise. He is named Yehuda because she wants to praise God. Leah is happy! What happened to cause this shift? Likely, it was some combination between having finally gained Yaakov's love[1] and feeling the affection from her numerous children.[2]

In fact, other evidence exists suggesting that the situation at home has improved. Immediately after Leah names Yehuda, the Torah states, "then she stopped bearing." In order to understand the significance of these words, we can connect it to an earlier verse describing the state of her fertility. "God saw that Leah was hated, and he opened her womb, but Raḥel was barren" (Gen. 29:31). Radak here writes that this verse suggests that *both* Raḥel and Leah were naturally barren, but God performed a miracle and opened Leah's womb *because* she was hated by Yaakov. If so, then now ceasing to bear children may reflect a new reality, and now that she is no longer hated by Yaakov, she resumes her "natural state" of being barren like her sister.[3]

Further proof that there has been a change is that only after Yehuda is born does Raḥel react.

> When Raḥel saw that she bore Yaakov no children, Raḥel envied her sister. She said to Yaakov, "Give me children, or else I will die." (Gen. 30:1)

---

1. Abarbanel on Gen. 29:31 describes how with each child, Yaakov gains more affection for Leah. By the time of Yehuda's birth, he begins to show her love. She praises God because now she feels loved.
2. See Ibn Ezra and Radak on Gen. 29:35. Rashi there views Leah's happiness as a function of attaining success in her competition with her sister Raḥel: "God has given me more than my portion." Abarbanel on Gen. 29:31 explains that Rashi's comment is based on the midrashic view that Leah knew there would be four wives and twelve sons, and each wife would presumably have three sons. When she had her fourth son, she realized that she would have more children than the rest of the wives, including Raḥel, and she thanks God.
3. Alternatively, this clause may be needed to explain why Leah will give her maidservant to Yaakov as a wife instead of having more children on her own.

Raḥel was barren this entire time throughout the births of Reuven, Shimon, and Levi, but she never before reacted negatively to the birth of her nephews. Why only after the birth of Yehuda does Raḥel become jealous of her sister and make demands of her husband? After Yehuda's birth, Raḥel perceives that her status has changed, so her infertility takes center stage. By now, Yaakov likely spends more time with Leah and her sons. Perhaps he now even loves Leah. This leaves Raḥel feeling agonizingly isolated and alone! It is at this moment, after the birth of Yehuda, that she shares her agony with Yaakov.

Evidently, this is the extent of the strain in the bond between Yaakov and Raḥel. This transformation is exhibited in Yaakov's response to Raḥel's painful comments; he gets annoyed and responds seemingly insensitively. Yaakov's anger is kindled against Raḥel, and he says, "Am I in God's place, who has withheld from you the fruit of the womb?" (Gen. 30:2). This is the first time that we know about Yaakov being angry at Raḥel, his favorite wife. He seems content with having children only with Leah, leaving Raḥel on her own to mourn her childlessness.

In spite of Yaakov's ostensible increased involvement with Leah and her children, the Torah does not record any stories that show direct contact between Yaakov and the young Yehuda. There is nothing written about their interactions, either positive or negative. However, as a result of Yehuda being born into a happier home, he does not exhibit any of the anger found in his older brothers. Unlike with Reuven, Shimon, and Levi, there are no stories of direct confrontation between Yehuda and his father. Therefore, it seems reasonable to presume that of the four older sons of Leah, Yehuda would likely be Yaakov's favorite.

## THE SALE OF YOSEF

> Yehuda said to his brothers, "What profit is it if we kill our brother and conceal his blood? Come, and let's sell him to the Ishmaelites, and not let our hand be on him; for he is our brother, our flesh." His brothers listened to him. (Gen. 37:26–27)

The first time that Yehuda comes to the forefront is during the sale of Yosef. As discussed in Chapter 2, when Yosef arrives in the field, far from their father's watchful eye, his brothers' immediate reaction is to express their desire to murder him. In Chapter 4, we observed that the Sages attribute this idea to Shimon and Levi. Reuven then steps up and suggests an alternative: The brothers should throw Yosef into a pit and leave him to die of natural causes, as opposed to murdering him with their own hands. Both of these ideas suggested by the three older brothers – murder or leaving him in the pit – would kill Yosef.[4] Yehuda suggests an alternative – sell Yosef to passing merchants. Amazingly, the brothers listen to him. There are two competing ways to understand Yehuda's motivations: Was Yehuda acting nobly to save Yosef or was he simply offering an alternative way to "dispose" of him?

### Virtuous Yehuda

The first option is that Yehuda was defending Yosef and saving him from the rest of the brothers. This seems clear, especially when comparing Yehuda's idea to his brothers' plans. His suggestion would allow Yosef to live.[5] Yehuda was trying to protect and save his younger brother.

However, if this is true, then why doesn't Yehuda go all the way and tell his brothers to leave Yosef alone? Why the need to sell him? The answer is obvious. If he takes Yosef home, he would have saved Yosef on *that* day in the field. However, Yehuda knew what could happen the next time that Yosef would be alone with his other brothers but without Yehuda there to save him. Yehuda knew that Yosef would be safe only if he was to be sent far away from the house of Yaakov, far away from his brothers who hated him.[6]

---

4. It is true that Reuven's intention was to return to the pit to save him. However, since he never told his brothers this plan, they thought his plan was to allow Yosef to die of starvation or from being eaten by an animal inside the pit.
5. See Radak on Gen. 37:26, who argues that Yehuda's plan is the most humane of all of the brothers', since it allows Yosef to live. Abarbanel on Gen. 37 also writes that Yehuda's idea to sell Yosef was intended as a way to save him from his brothers.
6. See Abarbanel's answer to his first question on Gen. 38. On the other hand, *Meshekh Ḥokhma* on Gen. 37:26 argues that Yehuda should have attempted to stop the brothers. Had Yehuda tried to stop them, he would have had the support of Reuven, who secretly also wanted to save Yosef, and the maidservant children, with whom Yosef played and who may have liked him. Therefore, if Yehuda had tried to fight for Yosef,

**Malicious Yehuda**

On the other hand, it seems equally plausible that Yehuda may have disliked Yosef and wanted to harm him (perhaps because of Yosef's constant showing off and tattling). Like his brothers, Yehuda may have wanted to remove Yosef from their father's home, but just didn't want to kill him. He was willing to send him permanently to a faraway land to be a slave. Yosef would be in a terrible situation with no hope of return, and Yehuda was comfortable with this outcome. As opposed to Reuven, who planned to go back to the pit and save Yosef, Yehuda has no intention of saving him. His plan would permanently rid Yosef from the house of Yaakov. Interestingly, this might be consistent with what the brothers meant when they originally spoke of killing him. Do we really think that they actually wanted to murder him? More likely, they were threatening and teasing Yosef. Unlike killing him outright, Yehuda's plan is just humane enough that the brothers were comfortable with it.

Whatever Yehuda's motivations, the brothers listen to him. They easily reject the plan of Reuven, the eldest brother, and possibly the plan of Shimon and Levi, the next oldest brothers, and replace it with the idea of the fourth brother. Why is this so? It is because everyone listens to Yehuda![7] This story – our introduction to Yehuda – gives us insight into his true role in the family: Yehuda is the natural leader of the family. Evidently, although he is not the oldest or the most assertive (recall that his was not the first idea presented), he is the one to whom they listen. His personality has a quality of leadership that resonates with the people around him.

## YEHUDA AND TAMAR

The next episode with Yehuda is surprisingly scandalous, thus compelling the reader to think hard to understand what the message of this incident might be. We will focus on how it might inform us about Yehuda. After a tragic period in his life, Yehuda's daughter-in-law (whom he had confused

---

it would have been six brothers standing up to save him against four brothers who wanted to hurt him. Yehuda could have prevailed!

7. Rashi on Gen. 38:1 writes that the brothers would have listened to anything Yehuda said. Had he said to save Yosef, they would have listened. Because he said to sell him, they sold him. For this reason, Yehuda is held accountable for the sale of Yosef: he had the power to prevent it.

for a prostitute) gives birth to twin sons fathered by Yehuda. This sounds like a wild tale that reflects on Yehuda terribly. However, what is most remarkable about this story is that it may not necessarily reflect a bad or evil man. He may simply be a sad, almost pathetic man who makes a number of poor decisions while wallowing in his sorrow. To further understand this episode, let us begin with the background to the story as understood by the conventional view that Yehuda was acting inappropriately, and maybe even maliciously, in his misbehavior with Tamar.

**Evil Yehuda**

> And Yehuda went down [*vayered*] from amongst his brothers. (Gen. 38:1)

Yehuda's life outside of the house of Yaakov begins on a bad note. His story starts with the language of "*yerida,*" going down, implying a lowering of status or a betrayal of values. Yehuda starts a new life with a new set of standards and morals. He befriends a man named Ḥira, who becomes a negative influence on him.[8] Consistent with behavior that is different from the house of Yaakov, Yehuda marries the daughter of a Canaanite man.[9]

Yehuda and his unnamed wife[10] produce three sons who go down an evil path, making us question if they are learning these ways from

8. Ḥira will later introduce Yehuda to the underworld of prostitution, and has no shame returning there afterward on Yehuda's behalf in order to pay the woman to whom Yehuda has become indebted.
9. As discussed in Chapter 4, the patriarchs were forbidden from marrying Canaanite women, but it is unclear if this command applied to the twelve sons of Yaakov. If the underlying concern for the original prohibition is the evil values espoused by Canaanites, it would logically follow that this prohibition applies to Yaakov's twelve sons. In fact, this is the view of R. Yehuda in Genesis Rabba 84:19. If so, then Yehuda's behavior violates this prohibition since she is the daughter of a Canaanite man. Similarly, in I Chr. 2:3, Yehuda's wife is called a Canaanite woman. Ibn Ezra on Gen. 38:2 concurs that the verse should be read literally and therefore one aspect of Er and Onan's death is punishment to Yehuda for marrying a Canaanite.
10. Unimportant characters don't have their names written down in the text of the Torah. This is similar to the case of *Ploni Almoni* in the story of Ruth. *Ploni Almoni* is understood to be an anonym, as this individual doesn't deserve to have his real name written because he doesn't step up to marry Ruth and fulfill his family obligation of *yibum* (Ruth 4:1).

their father's new lifestyle. His two oldest sons do "*ra be'einei Hashem,*" an act that is evil in the eyes of God, and die as a result (Gen. 38:7, 10).

What was their evil act?

The exact misdeed of the older brother, Er, goes unmentioned in the Torah. However, there is a hint in the description of his brother's death: "And He killed him also" (v. 10). The Sages point out that the word "also" implies that both brothers are guilty of the same misdeed. As we will see soon, Onan, the second brother, is punished for ensuring that his wife cannot become pregnant. Therefore, if Er is guilty of the same transgression, we want to understand why he would act in such a way. Rabbinic tradition asserts that he feared that if she became pregnant, his wife's beauty might be diminished.[11]

As noted above, the sin of Onan, Yehuda's second son, is explicit in the Torah. After the death of Er, Yehuda's firstborn, Yehuda commands his second son to fulfill the tradition of levirate marriage: "Go in to your brother's wife, and perform the duty of a husband's brother to her, and raise up seed to your brother" (Gen. 38:8). Onan obeys only the first half of his father's command: he marries Tamar, his brother's widow, but refuses to have a child in Er's name: "When he went in to his brother's wife... he spilled [the seed] on the ground, lest he should give seed to his brother" (Gen. 38:9). He intentionally ensures that his new wife cannot become pregnant; thus, she is unable to bear a child in his brother's name. This act is so wicked in the eyes of God that Er is deserving of death.

What does their misbehavior tell us about Yehuda? One might presume that Yehuda, whose values we know have descended since the time he left his father's house, shares some of the blame for the corrupt values of his sons or, at least, for not rebuking their actions.[12]

---

11. See Yevamot 34b quoted in Rashi on Gen. 38:7. Interestingly, this story shares significant similarities to that of Lemekh, a descendant of Kayin, who had two wives, Ada and Tzila (Gen. 4:19). According to Rashi on 4:19, Lemekh had this arrangement so that one could bear children and the other could remain beautiful and childless.
12. This is reminiscent of the story of Eli, the high priest, who is punished by God for not rebuking his corrupt sons (I Sam. 3:12). God yells at Eli and blames him, saying, "You didn't rebuke them." As a result, Eli and both his sons die on the same day.

After the death of the two brothers, Er and Onan, Tamar waits to marry the third brother, Shela. During this time, Yehuda instructs Tamar to go to her father's home to wait until Shela grows up. He implies that in a few years he will call her back to marry Shela. However, as time passes and he doesn't contact her, she is left in limbo. She is expected to marry back into the family but has not been invited to marry Shela. In fact, Rashi on 38:11 writes that Yehuda never intended to allow her to marry Shela. If so, she would be left in this tenuous situation forever!

For Yehuda, the story only deteriorates from there. In the company of his friend Ḥira, Yehuda is approached by Tamar dressed in the disguise of a harlot. Yehuda thus unknowingly ends up having relations with his daughter-in-law, and she becomes pregnant with twins.

Three months later, Tamar's pregnancy becomes public. Yehuda, clueless that he is the father, reacts forcefully. He asserts that she should be burnt at the stake for her infidelity. The saddest irony is that Yehuda is oblivious to the implications of his decree. By condemning her to death, he is about to kill his daughter in-law and his own babies! Why was he so sure of her punishment? Certainly, her death would be convenient for him, as then Shela could avoid marrying her, and would satisfy an element of resentment he might bear towards her for the death of his first two sons. In other words, his strong response may not be a direct reaction to the exact act that she is now guilty of. It might just be a function of previously developed anger against her and a desire for revenge.

Let us step back from the story to grasp what this all means for our understanding of Yehuda. This is a pathetic story, describing a low point in Yehuda's life. This story represents how much Yehuda has strayed from the ethics and principles of his father, Yaakov. However, there is another way to view Yehuda's role in this story.

**Sad Yehuda**

According to this view, Yehuda left his home out of a sense of guilt. Yehuda is living with guilt for his role in the sale of Yosef, as Yosef's disappearance has caused his father's endless sorrow.[13] This guilt might be coupled with the fact that he was living with the other sons of Yaakov,

13. See Rashi and *Ḥizkuni* on Gen. 38:1.

men who were willing to kill Yosef. Maybe he felt that the other brothers were a negative influence from which he needed to flee.[14] Or he might have left home for a much simpler reason: He had grown up and was ready to start a family of his own.[15] If he left to marry and have children, as any child would do when he or she is grown, there is nothing negative about these actions.

Previously, we contemplated the negative implications of Yehuda marrying a Canaanite woman. However, we need to recognize that for Yehuda, as one of the *sons* of Yaakov, this may have been permitted.[16] Alternatively, the word Canaanite might mean merchant, informing us that she was the daughter of a merchant, not necessarily a native of Canaan.[17]

---

14. See Abarbanel in his answer to his first question on Gen. 38.
15. In fact, the timing suggests that it is less likely that Yehuda's leaving was precipitated by the sale of Yosef. How so? Yosef was seventeen when he was sold (Gen. 37:2), and thirty when he met up with Pharaoh (Gen. 41:46). Therefore, thirteen years have passed. The story culminates when Yaakov comes down to Egypt in the second year of the famine (Gen. 47:18), which is nine years later (seven years of plenty plus two years of famine). This implies that there are no more than twenty-two years from Yosef's sale until he is reunited with his father. Let's now consider Yehuda's family. We know that after he leaves the family, Yehuda gets married, has three sons, two of whom die, and that he then wants to defer the marriage of this third son to Tamar. After some time, he has two sons with Tamar, and then two grandchildren. All of this happens before Yaakov's family comes down to Egypt (Gen. 46:12). It seems highly unlikely that all of this occurred during the limited period of twenty-two years. *Ḥizkuni* on 38:1 defends the approach, which is presented by Rashi, that Yehuda left home in reaction to the sale of Yosef. To ensure that the calculations (described above) are consistent with this explanation, he suggests that each of Yehuda's sons got married at the age of seven. In contrast, Ibn Ezra on Gen. 38:1 explains that Yehuda left home, married his wife, and had his children years *before* the sale of Yosef, but that even after he had left home and was married with children, Yehuda would still meet back up with his brothers to shepherd their father's sheep. There is a middle option: Yehuda left home before the sale, got married and had children, and it is right after the sale of Yosef that his own sons die. This idea is alluded to by Sforno on Gen. 38:1 who writes that the death of Yehuda's sons is punishment for what he did to Yosef.
16. This is R. Neḥemia's opinion in Genesis Rabba 84:19. See Chapter 4, which states that only Avraham, Yitzḥak, and Yaakov were warned against Canaanite women, but the twelve sons of Yaakov had no such prohibition.
17. The Talmud in Pesaḥim 50a suggests that Canaanite must mean merchant because otherwise, Yehuda would have violated a command of Avraham and Yitzḥak. Rashi

Furthermore, while we previously considered Yehuda culpable for his sons' deaths, this in fact may not be the case. The Torah informs us that both men die because of their own evil actions, not because of their father's deeds. Amazingly, Ramban on Gen. 38:7 writes that the Torah anticipates our confusion and therefore clearly states that their deaths are a result of their behavior and not a punishment for Yehuda's role in selling Yosef. How can their father be expected to rebuke his sons for something that happens in the privacy of their homes?[18] Further, Abarbanel[19] suggests that his two additional sons (the ones born to Tamar) are righteous. Their birth and virtue are evidence, suggests Abarbanel, that Yehuda was not to blame in the death of the first two sons. Those sons died because of their own evil actions, not due to anything about their father or the environment that he fostered.

In the next part of the story, there are two possible reasons that Yehuda instructs Tamar to go home to wait for Shela. The first is simple – he is afraid that if she marries Shela, he'll die too. In other words, he is afraid that Tamar has responsibility, either just as a jinx or due to a more active role, in the deaths of his first two sons, whose evil behavior was unknown to him. In his mind, she is a jinx, a wife who causes the death of her husbands, as he states, "Lest he also die like his brothers" (Gen. 38:11). Therefore, he feels forced to lie to protect the life of his only remaining son.[20] His treatment of Tamar may not have

---

and Radak on Gen. 38:2 both accept this translation of the text. Interestingly, while these commentators find it incongruous to suggest that Yehuda would sin in this way, they do not offer a comparable defense of Shimon!

18. Yehuda's sadness over the loss of his sons reminds us of Aharon's sadness when he loses his two sons Nadav and Avihu because of their own actions (Num. 26:61).
19. In his answer to his first question on Gen. 38.
20. The Talmud in Yevamot 64b questions what to do in the following situation: A woman marries a man and he dies; she marries a second man and he dies. May she marry a third man? R. Yehuda HaNasi says no and R. Shimon ben Gamliel says she may marry again. (However, even R. Shimon ben Gamliel says that if the third husband dies, she may not marry again.) Yehuda seems to operate according to R. Yehuda HaNasi's perspective – after the death of two husbands, a woman should not remarry, as she must worry that her presence is causing their deaths. Possibly, Yehuda was trying to prevent her from marrying anyone!

been kind, but is understandable, as he was simply trying to protect the life of his only living son.

Ramban on Gen. 38:11 has a different interpretation of the situation. He writes that Yehuda did intend to keep his promise and summon Tamar back after Shela grew up. However, she misunderstands him. She thinks that Yehuda meant to wait until Shela grew to the same age as Er and Onan at the time of their weddings. Thus, when Shela reaches that age and she is not asked to come back, she assumes that he has deserted her. However, Yehuda's perspective is that, evidently, his two older sons got married too young and were immature, leading them to sin. In order to protect Shela, he prefers to give him more time to mature and be influenced by his father's morals. Yehuda wants Tamar to return when Shela reaches an appropriate age (i.e., older than the age at which his brothers married). Miscommunication between Yehuda and Tamar caused the breakdown between them, not malice or anger on Yehuda's part.

Soon after the deaths of two of their sons, Yehuda's wife dies. He is all alone with only one remaining son, and he is sad and broken. One day, after the shearing of the sheep, which typically is a day of merriment and celebration,[21] Yehuda makes an enormous mistake. Sad, and possibly drunk, he hires a prostitute to comfort him. It is clear from the Torah that he has no idea this woman is his daughter-in-law, as the verse states: "He thought she was a prostitute" (Gen. 38:15). It is also clear that this is atypical behavior for him, as he does not bring money with him, and then he is too embarrassed to go back and find her to trade his items back for the money he owes her. After one attempt of sending his friend to locate her, he says, "Let her keep it, lest we be shamed" (Gen. 38:23), evidently feeling humiliated by his behavior.

Having sexual relations with a prostitute is certainly something to be ashamed of, but in the biblical period before the giving of the Torah it was not forbidden or uncommon.[22] Although Yehuda's actions with Tamar

21. Bekhor Shor on Gen. 38:13 provides this observation. This happens in the stories of Avshalom (II Sam. 13:23) and Naval (I Sam. 25:7), who both get drunk at parties following the shearing of the sheep. Thus, in our story, Yehuda might be drunk, and therefore acts differently than he would as a sober man.
22. Gen. 38:21 refers to her as a *kedeisha,* a woman who is unattached and is available to be with anyone. Only in Deut. 23:18 are the Jewish people commanded not to

are clearly not praiseworthy, given the context of his environment, they may not be abominable either.[23] Dejected, possibly inebriated, and miserable about the deaths of most of his family, Yehuda acts out of desperation. The story would have ended here, and assumedly not be recorded in the Torah, had Tamar not gotten pregnant from their sole encounter.

When Yehuda finds out that Tamar is pregnant, he sentences her to death. His rash response is consistent with the cultural norm of that time period, when it was normal to punish a cheating wife with the death penalty. Bekhor Shor on Gen. 38:24 posits that when a woman is waiting to enter into *yibum* (levirate marriage to her deceased husband's brother) – as Tamar was – she is tantamount to married, and therefore Yehuda's punishment choice was justified. Rashi on Gen. 38:24 adds an extra factor explaining why she was deserving of such a harsh punishment: She was the daughter of Shem, a priest, and royal lineage demands higher standards for intimate relationships.[24] Ramban on Gen. 38:24 adds two

---

allow a woman to be a *kedeisha,* and sexual relations with a *kedeisha* are forbidden. Rambam in his Guide for the Perplexed famously asserts that prior to the giving of the Torah this action was allowed (Guide for the Perplexed 2:49). Abarbanel on Gen. 38 (immediately following his answer to question 7) justifies Yehuda's behavior because it was technically permitted at that time. In fact, he says, the descendants of Noaḥ engaged prostitutes, especially after their wives died, to ease their loneliness. Yehuda was behaving in a manner consistent with the times.

Having relations with a prostitute or being in her house is found in a number of stories in the Torah, even after the revelation at Sinai. For example:

(1) The two spies sent to Israel by Yehoshua go to the house of Raḥav, a prostitute (Josh 2:1).
(2) Yiftaḥ, a judge from the book of Judges, was the child of a prostitute (Judges 11:1).
(3) Shimshon, a later judge in the book of Judges, spends the night at the home of a prostitute (Judges 16:1).
(4) Two prostitutes approach Shlomo, arguing over ownership of a baby (II Kings 3:16) and he answers them and gives them his judgment, treating them as he would any member of the Jewish people.

23. Many of the commentators offer alternative reasons to justify his actions. See *Ḥizkuni* on Gen. 38:7 for one suggestion. He also offers the observation that Yehuda's action led to Tamar's best possible outcome. By being with her, he was satisfying the rules of levirate marriage (as they were understood at that time) that any close relative can marry her, even the father.
24. In his presentation, Rashi seems to struggle with a basis to justify Yehuda's harsh judgment.

more considerations in favor of Yehuda's overall behavior. First, Yehuda, the leader of the land, had the status of king. Therefore, when she cheated on his family, her behavior was tantamount to rebellion against a king, and she was thus deserving of the death penalty.[25] Second, Ramban observes that in biblical times, when a woman was unfaithful to her husband, the custom was that he or his family had the right to determine her punishment. These approaches attempt to justify or at least contextualize Yehuda's decision to condemn Tamar to death.

### The Transformation of Yehuda

Amazingly, whatever Yehuda's motivation was throughout this story, whether he was acting out of malice or sadness or somewhere in between, Yehuda manifests a remarkable transformation as the episode with Tamar concludes. It is here that Yehuda's leadership qualities are revealed. His ability to admit his mistake and repent displays his tremendous strength of character.

As Tamar is being dragged to her death, she sends a message to Yehuda along with the items that he had left with her the night of their encounter. She says: "By the man whose these are, I am with child" (Gen. 38:25). At this moment, Yehuda has a life-altering choice. The easy option is to ignore her words, thereby allowing her to die and destroying all evidence of his misdeed. Alternatively, he can stop the demonstration and publicly admit that it was he who unknowingly had sexual relations with his daughter-in-law. How mortifying to admit this in front of all who were gathered, possibly including his brothers and father. Yet Yehuda immediately admits his guilt, stating: "She is more righteous than I, because I didn't give her to Shela, my son" (Gen. 38:26).

The story goes further in reflecting his turnaround. The verse states that "he knew her again no more" (v. 26). He didn't take advantage of the situation by continuing to engage in relations with Tamar. He realized that he did something wrong, and did not continue to act in this way.

Of course, Yehuda deserves credit for admitting his mistake and for now treating her with respect, but the most exceptional aspect of

---

25. Rambam, in *Hilkhot Melakhim* 3:9, writes that if one rebels against the king, the king has permission to kill that person.

his reversal is how he treats his children. As we noted earlier, Tamar gave birth to twins, Peretz and Zeraḥ, from their union. Since these two sons represent the low point in Yehuda's life, we might therefore expect him to send them away with Tamar, back to her father's home. However, Yehuda does the opposite. He raises and loves them as his sons, along with Shela. Inevitably, when he sees them every day, he is reminded of his lowest moment, yet he makes them part of his family. This is alluded to in Gen. 46, when the Torah lists the families of the twelve sons of Yaakov who come down to Egypt. There, Peretz and Zeraḥ and their children are included in the list of the sons of Yehuda: "All the sons of Yehuda are five: Er, Onan, Shela, Peretz, and Zeraḥ" (Gen. 46:12). Ironically, we eventually learn that Peretz, a product of the relationship between Yehuda and Tamar, is the progenitor of King David (Ruth 4:18–22).

## PROTECTOR OF BINYAMIN

### Standing Up to His Father

After the brothers return home from Egypt with the instructions to bring Binyamin on their next trip, Yehuda is forced to step forward. As discussed in Chapter 2, Yaakov rejects Reuven's offer to take responsibility for Binyamin. Yehuda realizes that he is going to have to take control to save his family from starvation. This story will reveal the striking differences between the personalities of Yehuda and Reuven. Unlike Reuven, Yehuda is considerate in his timing and wording. He understands how to influence people in order to attain the desired outcome.

In fact, much of Yehuda's leadership here seems to be a reaction to Reuven's mistakes. Reuven eagerly rushes to approach his father with his offer. As soon as the brothers come home from Egypt, he immediately gives his proposal. In contrast, Yehuda is patient and waits until they run out of food (Gen. 43:2–3). Yehuda knows that Yaakov would not allow them to take Binyamin to Egypt. However, once they are starving, he realizes that Yaakov's calculus might change. Even then, when their situation is dire, Yehuda has the presence of mind to wait for Yaakov to approach the brothers to return to Egypt for more food. Only then does Yehuda attempt to convince his father to trust him with Binyamin, as that is the only way to fulfill Yaakov's request.

Not only is Yehuda shrewder than Reuven in his timing, but he also shows more persistence. Reuven attempts to convince his father only once. After being rejected, Reuven immediately gives up (Gen. 42:37–38). In contrast, after Yehuda's first attempt is unsuccessful, he persists and tries again (Gen. 43:3, 8).

But the biggest difference between Yehuda and Reuven is neither timing nor effort; rather, it is the content of their words. Reuven said that he is willing to kill his sons if he fails to return. Clearly that is a ridiculous and thoughtless bargain! Of course, Yaakov would not want to lose two grandchildren after having already lost a son! In contrast, Yehuda's proposal, to accept responsibility, is sensible, sharp, and intelligent.[26]

Let us take a closer look at both of Yehuda's statements to his father to learn more about Yehuda. The two speeches are very different from each other, and examined together they reveal another talent of Yehuda's. He is able to read the reaction of his interlocutors and revise his words to bring them into agreement. He can interpret subtle cues from their response in order to know how to reply most productively. We will see this same skill when he speaks to Yosef, pleading for Binyamin's life in Gen. 44.

But let's first review these two presentations by Yehuda. His first speech is an attempt to rationally and calmly explain to his father the circumstances behind why they need to take Binyamin when they return to Egypt to buy food: "The man solemnly warned us, saying, 'You shall not see my face, unless your brother is with you.' If you send our brother with us, we will go down and buy you food, but if you do not send him, we will not go" (Gen. 43:3–5). With these words, Yehuda presents a very logical argument in a sensible and composed way. However, Yaakov does not react rationally. In an emotional tirade he berates his sons, blaming them for having revealed Binyamin's existence. The sons react by defending themselves and blaming the viceroy of Egypt for inquiring about their brother.

---

26. Ramban on Gen. 42:37 disagrees and believes that both offered the same thing, but that still, Yaakov trusts Yehuda more than Reuven. According to this explanation, it wasn't the content of what they said, as he was never going to trust Reuven. Yehuda has done nothing to lose his father's faith in him, and possibly the reason Yaakov trusts Yehuda is simply that Yaakov recognizes the leadership qualities in Yehuda and trusts that he would be able to keep Binyamin safe.

This is when Yehuda successfully de-escalates the situation. He tries a second, entirely different approach. He understands that his father is being emotional and not thinking rationally about Binyamin. Therefore, Yehuda realizes that he needs to emote and show passion in his argument: "Send the boy with me, and we will arise and go, so that we may live and not die, both we and you, and also our little ones. I will be collateral for him. From my hand will you require him. If I do not bring him to you and set him before you, then let me bear the blame forever, for unless we had lingered, surely we would have returned a second time by now" (Gen. 43:8–10). Yehuda is no longer asking docilely for permission; instead, he is forceful, commanding his father to send the boy with him. He appeals to his father's fears by assuring him that he will be responsible for Binyamin and offers himself as collateral for his brother.[27] This is a much more impassioned offer than the one presented by Reuven.

However, it should be noted that as he begins this speech, he starts with an obvious point – that not sending Binyamin would cause death to the entire family. He is manipulating Yaakov by using his own words and fears against him. Recall that Yaakov had told his sons when they went to Egypt for the first time that they should go so that "we will live and not die" (Gen. 42:2). Now Yehuda mimics his father's words and throws them back at him (Gen. 43:8). The only way that we can survive, he tells Yaakov, is if you let us take Binyamin, "so that we may live and not die"! In Yehuda's recycling of Yaakov's words he essentially accuses his father of caring about Binyamin more than the rest of the family. He explicitly notes the contradiction in Yaakov's view – forbidding Binyamin to leave would not be giving Yaakov more time with Binyamin in the long term because Yaakov himself would die of starvation along with Binyamin. Yehuda concludes by blaming Yaakov for the delay he is causing in their procuring more food. Had he allowed them to take Binyamin, they would already have returned from Egypt with food!

As opposed to Reuven, Yehuda is able to successfully manipulate their father. He manages to do this through a combination of the force of his personality and his ability to twist Yaakov's words against him.

27. Rashi and Rabbenu Baḥya on Gen. 43:9 each understand Yehuda's offer as an acceptance of responsibility in the World to Come were something bad to happen to Binyamin.

He then presents the only possible solution to all these issues, which is entrusting himself with Binyamin. It should not surprise the reader that Yaakov acquiesces to Yehuda's demand.

**Standing Up to Yosef**

The brothers return to Egypt with Binyamin to face their brother Yosef for the second time. Yosef commands one of his servants to place his goblet into Binyamin's sack, after which Yosef accuses Binyamin of stealing and sentences him to a life of servitude. At this point, Yehuda asserts his leadership once again. His qualities of persistence, power, and fearlessness, as well as the strength of his argument, will allow him to prevail against the Egyptian viceroy. Let us review the unfolding narrative.

After Binyamin is caught with the goblet, his brothers accompany him back to the palace to face Yosef. The verse here mentions Yehuda's name separately, implying that he has already stepped into his leadership position: "And Yehuda and his brothers came to the house of Yosef…" (Gen. 44:14).

Yehuda prepares to engage with the second most powerful man in the world. Just as he did with his father, Yehuda begins with a gentle tone, and then switches his strategy when the plan fails. At first, Yehuda expresses flattery and praise for the viceroy. All the brothers fall on their faces, bowing to Yosef to show their respect. Yehuda, still on the floor, speaks: "Yehuda said, 'What will we tell my lord? What will we speak? Or how will we clear ourselves? God has found out the iniquity of your servants. Behold, we are my lord's bondservants, both we, and he also in whose hand the cup is found'" (Gen. 44:16). Yehuda begins with flattery, referring to Yosef as "my master" and to himself and his brothers as "your servants." During this dialogue, he refers to Yosef as their master eight times, and to himself and his brothers as servants thirteen times. Yehuda's first strategy is to follow up his flattery with supplication, pleading for Binyamin's life. He attempts to appeal to Yosef's merciful side. Yosef responds by stoically reiterating that Binyamin will be his slave for life and the rest of them can go home.

Yehuda persists and tries again, this time with a different strategy. The verse states that "Yehuda approached him" (Gen. 44:18). Yehuda gets up from his prostration and comes face-to-face with Yosef, unafraid and determined to save his brother. He begins again with flattery, assuming that powerful people enjoy hearing their praises. As Yosef is second-in-command,

Yehuda suspects that Yosef likely aspires to absolute control. Therefore, Yehuda begins his oration with the ultimate compliment: "You are just like Pharaoh himself." After this flowery opening, Yehuda transitions swiftly to an altogether different, much harsher and stronger tone.

Yehuda begins innocently by recounting earlier events that explain why Binyamin is currently in Egypt. By the time he is done, Yehuda has so twisted the details that he has laid the blame for their situation with Yosef himself.

This is Yehuda's version of the story as he tells it:

> My lord asked his servants, saying, "Have you a father, or a brother?" We said to my lord, "We have a father, an old man, and a child of his old age, a little one; and his brother is dead, and he alone is left of his mother; and his father loves him." You said to your servants, "Bring him down to me, that I may set my eyes on him." (Gen. 44:19–21)

This is the actual narrative as presented in the Torah:

> Yosef remembered the dreams which he dreamed about them, and said to them, "You are spies! You have come to see the nakedness of the land." They said to him, "No, my lord, but your servants have come to buy food. We are all one man's sons; we are honest men. Your servants are not spies." He said to them, "No, but you have come to see the nakedness of the land." They said, "We, your servants, are twelve brothers, the sons of one man in the land of Canaan; and, behold, the youngest is this day with our father, and one is no more." Yosef said to them, "It is like I told you, saying, 'You are spies.' Hereby you shall be tested. By the life of Pharaoh, you shall not go forth from here, unless your youngest brother comes here… Bring your youngest brother to me; so will your words be verified, and you will not die." (Gen. 42:9–15, 20)

Yehuda manipulates the truth by leaving out important details and adding in subtle inaccuracies. What is the effect? Yosef feels guilty and responsible for the situation. How did Yehuda accomplish this? He presumed that with the passage of time, Yosef would not remember all the details of their first encounter. By maintaining as many accurate details as possible, and only changing the minimum number of details that are necessary for his objective, Yehuda hopes that Yosef will not realize the lies.

What were Yehuda's fabrications? The first is his explanation for why Binyamin is present: It was Yosef's doing, because he asked them if they had a father and brother.[28] He is pointing a finger at Yosef, saying that had he not asked about Binyamin, he would not have known about him and therefore wouldn't have asked the brothers to bring him down. Consequently, Binyamin would not have been in the position to take the goblet. Yehuda is claiming that it is entirely Yosef's fault that Binyamin is in Egypt and took the goblet!

In truth, Yosef had never even asked them these questions at all! Rather, the brothers had volunteered this information in their defense against the accusation of spying. In summary, Yehuda's lie assigns the blame to Yosef for asking them the questions that led to the discovery of Binyamin's existence.

His second fabrication consists of leaving out a significant element of the story that puts the brothers in a compromising position. Yehuda does not want to remind Yosef that he accused the brothers of being spies the first time he met them. Rather, his presentation focuses on their innocent intentions of coming to Egypt to collect food, a process during which Yosef had asked them gratuitous questions about

---

28. Ralbag on Gen. 43:7 argues that this was not, in fact, a lie at all. When Yosef accused them of being spies, he started asking questions in order to prove his suspicion and catch them in a lie. Among other questions, he asked "Do you have a father?" and "Do you have another brother?" Therefore, Yehuda is not lying when he says that Yosef asked him these questions. Furthermore, when the brothers report the story to their father, they also tell him that Yosef asked them these questions (Gen. 43:7).

    However, one could counter that the brothers repeat their experiences in Egypt twice to their father. The first time is soon after they return home, when they have no reason to lie. At that point, they don't mention Yosef asking them any questions (Gen. 42:30–32), but they do mention that they offered him information about their family to prove that they are not spies. Only in Gen. 43:7, after Yaakov yells at the brothers for telling Yosef about Binyamin, do they change their story. They say Yosef asked them if they had a brother, but deny that they offered him the information. It appears that Yaakov's sons lie to their father in an attempt to convince him about the necessity of taking Binyamin to Egypt.

their family. He skips the part of the story relating to their time in jail or Shimon's later incarceration. By ignoring the details relating to Yosef's earlier accusation about spying, Yehuda hopes to avoid the connection between that accusation and the new one leveled against Binyamin. If he had made that connection, Yosef would then have corroboration for his suspicion that this is a family of sinners, spies, and thieves.

Finally, Yehuda adds imagery that invokes mercy and sympathy. The details he adds that were not in the original narrative are about Binyamin's special status in the family as the only remaining child from his mother. This had never actually been told to Yosef in Gen. 42. They had simply told Yosef earlier about Binyamin that he is "younger… [and] at home with our father" (Gen. 42:13). Yehuda is trying to engender compassion from Yosef, focusing on Binyamin's special status as his father's favorite child.

To review, in only three verses, Yehuda changes the entire content and emotional cadence of the brothers' first encounter with Yosef. In his version of the story, Yehuda depicts an overbearing, cruel leader who asked unnecessary questions and forced Binyamin to appear, even given his distinctive role in the family.

But Yehuda does not stop there. He fabricates an alternative conclusion to the story. He makes up a completely new ending, where the brothers argue against Yosef's request: "We said to my lord, 'The boy can't leave his father: for if he should leave his father, his father would die.' You said to your servants, 'Unless your youngest brother comes down with you, you will see my face no more'" (Gen. 44:22–23). During the original story in Gen. 42, the brothers never imply anything even remotely similar to this! They don't react to Yosef's command at all, but just accept it as their fate. Here, Yehuda is exaggerating to burden Yosef with the implications of this version of the story. He is positioning Yosef as a tyrannical leader who has no pity for their sad state. By doing so, he is also branding the brothers as selfless pawns who are coerced by Yosef, but who really care only about their father's welfare. In this version, Yosef is portrayed as an ogre who ignores their pleas for the life of their father. Still, Yehuda is not finished! He furthers his rendition of history by describing an almost-truthful version of the interactions between the brothers and Yaakov upon their return from Egypt.

In the rest of his speech, Yehuda continues to use these tools to accomplish his goal of manipulating Yosef and reversing the fate of Binyamin. First, he changes actual details of the story and twists the details of the original narrative to make Yosef feel partially accountable and to pity their aging father. Second, he leaves out important details that would take the focus away from Yehuda's goal.

His first method of creating fabrications is clearly seen when he rewrites the story of the brothers' negotiation with their father. He depicts his father as a frail old man who is hungry and just wants a little food to eat. Yehuda hides the truth that Yaakov waits until they are almost completely out of food before he requests that their return to Egypt, insensitive to the fact that the rest of his family is starving (Gen. 43:2). Yaakov puts the welfare of Binyamin over that of the rest of the family. But Yehuda changes all of Yaakov's outcries and accusations towards his sons[29] into passionate and sorrowful speeches. He rewrites Yaakov's words to be more sympathetic, quoting him as saying, "You know that my wife bore me two sons, and the one went out from me, and I said, 'Surely he is torn in pieces,' and I have not seen him since" (Gen. 44:27–28). Although in both versions Yaakov cries about Yosef, in Yehuda's version Yaakov's plea evokes much more sympathy as he cries over losing his two sons from his favorite wife. Yehuda is manipulating the truth to create an image of a pitiful old man whose life is now dependent on Yosef.

But changing details isn't enough to convince Yosef. Yehuda must also delete all the details of the story that incriminate the family or that call their innocence into question. Yehuda never mentions telling their father about Yosef's accusation of them being spies and his keeping Shimon in jail. Actually, he omits Shimon's name from this entire speech because he doesn't want Yosef to be reminded of the brother he threw in jail, who has already been released.[30] He also leaves

29. Yaakov's version was: "You have bereaved me of my children! Yosef is no more, Shimon is no more, and you want to take Binyamin away. All these things are against me" (Gen. 42:36).
30. Shimon is released in Gen. 43:23, when the brothers come back to Egypt and are brought to Yosef's house for a meal.

out Reuven's attempt to convince his father to let him be responsible for Binyamin, as well as Yaakov's refusal, since that would make Yaakov sound stubborn and unsympathetic to his starving family. Additionally, Yehuda doesn't say that he twice attempted to convince his father to permit Binyamin's travel to Egypt, nor does he say anything about his father's outburst when he found out that the brothers told Yosef they had a younger brother.

Yehuda's reason for changing and removing details of the story is to depict his father as a sympathetic, starving old man who so desperately loved his deceased wife Raḥel and her two sons that he won't survive losing the last remnant of their union.[31] By describing Yaakov as a kindhearted person who has already experienced too much tragedy in his life, Yehuda is implying that it would be cruel to make such a dejected man go through more pain and sorrow.

His grand finale is when he explicitly blames Yosef for murdering his father by saying, "It will happen, when he sees that the boy is no more, that he will die. Your servants will bring down the gray hairs of your servant, our father, with sorrow to the grave" (Gen. 44:31). Yehuda is stating outright that their father will die from misery, and it will be Yosef's fault, as he was forewarned of this outcome. He is blaming Yosef for something there would have been no way for Yosef to know. When looking at the original story, never did the brothers communicate that Binyamin is so precious that their father's life depends on his welfare. However, in Yehuda's version, Yosef did know but didn't care. Yosef is being accused of being cold and callous!

---

31. Yehuda also changes his description of the status of Raḥel's oldest son. When they initially came down to Egypt, the brothers said that Yosef was missing (Gen. 42:13), whereas in Yehuda's summary he says that Yosef is dead (Gen. 44:20). Why might he have switched the description? Perhaps he did this because Binyamin was present, so Yehuda had to maintain the pretense that Yosef is dead. Alternatively, as Rashi on Gen. 44:20 points out, Yehuda was concerned that if he said Yosef was missing, the viceroy of Egypt would command them to find him in order to redeem Binyamin from slavery. Finally, and most simply, saying a brother is missing raises greater suspicion and foments more distrust of the family.

## The Culmination of Yehuda's Oration

> Now therefore, please let your servant stay instead of the boy, a bondservant to my lord; and let the boy go up with his brothers. For how will I go up to my father if the boy is not with me? Lest I see the evil that will come on my father. (Gen. 44:33–34)

Yehuda ends his pitch by offering the ultimate personal sacrifice. He is willing to martyr himself for his brother Binyamin for the sake of his fragile, elderly father. This proposition confirms his credibility and shines the focus brightly on his father, Yaakov.

What was the goal of Yehuda's whole speech? Clearly, he wanted to frame this oration, which should have been about the goblet in Binyamin's sack, as a reflection of Yaakov's heartache. He focuses on his father as an innocent figure sitting at home, waiting anxiously for the return of his sons. He is delicate and starving, on the brink of death. He is miserable and sorrowful from the tragedies he has lived through. The speech is not about Binyamin. In fact, Binyamin is never even mentioned by name. He is only described in sympathetic language: he is referred to as a "young boy" (43:8), implying his innocence. Why did Yehuda do this? Clearly, Yehuda thinks that focusing on Binyamin's behavior would have been ineffective (apparently he sees it as being worthy of guilt). Rather, Yehuda reframes the narrative to focus on the one factor that Yosef has already shown an interest in – Yaakov, their father. Yehuda noted that when the brothers returned to Egypt, Yosef immediately asked about the welfare of their father. "He asked them of their welfare and said, 'Is your father well, the old man of whom you spoke? Is he yet alive?'" (Gen. 43:27). He seemed to care about the old man's health and well-being. Yehuda uses this hint of kindness and interest in his family to redirect the narrative and manipulate Yosef.

As we have observed, Yehuda is very successful at manipulation! But do his efforts successfully impact Yosef? After Yehuda finishes his oration, Yosef breaks down and cries out. He is so overcome with emotion that his cries are heard throughout the palace. Yehuda, with his strength, conviction, intelligence, and ingenuity, deflects the harsh punishment of the viceroy of Egypt!

This episode encapsulates Yehuda's unique leadership traits. He is fearless in the face of confronting authority. He knows how to control the dialogue and get into the heads and hearts of his audience. And he persists until he attains his desired result. This is Yehuda!

However, this story is even more powerful when viewing it in comparison to Yehuda's actions during the sale of Yosef, Raḥel's older son. His absolute commitment to protecting Binyamin in Egypt may indicate Yehuda's repentance for the sin of selling Yosef. Unlike that ordeal from his past, when he allowed Yosef to be sold and lost presumably forever – Yehuda now fearlessly stands up for Binyamin even at the risk of his own life. He recognizes that the children of Raḥel are irreplaceable to his father, and therefore he must fight for their safety. Yehuda accomplishes here what he was unable to do in Gen. 37: he prevents Yaakov from losing a son of his favorite wife, Raḥel.

## RECOGNIZED AS LEADER BY HIS FATHER

### Sent First to Goshen

> He sent Yehuda before him to Yosef, to show the way before him to Goshen, and they came into the land of Goshen. (Gen. 46:28)

When Yaakov is about to descend to Egypt and reunite with his son Yosef, he waits until he receives God's encouragement and permission to leave the land of Israel. Yaakov wants to see Yosef but is afraid of the implications of leaving Israel. Recognizing that Yehuda is the son whom he can rely on before arriving in Egypt, Yaakov sends Yehuda to his newly allocated land of Goshen. What was Yehuda's task? The commentators debate whether Yaakov's instruction to prepare the land related to its physical or to its spiritual character.[32] Interestingly, it is Yehuda – not

32. Rashi on Gen. 46:28 quotes both views. Concerning the view that Yaakov wanted Yehuda to prepare Goshen physically, Rashi says this is the literal reading of the text, whereas the view that he wanted him to prepare Goshen spiritually is the midrashic view of the Sages (see Gen. Rabba 95:3). Radak and *Ḥizkuni* on Gen. 46:28 write that Yaakov wanted Yehuda to ask Yosef for the most direct path to Goshen, thus avoiding traveling through Egypt. Sforno ad loc. adds that Yehuda was sent ahead to set up their homes.

Yosef – who is selected for this mission. Rabbenu Baḥya on Gen. 46:28 writes that by sending Yehuda, Yaakov demonstrates his belief that Yehuda is the strongest and most clever of all the brothers.

## The Blessing of Leadership

> "Yehuda, your brothers will praise you: Your hand will be on the neck of your enemies; your father's sons will bow down before you. Yehuda is a lion's cub. From the prey, my son, you have gone up. He stooped down, he crouched as a lion, as a lioness. Who will rouse him up? The scepter will not depart from Yehuda, nor the ruler's staff from between his feet, until he comes to whom it belongs. To him will the obedience of the peoples be. Binding his foal to the vine, his donkey's colt to the choice vine; he has washed his garments in wine, his robes in the blood of grapes: His eyes will be red with wine, his teeth white with milk." (Gen. 49:8–12)

Yaakov thus blesses Yehuda with leadership. On his deathbed, Yaakov tells Yehuda that he is destined to be the king of the Jewish people; all of his brothers will bow to him. This blessing is the natural trajectory for the Yehuda whom we've learned about in Genesis. The brothers listened to him at the sale of Yosef; he represented them successfully regarding Binyamin, both to Yaakov and to Yosef; he is the brother who prepares Goshen for the family. Yehuda is born a leader and will continue to lead throughout Jewish history.

Yaakov's blessing captures Yehuda's specific qualities of leadership. He compares Yehuda to a lion, the fiercest of all animals, representing his strength and fearlessness.[33] Yehuda is strong in the confident way he speaks to his father and to the viceroy of Egypt. His strength of character is equally evident in his ability to publicly admit his mistake with

33. The mention of wine in Yaakov's blessing can be understood to be foretelling that in the land of Yehuda there will be vineyards that will produce a tremendous amount of wine. Alternatively, it may refer to the numerous righteous people who will be born into his tribe (see Rashi on Gen. 49:11). Lastly, it may hint to the wealth of the future kings who come from this tribe.

Tamar. He is also comparable to a lioness who crouches as she waits for prey. Yehuda shows tremendous patience and timing, as he waits to speak to Yaakov until after Reuven has tried. He waits patiently, like a lioness, until he knows that he has found the opportune time and best way to approach his target.

Concluding the stories about Yehuda in Genesis, we note that we have been exposed to an awe-inspiring character. His intelligence, fearlessness, and leadership are unparalleled by any of his brothers. In the next chapter, we will see these traits on display in his descendants. Unfortunately, we will also observe that just like Yehuda, there are progeny from this tribe who fail to control their temptation for beautiful women.

*Chapter 7*

# Yehuda in Tanakh

As we saw in the last chapter, Yehuda is a natural leader. He exhibits wisdom, bravery, and inner strength when he leads his family through very challenging circumstances. Yaakov's deathbed blessing to Yehuda reaffirms Yehuda's role as leader over his brothers. In fact, throughout Tanakh, Yehuda's progeny take on a disproportionately large share of responsibility for and management of the Jewish nation. Not only will individuals from Yehuda rise to leadership positions, but the tribe as a whole will guide and direct the Jewish people.

## THE LEADERSHIP TRIBE

The tribe of Yehuda leads the nation in their travel configuration during the forty-year trek through the desert. In Numbers chapter 2, where the tribes are divided into encampments, Yehuda is not only the leader of his local three-tribe encampment, going ahead of the tribes of Yissakhar and Zevulun, but Yehuda's encampment is also at the forefront of the other three encampments (Num. 2:3–9). Traveling in the front, Yehuda blazes the trail, leading the way for the entire nation. As a result of its unique status, the tribe of Yehuda is the first to be allocated land in Israel. Years later, when Yehoshua earmarks the land by lottery, the first drawing is – amazingly – the tribe of Yehuda (Josh. 15).

Twice in the book of Judges when the Jewish people ask for a leader, God responds, "Yehuda will lead" (Judges 1:2, 20:18). The first instance is after the death of Yehoshua, when no individual successor is appointed. God tells the people that the new leader will be the tribe of Yehuda, who will be at their head to capture the new land in Israel. Immediately following this appointment, we learn about Yehuda's military successes against the Canaanites in their land. Yehuda is the only tribe to capture its entire territory (Judges 1). It is fitting that during that period, the first judge of the Jewish people is Otniel son of Kenaz from the tribe of Yehuda. Similarly, years later when the nation needs a leader for a civil war against the tribe of Binyamin, God answers the nation's second request for leadership, and the tribe of Yehuda becomes their guide (Judges 20:18). Eventually, a Jewish monarchy is established, and after the short reign of Shaul from the tribe of Binyamin, Yehuda rules until the Jewish nation is exiled from the land. In summary, the tribe of Yehuda plays a central leadership role throughout this early period of Jewish history. Members of this tribe step into unique roles of leadership that reflect the attributes of their patriarch, Yehuda – both the positive and negative aspects.

## SHARED STRENGTHS FOUND IN YEHUDA'S DESCENDANTS

### Fearlessness

Many of Yehuda's descendants exhibit the boldness and courage that remind us of their ancestor Yehuda in Genesis. Specifically, they share his capacity to stand up to people of power, acting fearlessly when others are afraid to engage.

#### *Naḥshon Son of Aminadav*

Naḥshon leads the tribe of Yehuda during the journey through the desert (Num. 1:7). This may explain why Aharon chooses to marry his sister Elisheva. The verse states, "And Aharon took Elisheva the daughter of Aminadav, sister of Naḥshon, as a wife" (Ex. 6:23). The text highlights that he is Elisheva's brother, implying that his stature may have been a factor for Aharon's consideration in selecting Elisheva as a wife. The

Talmud adds a dimension to Aharon's decision to marry Naḥshon's sister by providing background about who he is. The Talmud in Sota 37a states that when the Jewish people were standing at the banks of the Red Sea, they were frozen in fear of the approaching Egyptians. At that point, Naḥshon jumped into the waters, precipitating the splitting of the sea. Naḥshon exhibited courage and full faith in God, demonstrating to the Jewish people that they had no reason to be afraid. He led the Jewish people by example into the water, where they witnessed the final stage of their miraculous freedom from their oppressors. The sea split, allowing them to cross it on dry land as the Egyptians drowned in the water. It is fitting that the Sages attribute this fearless action to a man from the tribe of Yehuda.

### *Kalev Son of Yefuneh*

Kalev demonstrates heroism and bravery on numerous occasions. He is introduced to us as one of the spies whom Moshe sends to scout out the land of Israel (Num. 13:6). Kalev, along with Yehoshua, are the only two spies to return with a positive report about the land. After the other ten spies terrify the nation by reporting sightings of giants and warriors, Kalev counters their claim.[1] Kalev, from the tribe of Yehuda, is strong enough to dispute the words of the ten princes. He quiets the nation and argues that the Jewish people are entirely capable of going into Israel and possessing it (Num. 13:30).[2] After his report, the other spies attempt to contradict him, leading the people to start crying and

---

1. Moshe, Aharon, and Yehoshua stand quietly as Kalev speaks up. After Kalev's speech does not succeed, Moshe and Aharon fall on their faces, unable to speak.
2. The Talmud in Sota 35a states that Kalev quieted the people by first seemingly insulting Moshe, thus convincing the people to listen to him. He began as follows: "Look what the son of Amram has done to us." They all stopped to listen, and then instead of speaking critically he said, "We can do it! We can go in!" Kalev, like Yeḥuda in Genesis, knew the right words to say to make those around him listen. He understood them and knew how to make his words resonate with them. (Rashi on Num. 13:30 also cites this view from a midrash.) Rashi on Num. 14:24 adds that Kalev deceived the ten spies into thinking that he was on their side and was against entering the land of Israel. Therefore, they allowed him to speak. He was able to use his charisma and powers of persuasion to control the ten spies and the Jewish people, embodying the personality of his ancestor Yehuda.

complaining. This time, Kalev and Yehoshua together try to silence them. They say, "The land, which we passed through to spy it out, is an exceedingly good land. If God delights in us, then He will bring us into this land, and give it to us, a land that flows with milk and honey. Only do not rebel against God, neither fear the people of the land; for they are bread for us: their defense is removed from over them, and God is with us. Do not fear them" (Num. 14:7–9).

In both of his orations, Kalev shares his strong belief that, against all odds, the Jewish people can overcome their enemies. We are strong, he argues. There is no reason to fear, for God will protect us! As a result, God publicly recognizes and praises the fearlessness of Kalev and describes it as otherworldly: "My servant Kalev... had another spirit with him, and has followed Me fully" (Num. 14:24). God singles him out for his exceptional bravery in this story. By standing up against the spies, and then standing up against the cries of the nation who were being swayed by the lies, Kalev merits special recognition and praise from God. Kalev is rewarded for his deeds with permission to enter the land of Israel and is given a special plot of land in Israel, the land of Hebron.[3]

Beyond expressing fearlessness when he speaks, Kalev is also brave in battle. In the story of the spies, Kalev tells the Jewish people not to fear the giants. Years later, in the book of Joshua, it is none other than Kalev who kills the giants: "Kalev drove out there the three sons of the giant: Sheshai, and Aḥiman, and Talmai, the children of the giant" (Josh. 15:14). As noted earlier, the tribe of Yehuda is the first one to obliterate all the Canaanites in their land, and this is to the credit of their leader, Kalev, who leads them in battle against the Canaanites in their land. They are even successful in overpowering the terrifying King Adoni Bezek, who was known for conquering seventy kings and for the cruelty of cutting off the thumbs and big toes of his enemies (Judges 1:5–7).

3. The tribe of Yehuda ensures that Yehoshua allocates this land to Kalev in Josh. 14. It is especially fitting that Yehoshua, the other "good spy," is the one to award this land to Kalev. The verse states: "And Yehoshua blessed him and gave the land of Hebron to Kalev son of Yefuneh as his inheritance" (Josh. 14:13).

Just as Kalev has the qualities of a leader, he inculcates these attributes in his son Ḥur.[4]

### *Ḥur*

Ḥur is introduced to us as a member of Moshe's leadership team. In the initial battle after leaving Egypt, the war against Amalek, Aharon and Ḥur are selected to join Moshe on the top of a mountain. They are trusted to hold up Moshe hands, thus inspiring the Jewish people to turn to God (Ex. 17:10–12). Later, when Moshe goes up on Mount Sinai to receive the Torah, he places Aharon and Ḥur in control of the nation. "Behold, Aharon and Ḥur are with you. Whoever is involved in a dispute can go to them" (Ex. 24:14). Ḥur, representing the tribe of Yehuda, helps lead the nation along with Moshe's other partners, Aharon, from the tribe of Levi, and Yehoshua, from the tribe of Yosef's son Ephraim.

Despite Ḥur serving critical roles in the early stages of the Jewish people, he does not reappear in the Torah after the revelation. To help understand this omission, the Sages presume that he has died.[5] How so? Before Moshe belatedly descends from the mountain at Mount Sinai, the nation approaches Ḥur, asking to build a golden calf. Fearless and strong, Ḥur says no; he refuses to enable such an atrocity. In retribution, the people murder him.[6] His reaction demonstrates the quality of standing up for what one believes in for the sake of God, even at the risk of one's life. Showing the same courage seen in Yehuda and his other descendants, Ḥur does not fear the maddened throngs, even under danger of giving up his life in defense of God.

---

4. Evidence that Ḥur is Kalev's son is found in the following verse: "And Kalev took a wife, Efrat, and she bore him a child named Ḥur" (I Chr. 2:19).
5. See Leviticus Rabba 10:3.
6. Rashi on Ex. 32:5 presents this midrash to explain the words "and Aharon saw." Rashi there asks: what did Aharon see that would convince him to agree to collect jewelry and build the calf? According to the midrash, Aharon saw the people murder Ḥur. Therefore, Aharon recognized that refusing their demands was not an option.

### *Otniel Son of Kenaz*

> When the children of Israel cried to God, God gave the children of Israel a savior: Otniel the son of Kenaz, Kalev's younger brother, who saved them. The spirit of God came on him, and he judged Israel; and he went out to war, and God delivered Kushan Rishataim, king of Mesopotamia, into his hand: and his hand prevailed against Kushan Rishataim. (Judges 3:9–10)

Kalev has another close relative who leads the Jewish people. Three times in Tanakh, we are told that Otniel is the brother of Kalev (Josh. 15:17, Judges, 1:13, 3:9),[7] highlighting the familial bond of fearlessness and strength, especially in conquering the land of Israel. But as an individual, who is Otniel?

Otniel is the first judge of the Jewish people after the death of Yehoshua. An earlier story illustrates his bravery and strength and explains why he deserves this distinguished role in the Jewish nation. This story about Otniel is so significant that it is recorded twice, once in the book of Joshua and again in the book of Judges. The book of Joshua records that "Kalev said, 'He who strikes Kiryat Sefer, and conquers it, I give to him Akhsa, my daughter, as a wife.'" (Josh. 15:16). The book of Judges then relates that "Otniel the son of Kenaz, the brother of Kalev, took it: and he gave him Akhsa, his daughter, as a wife" (Judges 1:13).

Kalev had led the tribe of Yehuda in fighting for their land. However, he left one parcel of land unconquered at the southern border of Yehuda's territory. Presumably, this land was an intimidating and difficult place to fight, as he offers his daughter in marriage to anyone who is brave

7. One may wonder how it is possible that Kalev, the son of Yefuneh, is the brother of Otniel, son of Kenaz. The Talmud in Sota 11b writes that they shared the same mother but had different fathers. Abarbanel, in his introduction to the book of Judges, writes that they had the same mother and father; Kenaz was really their grandfather, and Yefuneh their father. He writes that there are other people who are called the sons of their grandfathers instead of their fathers – for example, Akhan son of Zeraḥ (Josh. 7:24), even when we know that Zeraḥ is his great-grandfather (Josh. 7:18).

enough to conquer it.[8] Without flinching, Otniel fights for this land and marries his niece, Akhsa.

Later, when Otniel ascends to become the first judge of the Jewish people, he is victorious in his battle against the oppressive enemy, Aram.[9] The text offers very limited details about this battle, simply stating that "he goes out to war and God gives them over into his hand" (Judges 3:10). In contrast to the other judges who succeed him, Otniel needs no special encouragement. He is brave! The others will need reassurance, detailed battle plans, and oversized armies. He is fearless in battle and is armed only with the knowledge that God is on his side: "And the spirit of God came on him, causing his victory, and God gave into his hands Kushan Rishataim the king of Aram" (Judges 3:10).

### *King David*

A few generations after Otniel, we are introduced to arguably the most courageous and fearless person in all of Tanakh, King David. As a young boy,[10] he confronts Goliat the giant, armed with only a slingshot and a few rocks, and no armor. There is no other soldier in the Jewish army, including King Shaul, brave enough to face the terrifying giant. The text summarizes the scene as follows: "All the men of Israel, when they saw the man, fled from him and were extremely afraid" (I Sam. 17:24). Shaul offers his daughter's hand in marriage as well as a tax exemption to any man who fights and kills the giant.[11] Why the need for such an excessive incentive? Clearly,

8. Similarly, Shaul offers his daughter to anyone who successfully defeats the intimidating warrior Goliat. In that context, it seems that Shaul is too scared to fight the enemy. He bribes someone else to fight the giant in his place, by offering marriage to his daughter (I Sam. 17:25). It appears that Otniel is being offered the same arrangement by Kalev. Why would Kalev offer such an arrangement if he himself is a brave warrior? Evidently, the only reason he would pass off this piece of land to his brother is that the people living there are so terrifying. Even Kalev is too scared to fight! This highlights the exceptional fearlessness of Otniel.
9. Judges 3:9–10.
10. He is too young to be drafted into the army. Why, then, is he present at the battlefield? His father sends him to check on his older brothers, who are soldiers, and to bring them food. For this reason, Shaul initially refuses to let David fight, saying, "I cannot let you fight because you are a boy" (I Sam. 17:33).
11. This is similar to the reward offered by Kalev to the man who fights and conquers Kiryat Sefer, as discussed above.

the chances of survival must have been slim. In spite of these risks, David is full of bravery and faith in God. Therefore, he immediately volunteers for the task. Yet, the offer is so outrageous that Shaul initially rejects it because of David's young age. However, David insists that he is perfect for the job. This persistent refusal to accept rejection resembles his ancestor Yehuda's refusal to accept rejection from his father with regard to taking Binyamin to Egypt. David reaffirms his desire to fight and insists that despite his age, he is strong enough. To prove himself, he shares with Shaul a story about his fearlessness. He claims that on one occasion when he was shepherding his father's sheep, a lion and bear attacked one of the sheep. David describes how he chased down the bear and slayed it, removing the sheep from its mouth. When the lion pounced on him, he grabbed its mane and killed it as well (I Sam. 17:34–35). This famous incident highlights the bravery of the young future king.

Also, in spite of the unique reward offered by Shaul, David is clear that the reward is not the motivating factor in his desire to fight Goliat. Rather, he wants to kill the giant as a demonstration of his faith in God. He states: "God, who delivered me out of the paw of the lion, and out of the paw of the bear, He will deliver me out of the hand of this Philistine" (I Sam. 17:37).

So too, when Goliat laughs at David and curses him, David responds: "Then said David to the Philistine, 'You come to me with a sword, and with a spear, and with a javelin, but I come to you in the name of God, the God of the armies of Israel, whom you have defied. This day will God deliver you into my hand; and I will strike you and take your head from off you; and I will give the dead bodies of the host of the Philistines this day to the birds of the sky, and to the wild animals of the earth; that all the earth may know that there is a God in Israel'" (I Sam. 17:45–46).

The key factor that demonstrates David's heroism in this episode is his battle strategy against Goliat. When the giant charges at him, instead of receding in fear, David bravely charges directly at him! He hits Goliat with a rock from his slingshot, toppling him over. David then rushes over and chops off Goliat's head using the giant's own sword. This is an utterly incredible act of physical bravery and inner strength!

### *Daniel, Ḥananya, Mishael, and Azarya*

Moving hundreds of years forward to the first exile to Babylon, where the book of Daniel takes place, we encounter two remarkable stories of bravery and faith in God even in the face of likely death.[12]

In Daniel chapter 3, Daniel's three friends (Ḥananya, Mishael, and Azarya) are told (twice!) to bow to a giant golden image. They refuse, even under threat of being thrown into a fiery furnace. In chapter 6, Daniel violates the law of the land by praying to his God and is thrown into a lion's den. In both stories, the heroes refuse to relinquish their values, and prefer to receive a horrible death penalty. When they miraculously survive, they gain tremendous respect from all who witness the events. King Nevukhadnetzar promotes them and publicly declares "that every people, nation, and language that speak anything evil against the God of Ḥananya, Mishael, and Azarya, shall be cut in pieces because there is no other god who is able to deliver in this way" (Dan. 3:31–33).

To summarize, fearlessness is a recurring attribute among Yehuda's descendants. Because of their dual belief in God and their mission, they are willing to fight while everyone around them is scared and hiding. Clearly, this is a core attribute for leadership.

## Superior Intelligence

Yehuda in Genesis demonstrated his superior intellect in the way he spoke to and manipulated those around him to concede to his plans. Hence, he was able to convince his father to permit Binyamin to go to Egypt. Once in Egypt, he used this skill when speaking with Yosef, culminating with Yosef revealing his identity. Yehuda's intelligence is unparalleled among his brothers and is a vital attribute in the leadership of his descendants in Tanakh.

### *Betzalel*

Betzalel, the grandson of Ḥur and great-grandson of Kalev, is chosen for the honor of building the Tabernacle and its utensils. He earns this role specifically because of his unique intelligence:

---

12. These four individuals are introduced to the reader as members of the tribe of Yehuda: "And it was amongst them, from the tribe of Yehuda, Daniel, Ḥananya, Mishael, and Azarya" (Dan. 1:6).

> Behold, I have called by name Betzalel the son of Uri, the son of Ḥur, of the tribe of Yehuda: I have filled him with the spirit of God, in wisdom, and in understanding, and in knowledge, and in all manner of workmanship, to devise skillful works, to work in gold, and in silver, and in brass, and in cutting of stones for setting, and in carving of wood, to work in all manner of workmanship. (Ex. 31:2–5)

This emphasis on his wisdom is repeated again later (Ex. 35:30–33). It is clear that to undertake the role of building a house of worship for God, Betzalel requires an additional dose of wisdom.

### *Otniel Son of Kenaz*

The Sages struggle to understand why the story of Otniel fighting in Kiryat Sefer (described above) is included twice in Tanakh, first in Josh. 15 and again in Judges 1. Further, they struggle to understand the nature of this place. One suggestion to the latter point is that the name of the city, Kiryat Sefer is not actually its name, but is rather an allusion to his conquest of the most valuable and precious Jewish *sefer*, i.e., book: the Torah. The Talmud in Temura 15a presents an approach in line with this view, which explains that this story of Otniel conquering Kiryat Sefer is intended to enlighten the reader about his intellectual conquest. Otniel is able to learn the 1,700 Torah secrets that were forgotten during the mourning period for Moshe. Accordingly, the repetition of this story reinforces the unique significance of this event and this person. Malbim on Judges 1:11 offers textual evidence for the Sages' perspective to address why this battle is followed by the seemingly irrelevant detail that the sons of Keini moved to the land of Yehuda. He suggests that this detail is added to highlight that they were coming to learn these new Torah insights from Otniel, the "*Rosh Yeshiva*," i.e., head of the study house. According to this rabbinic tradition, the focus of this story is not just on the literal battle in a place called Kiryat Sefer, but also on Otniel's role as a generational link in passing the traditions and teachings of Moshe to a new generation.

### *King Shlomo*

King Shlomo is famous for his unparalleled wisdom. After being anointed as king, Shlomo hears the word of God in a dream, offering him a special gift. Shlomo chooses wisdom: "Give your servant therefore an understanding heart to judge your people, so that I may discern between good and evil; for who is able to judge this, your great people?" (I Kings 3:9). God grants him understanding and wisdom, and the gift is described in much the same way as the account of Betzalel:[13] "Behold, I have done according to your word: behold, I have given you a wise and an understanding heart, so that there has been none like you before you, neither after you shall any arise like you" (I Kings 3:12).

This blessing is immediately followed by a story that tests and ultimately exposes Shlomo's wisdom. Two women come to King Shlomo, each claiming to be the mother of the same baby. His response: Cut the baby in half! What motivated this answer? He knew that the actual mother would do anything, even give her baby to another woman, to save his life. This story serves as Shlomo's introduction to the world stage as a sagacious leader. And indeed, the world took notice: "They saw that the wisdom of God was in him, to do justice" (I Kings 3:28).

A few chapters later, the Torah reiterates the superiority of Shlomo's wisdom:

> God gave Shlomo wisdom and understanding exceeding much, and very great understanding, even as the sand that is on the seashore. For he was wiser than all men, and his fame was in all the nations round about. He spoke three thousand proverbs; and his songs were one thousand and five. He spoke of trees, from the cedar that is in Lebanon even to the hyssop that springs out of the wall; he spoke also of animals, and of birds, and of creeping things, and of fish. There came of all peoples to hear the wisdom of Shlomo, from all kings of the earth, who had heard of his wisdom. (I Kings 5:9–14)

In fact, the prophet Yeshayahu utilizes the imagery of the wisdom of Shlomo when he attempts to describe the ideal king: "A spirit of wisdom

13. The description for Betzalel is "wisdom, understanding, and knowledge" (Ex. 31:3, 35:31). Similarly, for Shlomo the description is "a heart of wisdom and understanding" (I Kings 3:12). In both cases, these traits were explicitly given to them by God.

and understanding, the spirit of counsel and might, the spirit of knowledge and of the fear of God, he shall not judge after the sight of his eyes, neither decide after the hearing of his ears; but with righteousness shall he judge the poor, and decide with equity for the humble of the earth" (Is. 11:2–4).

However, the awareness of Shlomo's wisdom is not limited to the prophets or even the Jewish nation. Respect for Shlomo's wisdom impacts his national enemies, precipitating a period of peace and serenity, as seen in his interaction with King Ḥiram: "And God gave wisdom to Shlomo as He told him, and there was peace between Ḥiram and Shlomo and they made a covenant together" (I Kings 5:26). Similarly, Shlomo impresses the Queen of Sheba, who tests Shlomo's wisdom with riddles. She concludes by stating: "Your wisdom is even greater than what I had heard" (I Kings 10:7).

Shlomo's enhanced standing in the world leads to a period when the Jewish people flourish and multiply, thus fulfilling the promise God had made to Avraham so many years earlier: "I will multiply your seed... as the sand which is on the seashore" (Gen. 22:17). In the past, these words described the enemies attacking us. For instance, during the time of Yehoshua, the army of Canaan is described as "even as the sand that is on the seashore in multitude" (Josh. 11:4). Similarly, during the time of King Shaul, the Philistines are described as "people as the sand that is on the seashore in multitude" (I Sam. 13:5). Now, for the first time, during Shlomo's rule, these words describe the Jewish people: "Yehuda and Yisrael were as numerous as the sands of the seashore" (I Kings 4:20).

### *Daniel, Mishael, Ḥananya, and Azarya*

In the last year of King Yehoyakim's reign (he, too, was from the tribe of Yehuda), Nevukhadnetzar attacked Jerusalem, taking the brightest Jewish boys to Babylonia as his future advisors. Daniel, Ḥananya, Mishael, and Azarya, all from Yehuda, are among those taken because of their exceptional intellect.[14] During their fourth year in Babylonia, they are

14. The description of their intelligence resembles the language regarding Betzalel and King Shlomo: "And skillful in all wisdom, and endowed with knowledge, and understanding science" (Dan. 1:4). Similar to the blessing bestowed on Betzalel and Shlomo, their intelligence is an explicit gift from God: "Now as for these four

tested and found to be smarter than the king's wise men and astrologers. In the second chapter of Daniel, these men are able to interpret King Nevukhadnetzar's dream that he forgets upon awakening. None of his wise men or astrologers can figure out how to interpret a forgotten dream. With the help of God, Daniel and his friends are able to remind Nevukhadnetzar of his dream and tell him its interpretation.

Exceptional intelligence is a common attribute found in descendants of Yehuda. Their ability to lead is in many ways connected to their situational awareness and ability to understand people. The stories of Betzalel, Otniel, Shlomo, and Daniel are examples that reflect this trait found in abundance in the tribe of Yehuda.

### Persistence

Another of Yehuda's special qualities is his persistence. Recall that Yaakov initially refused Yehuda's request to take Binyamin down to Egypt. Unlike Reuven, Yehuda persists until his father relents. Similarly, after Yosef refused to allow Binyamin to return to Yaakov, Yehuda persists until his brother is freed from slavery. He never gives up! Instead, he adapts his strategy to attain his desired outcome. In the prior chapter, we observed how Yehuda uses this characteristic when he switches tones with Yaakov, going from respectful to demanding. When interacting with Yosef, Yehuda switches from desperate to strong. The trait of persistence is also apparent in his descendants; they persist until attaining the outcomes they desire.

#### *Tribe of Yehuda*

As the book of Judges concludes, Yehuda is selected to lead the Jewish people in a civil war against the tribe of Binyamin.[15] Shockingly, Yehuda and the eleven tribes lose the first battle, with a death toll of 22,000 soldiers. Led by the tribe of Yehuda, the Jewish nation does not give up. Rather, the tribe coordinates another battle, where it loses

youths, God gave them knowledge and skill in all learning and wisdom: and Daniel had understanding in all visions and dreams" (Dan 1:17).

15. Judges 20:18–48. This war is a reaction to Binyamin's refusal to hand over the men from their tribe who were responsible for raping and murdering a concubine passing through their land.

another 18,000 soldiers. Amazingly, Yehuda still does not give up! This time, the tribe turns to God in prayer and fasting. The tribes seek guidance from Pinḥas, the grandson of Aharon, who informs them that God grants them permission to keep fighting. The tribe pulls together its army to fight a third battle; this time, it is successful, killing 18,000 soldiers and destroying much of the tribe of Binyamin (Judges 20:44).[16]

### *King David*

Just like when he was a boy,[17] King David never allows a momentary setback to prevent him from accomplishing a goal. Once appointed king, David wants to bring the Ark, which has inside it the holy tablets, to the City of David (Jerusalem). Understanding David's challenge in achieving this objective requires background information about the travels of the ark. Prior to this point, the ark had been in limbo since the times of Eli the high priest, when it was in Shiloh. Eli's sons, Ḥofni and Pinḥas, had removed the ark from the Tabernacle to bring it with them to battle against the Philistines. That war ends tragically. Ḥofni and Pinḥas are killed and the ark is stolen (I Sam. 4). The Philistines take the ark back with them, but

---

16. There is much discussion in the commentaries about why they lose the first two battles. Malbim on Judges 20:18–28 offers three possibilities:
    (1) Permission: They did not request permission from God to go to battle until the third fight.
    (2) Repentance: In a similar approach, they may not have repented before battle until the third time.
    (3) Implications: By losing the first two battles, they were made sensitive to the implications of a civil war.
17. As a lad, David approaches King Shaul to volunteer to fight the giant Goliat. As we noted earlier, Shaul's initial reaction is to refuse the offer because young David does not look old enough to be a soldier. He states, "You are not able to go against this Philistine to fight with him; for you are but a youth, and he a man of war from his youth" (I Sam. 17:33). David does not give up! Rather, he tries again to convince Shaul to let him fight Goliat. He shares a story about how he killed a lion and a bear that attacked a sheep from his father's flock while the sheep were under his watch. He concludes by stating, "God who delivered me out of the paw of the lion, and out of the paw of the bear, he will deliver me out of the hand of this Philistine" (17:37). It is unclear whether his story is factual, or contrived to convince Shaul to let him fight. This story is representative of someone from the tribe of Yehuda, not only in David's refusal to give up, but also in his ability to contextualize his argument, perhaps even lying, to get his way.

its presence leads to people dying. The Philistines move it to another city, but death follows the ark. After numerous attempts to move the ark, each time leading to death in the new location, the Philistines decide to return it to the Jewish people. When they reach the Jewish city of Beit Shemesh, Jewish people start dying as well (I Sam. 6). It is decided to place the ark in hiding, inside the home of Avinadav from the tribe of Binyamin, where it remains until the reign of King David (I Sam. 7:1, II Sam 6:3).

King David decides it is time to bring the ark to the center of the monarchy, Jerusalem. However, his initial attempt fails because during the attempted move Avinadav's son Uzza touches it, leading to his death (II Sam. 6:6–7). King David does not give up. He tries again to bring the ark out of hiding. This time he is successful (II Sam. 6:12)! He marks the event with a major celebration, including sacrifices to God and public dancing in the name of God (II Sam. 6:17–19).

Similarly, in II Sam. 7, we learn about David's primary goal for his reign. David desires to build a house for God as a permanent structure to house the ark and God's presence. How does King David attempt this? Simple: he approaches the prophet Natan for permission to build a house for God, i.e., the Holy Temple. Natan initially says yes, but God appears to Natan and demands that he renege on his approval for this request.[18] Once again, David does not accept "no" for an answer. He begs

18. The exact reason God refused to allow King David to build the Holy Temple is unclear. There are three distinct times where this topic is addressed in Tanakh.
   (1) In II Samuel, God cryptically explains to Natan that it is because of David's unique mission. The Temple must be built during a time where "I will cause you to rest from all your enemies" (7:11). Therefore, building the House of God will be the mission of the next generation.
   (2) In I Kings, King Shlomo explains to Ḥiram, the provider of wood for the Holy Temple: "You know how David my father could not build a house for the name of his God for the wars which were about him on every side, until God put them under the soles of his feet. But now God has given me rest on every side; there is neither adversary nor evil occurrence" (5:17–18). Shlomo explains that David's reputation for shedding blood in battle seems to be why he could not build the Holy Temple.
   (3) This is further explained in I Chronicles, where we are told that "David said to Shlomo his son, 'As for me, it was in my heart to build a house to the name of the Lord my God. But the word of God came to me, saying, "You have shed blood abundantly, and have made great wars: you shall not build a house to My Name because you have shed much blood on the earth in My sight. Behold, a son shall

God to allow him this honor. Even after being rejected again, David still does not despair. Instead, he changes his goal. He decides to prepare the infrastructure so that his son Shlomo would be able to build the Temple during his reign. King David collects gold, silver, and other materials, and builds all the vessels for the Temple. Years later, when his son Shlomo is ready to build the First Temple, he utilizes all the vessels that his father had prepared for him: "Thus all the work that King Shlomo worked in the house of God was finished. Shlomo brought in the things that David his father had dedicated, even the silver, and the gold, and the vessels, and put them in the treasuries of the house of God" (I Kings 7:51).

David could have accepted his fate of not being the one to build the Holy Temple and given up on that dream. Instead, he persevered, doing as much he possibly could in anticipation of Shlomo's future role.

***Daniel, Ḥananya, Mishael, and Azarya***

In the first chapter of the book of Daniel, the four captive boys (whom we met earlier in this chapter) arrive in Babylonia to work in the palace, where they are offered non-kosher meat and wine to eat and drink. They approach the commanding officer to ask for different food. He responded to them saying that they must eat the non-kosher food to ensure they stay in the same physical condition as all other boys taken by the king, because if these four were to be found looking even slightly more malnourished, this officer would fear for his own life. Daniel and

---

be born to you, who shall be a man of rest; and I will give him rest from all his enemies round about; for his name shall be Shlomo, and I will give peace and quietness to Israel in his days. He shall build a house for My Name, and he shall be my son, and I will be his father; and I will establish the throne of his kingdom over Israel forever." Now, my son, God be with you; and you should prosper, and build the house of the Lord your God, as He has spoken concerning you'" (22:7–11). God's home on earth must represent peace and unity of all nations; it cannot have a builder who is associated with bloodshed.

*Midrash Soḥer Tov* 62:4 provides an alternative, non-textual basis for God's refusal to allow David to build the Holy Temple. Given his extreme holiness and righteousness, if David had built the Temple, God would never want to destroy it. Therefore, when the Jewish people sin in the future, God would destroy them instead of the Temple. Thus, God forbade David from building it so that He could retain the possibility of destroying it in the future.

his friends persist and propose that they eat only raw vegetables and herbs for ten days as an experiment. If their health remains equal to the others, then they should be allowed to continue with their diet of vegetables. But if they lose weight, they are to be killed. The officer accepts this proposition. How does it end? God rewards their faith and ensures that they are even healthier and heftier than those who ate the meat and drank the wine.

The ability to persevere and to push the limits of what is possible is evidently a common characteristic found in the descendants of Yehuda. Their ability to fight through perceived obstacles helps them accomplish what others might not. This is another important trait for a leader: to persist in attempting to achieve his national goals.

### Strength to Admit a Mistake

A peak in Yehuda's life and a special moment of moral leadership is his public pronouncement of "she is more righteous than me" (Gen. 38:26). He admits that he erred in his accusation of Tamar and identifies himself as the one who had relations with her. He explains that by avoiding a levirate marriage between his twice-widowed daughter-in-law, Tamar, and his third son Shela, he is at fault and she is innocent. It is human nature to defend ourselves and to rationalize our misdeeds. Yehuda overcomes these natural tendencies and stands up to proclaim that he was in the wrong. This ability to admit wrongdoing reappears throughout the lives of Yehuda's descendants. All humans have flaws, but only the strongest ones are able to admit to them.

#### *Akhan*

> Akhan answered Yehoshua and said, "Of a truth I have sinned against the God of Israel, and thus and thus have I done." (Josh. 7:20)

Twice in Tanakh the following words are uttered: "I have sinned against God." The first person to make this confession is Akhan, from the tribe of Yehuda, in the seventh chapter of the book of Joshua. What led to his declaration of guilt? The Jewish people were beginning to gain a foothold in the land of Israel. Before their initial battle inside Israel, against the inhabitants of Jericho, they are instructed to burn the entire city and everything within it. Akhan defies the command and hides some of the loot inside his tent. As a consequence, God punishes the people in their next battle. The Jewish people lose their fight against the city of Ai, and thirty-six men are killed. Utilizing a lottery system, Yehoshua determines that Akhan is responsible. It is at this point in the story that Akhan steps forward and admits, "I have sinned against God, the God of Israel, and thus have I done" (Josh. 7:20). Akhan does not try to give excuses or justify his misbehavior prior to being condemned to death.

### *Boaz*

> Boaz said, "Blessed are you by God, my daughter: you have shown more kindness in the latter end than at the beginning." (Ruth 3:10)

The book of Ruth depicts a story that takes place during the time of the judges,[19] about a family from the tribe of Yehuda. The family patriarch, Elimelekh, and his two sons Maḥlon and Kilyon die, leaving Naomi and her daughters-in-law, Ruth and Orpah, to consider their respective futures. While Orpah returns to her family in Moab, Ruth returns to Israel in abject poverty with Naomi. (Except for Ruth's willingness to beg for food, they have no source of livelihood.) Ruth ventures into the fields of Naomi's relative, Boaz, to forage for leftover fruits and vegetables to take to her mother in-law. Naomi recognizes that Boaz might be their best chance for survival and asks Ruth to seek his hand in marriage, thus fulfilling the biblical tradition of levirate marriage, i.e., marrying the wife of a close relative who died without children.

This episode is reminiscent of the levirate marriage story between Yehuda and Tamar from the book of Genesis. Recall that Tamar was Yehuda's daughter-in-law; her first two husbands – each a son of Yehuda – die without children. Tamar manipulates Yehuda into having relations with her for the purpose of bearing children according to the laws of

19. In fact, the book of Ruth begins by establishing this context: "It happened in the days when the judges judged…" (Ruth 1:1).

levirate marriage. In both narratives, two brothers die, leaving no children and an obligation of levirate marriage for the widow – Ruth and Tamar, respectively. In both stories, the relatives do not initially fulfill their obligation. It therefore doesn't surprise us when Ruth uses strategies that are somewhat similar to Tamar's (who manipulated Yehuda by dressing up as a prostitute), with the intention of convincing the deceased husband's relative to have relations with her in order to bear his children. How does Ruth do this? She dresses up and perfumes herself in order to convince Boaz to marry her, thus fulfilling this mitzva. Boaz, like Yehuda, admits his mistake of not fulfilling his responsibility to Ruth earlier. Boaz admits, "Blessed are you by God" (Ruth 3:10), similar to Yehuda's words, "She is more righteous than I" (Gen. 38:26). These stories depict the growth of Yehuda and Boaz from abdicators to assumers of their unique responsibilities. They each publicly admit their errors, take responsibility, and repair their past mistakes. Not surprisingly, the unions created by these two episodes ultimately lead to the birth of King David.[20]

### *King David*

> David said to Natan, "I have sinned to God." (II Sam. 12:13)

King David is the second person to exclaim, "I have sinned to God."[21] What led to his confession? David had sexual relations with Batsheva, wife of Uriah, and impregnated her. With that background, King David sends Uriah to the front lines of the battlefield; essentially, he sends him

20. This biological chain is summarized by the final verses of the book of Ruth, which begins with a son from the union of Yehuda and Tamar: "Now this is the history of the generations of Peretz: Peretz became the father of Ḥetzron, and Ḥetzron became the father of Ram, and Ram became the father of Aminadav, and Aminadav became the father of Naḥshon, and Naḥshon became the father of Salma, and Salma became the father of Boaz, and Boaz became the father of Oved, and Oved became the father of Yishai, and Yishai became the father of David" (Ruth 4:18–22).
21. Akhan and David both use the specific words "*ḥatati Lashem.*" Interestingly, this term reminds us of Yehuda's language to his father when taking responsibility for Binyamin: "*ḥatati lekha kol hayamim,*" "I will have sinned to you all my life" (Gen. 43:9), and to Yosef when explaining why he can't leave Binyamin in Egypt: "*ḥatati le'avi kol hayamim,*" "I will have sinned to my father all my life" (Gen. 44:32).

to be killed. In response, the prophet Natan visits David and recounts a parable about a rich man who seizes the poor man's only sheep to feed to his guest. David instinctively condemns the rich man's behavior, at which point Natan compares the rich man to David, who has numerous wives, and the poor man to Uriah, who has one wife. Natan reprimands David for seizing Batsheva from her husband and having him killed. King David immediately recognizes his mistake. He confesses without trying to conceal the nature of his error or cover it with excuses disguised as justifications, despite his position as king. It is the quality of his admission that ensures he is still able to remain king.[22] However, his misdeeds result in punishments, including the death of Batsheva's first child and many troubles from his sons.

The second time David admits to a sin is at the end of his reign, when he counts the Jewish people. He immediately regrets this action and admits, "I have sinned greatly in that which I have done" (II Sam. 24:10). What did he do wrong? One suggestion is simply that he counted the people unnecessarily;[23] another is that by counting them, he implied that he was relying on the large number of men for victory instead of depending on God.[24]

---

22. David's willingness to own up to his mistake when confronted by the local prophet is in contrast to his father-in-law, Shaul, who twice denies his sins when approached by the prophet Shmuel. The first time that occurs is when Shmuel commands Shaul to wait seven days for him, then give sacrifices to God, and only then to fight the enemy. Shaul blames the nation for pressuring him into fighting before Shmuel arrives, and blames Shmuel for being late (I Sam. 13:11–12). The second time is when he does not fulfill the command to annihilate Amalek, by allowing the king and certain animals to live. Instead of taking responsibility, he blames the people for influencing him. Even though Shaul does say "I sinned," he follows the confession with blaming others and trying to justify his actions (I Sam. 15:24). It is Shaul's inability to take full responsibility that leads him to lose his kingdom to David (see Ralbag on II Sam. 22:26, 24:25). This idea is captured in a verse in Proverbs: "He that covers up his sins shall not prosper; but whoever confesses and forsakes them shall have mercy" (28:13).
23. See Rabbi Yeshaya di Trani's commentary on II Sam. 24:10, where he writes that counting the Jewish people is permitted only when the nation is preparing for battle. Here David is being blamed for counting them without needing to know this information for battle.
24. See Ralbag on II Sam. 24:10.

### *King Ḥizkiyahu*

Many generations later, after the division of the Jewish nation between the kingdom of Yehuda and kingdom of Israel, led by Ephraim, Ḥizkiyahu becomes the king of Yehuda.[25] He is righteous. The verse says about him that "he did that which was right in the eyes of God, according to all that David his father had done" (II Kings 18:3). He removes all the foreign gods and houses of idol worship in Yehuda and re-establishes the worship of Hashem and the laws of the Torah. The Tanakh praises him for his efforts: "For he stuck with God; he did not depart from following Him, but kept His commandments, which God commanded Moshe" (II Kings 18:6). In return, God protects Ḥizkiyahu from his enemies and blesses him with military success. Sadly, in II Kings 20, King Ḥizkiyahu becomes deathly ill. He is visited by the prophet Yeshayahu, who warns him about his impending death. King Ḥizkiyahu turns to God in prayer, and God heals him. The Talmud in Berakhot 10a offers the rabbinic tradition for the missing details in this episode. What had Ḥizkiyahu done to warrant being punished so severely? According to the Talmud, he chose to remain unmarried to avoid fulfilling a prophecy that he would produce evil children. Yeshayahu refuses to help him as he believes the judgment was set in stone, and he therefore rejects Ḥizkiyahu's request to marry the prophet's daughter. To this Ḥizkiyahu replies in the Talmud, "Even if a sharp sword is resting on a person's neck, he should not refrain from praying for mercy." Ḥizkiyahu refuses to believe that he should allow himself to die. Rather, he will scream out to God for mercy and admit his sins. This episode highlights the pattern of Yehuda and his progeny to admit their mistakes and improve their ways.

### *King Yoshiyahu*

> He did that which was right in the eyes of God, and walked in all the ways of David his father, and did not turn aside to the right hand or to the left. (II Kings 22:2)

Ḥizkiyahu's great-grandson Yoshiyahu is another righteous king of Yehuda. During his reign, a Torah scroll with many laws and

25. He becomes king in II Kings 18:1, replacing his father Aḥaz.

commands was discovered. These writings had previously been forgotten and therefore the laws therein had not been practiced for many years. Immediately upon the scroll's discovery, Yoshiyahu tears his clothing in mourning and declares that the Jewish nation must learn the laws in order to observe them. He offers no apologetics; he does not attempt to deny or rationalize their prior misdeeds. Rather, he initiates a massive repentance campaign. He reads the Torah to the entire nation and renews the covenant with God, resolving to observe all the commandments in the Torah (II Kings 23).

This sampling of stories from the family of Yehuda highlights the inner strength of the tribe, which has the courage to admit its mistakes. This courage is coupled with physical bravery, usually apparent in battle, as we observed previously. The prophecy of Yaakov comparing Yehuda's strength to the strength of a lion is shown to be true throughout Jewish history.

## SHARED FLAWS FOUND IN YEHUDA'S DESCENDANTS

The patriarch Yehuda had flaws that are detectable in his descendants as well. Recall the challenges Yehuda faced. Yehuda demonstrated his susceptibility to be seduced by a woman (Tamar). He also stepped back during challenging situations, allowing the situation to develop until he was ready to step forward. This latter issue is clearly the reflection of a critical strength of Yehuda – he does not covet power, and he lets leadership come to him naturally. Regrettably, at times this can cause a leadership void which other, less qualified people may try to fill. Similarly, while Yehuda is a man of strength, we will see that his descendants must struggle to contain that strength.

### Susceptibility to Seduction

As noted, Yehuda fell prey to a beautiful woman, Tamar, who was waiting for him on the side of the road. Yehuda's descendants will sadly also succumb to a disproportionate number of inappropriate relationships.

#### *Maḥlon and Kilyon*

Earlier, we noted the deaths of Elimelekh, Maḥlon, and Kilyon in the first chapter of the book of Ruth. However, the text never reveals how or why they died. Was it because they had left Israel,[26] or because they abandoned their fellow brothers to starve during the famine,[27] or for choosing to live permanently in the land of Moab?[28] The reader does not know! However, we do know that Maḥlon and Kilyon not only remain in Moab after the death of their father, Elimelekh, but they choose to marry Moabite women. "They took them wives of the women of Moab; the name of the one was Orpah, and the name of the other Ruth" (Ruth 1:4).

---

26. The Talmud in Bava Batra 91a attributed their deaths to this reason. There are various textual allusions to it as well. Two times in the opening verses of the book of Ruth the text states that they left "*Beit Leḥem Yehuda*" (v. 1 and 2), highlighting their decision to leave their ancestral land in Israel. This decision to leave may have been their father's. However, after his death, they remain in Moab, thus making themselves equally culpable and deserving of the same punishment. Similarly, the text describes the permanence of their sojourn to Moab by using the phrase "and they were there" (v. 2). This is a clause used exclusively in our story plus three other instances in Tanakh; in the other three instances, there is no intent on leaving or moving (Deut. 10:5, Josh 4:9, I Kings 8:8). Consistent with this, Maḥlon and Kilyon are punished only after they remain outside of Israel for another ten years: "And they were there for about ten years" (Ruth 1:4). The implication is that this represents a period of permanence.
27. The Talmud in Bava Batra 91a quotes a rabbinic tradition that assumes Elimelekh, Maḥlon, and Kilyon were wealthy leaders of the Jewish people who could and should have supported them during a famine (Rashi on Ruth 1:1). There might be a supporting hint in the text: Elimelekh is called "*ish*," "a man," which Rashi on Numbers 13:3 writes is only used to highlight the importance of a person.
28. The text repeats four times that they specifically chose to live in the land of Moab (v. 1, 2, and 6), highlighting that their living in Moab and marrying Moabite women is the reason they were killed. The Torah in Deuteronomy 23:4 presents the rule that Jews are never allowed to marry someone from Moab because of all their terrible misdeeds towards the Jewish people in our past:
    (1) The Moabites forbade the Jewish nation to pass through their land and didn't give them food and drink on the way into the land of Israel.
    (2) The Moabites hired Bilam to curse and then destroy the Jewish people.
    (3) The Moabites sent women to seduce the Jewish men as a ploy to cause the Jewish people to sin and thus be vulnerable to defeat.

    Ruth Rabba 1 and Seder Olam Rabba 12 place this story at the time of Ehud (a judge in the book of Judges), who fights against the nation of Moab. If this is true, then Elimelekh and his sons are traitors for leaving the Jewish people and joining the enemy nation.

Presumably, their willingness to marry Moabite women played some role in their punishment.[29]

### *Boaz*

Boaz had a responsibility to marry his relative's widow, Ruth, and fulfill the mitzvah of levirate marriage. As we noted earlier, this realization did not come to him immediately upon Ruth's appearance from Moab. How did he recognize that he had this responsibility? It happened in a very Yehuda-like episode. Following Naomi's counsel, Ruth washes and anoints herself with sweet-smelling scents. She dresses up attractively (like Tamar in Yehuda's story). Ruth enters Boaz's tent in the middle of the night while he is sleeping, uncovers his legs, and lies there until he awakes. Somehow, she suggestively proposes that he should marry her, and then follows up by securing his commitment to marry her. This story therefore shares two elements of Yehuda's encounter with Tamar: the man's tendency to fall prey to an attractive woman's advances, and the woman utilizing this shortcoming to secure marriage.[30]

### *The Concubine at Giva*

At the end of the book of Judges, an unnamed woman from the tribe of Yehuda is raped and murdered. Although our sympathy is with her for the cruel behavior of her attackers, the story begins with her own misdeed against her husband. The verse states, "His concubine cheats on him" (Judges 19:2). This is another example of sexual misconduct in the tribe of Yehuda.

---

29. I Chr. 4:22 describes the sin of Yoash and Saraf from Yehuda. The Sages in Bava Batra 91b assume these two men are in fact Maḥlon and Kilyon. Their sin is described in the Talmud as marrying into Moab.

30. Whether or not Boaz and Ruth had relations in his tent is debated in rabbinic tradition. One perspective is presented in Ruth Rabba 6, where it is assumed that Boaz and Ruth overcame their physical desires. Alternatively, *HaKetav VeHakabbala* on Gen. 35:22, commenting on the episode of Reuven and Bilha, assumes that Boaz and Ruth had a sexual encounter in the tent. His understanding is derived from the repetition of the Hebrew root *shin, kaf, beit,* meaning "to lay," in Ruth 3:13–14, as that root often indicates sexual relations.

### *King David*

> David did that which was right in the eyes of God, and did not turn aside from anything that He commanded him all the days of his life, except only in the matter of Uriah the Hittite. (I Kings 15:5)

King David is praised for his many righteous acts and extraordinary leadership. His military prowess ensures that his son and successor, King Shlomo, will benefit from a peaceful reign. Unfortunately, in his personal life King David is disquieted by the same problematic attraction to women that befalls many of Yehuda's descendants. As we saw earlier, II Samuel 11 presents the backstory of David's relationship with Batsheva, the wife of Uriah. At the beginning of the chapter, King David is on his roof at night, where he suddenly observes Batsheva, a very beautiful woman, bathing. In spite of the warning he receives that she is married, he immediately sends messengers to summon her, which leads to intimate relations between them. When David discovers that Batsheva is pregnant as a result of their encounter, he sends for her husband, who is at the battlefront, and tries to subtly convince him to go home and be intimate with his wife so that everyone (Uriah included) would assume Batsheva's pregnancy is due to their evening together. However, Uriah refuses to go home; consequently, David devises an alternative plan. He sends Uriah back to the battlefront with a note to the general to put Uriah on the front lines for the next skirmish. Soon after, Uriah is killed in battle and David marries Batsheva.

The Talmud in Shabbat 56a presents the rabbinic tradition of R. Shmuel bar Naḥmani quoting R. Yonatan that David did not sin. According to this tradition, the David-Batsheva union was technically permissible. How? Once Uriah died in battle, Batsheva was retroactively divorced, based on a retroactive divorce document that warriors typically provided their wives before leaving for battle. Accordingly, David and Batsheva's union was not technically sinful.[31] Even so, this story

31. This view is quoted by Rashi on II Sam. 11:4 in the name of the Sages. In his commentary to the same verse, Rabbi Yeshaya di Trani adds evidence that David didn't

highlights the challenge facing the men from Yehuda's lineage with respect to beautiful women.

In spite of this rabbinic tradition, the text assumes she was a married woman and, therefore, strongly suggests that he transgressed. In fact, King David admits as much to the prophet Natan when he tells him "I have sinned to God" (II Sam. 12:13). How does Natan respond? He does not suggest that David was innocent of transgression; instead, Natan says that because of his meaningful and voluntary admission of wrongdoing, David will be spared an untimely death. As noted earlier, David's misbehavior is followed by punishments, including the death of his first child with Batsheva as well as many tribulations involving his sons. Shockingly, one of David's sons, Avshalom, rapes ten of David's wives on the roof of David's palace in the exact location where David originally saw Batsheva bathing.[32]

Further evidence to suggest that this encounter was wrong is the verse quoted at the opening of this section, which states clearly that David was free of all sins except for this episode.[33] And David himself admits to his sin in the book of Psalms. He writes:

---

sin by sleeping with a married woman, in that the parable told to David by Natan is about a rich man stealing from a poor man, not about forbidden relations. Therefore, it must be that David only stole something, but nothing worse. So too, he argues that a king is allowed to put his strongest soldiers on the front lines, so he did nothing wrong by sending Uriah to fight and consequently die.

32. The verse there states: "Avshalom spread a tent on the roof of the house; and Avshalom went in to his father's concubines in the sight of all Israel" (II Sam. 16:22). The use of the word "the roof" connects this story to the earlier one with David and Batsheva. Recall the description of that event: "It happened at evening, that David arose from off his bed, and walked on the roof of the king's house: and from the roof he saw a woman bathing; and the woman was very beautiful to look at" (II Sam. 11:2). Radak on II Sam. 22:11 asserts that Avshalom sinned in such a way because of David's encounter with Batsheva. As punishment for David's sin, God decreed that his son would rape his concubines.

33. Many commentators acknowledge that the text of the David-Batsheva story is filled with comments that acknowledge that David sinned. Rabbi Yosef Kaspi on II Sam. 11:2 writes that it is evident from the words "and it was bad what David did in the eyes of God" (II Sam 11:27), as well as the other sources noted earlier (Natan's accusation and David's confession in Psalms). Similarly, Ralbag on II Sam. 21:21 writes that David sinned by killing Uriah. Therefore, he was punished in a commensurate

> A psalm by David, when Natan the prophet came to him after he had gone in to Batsheva. Have mercy on me, God, according to Your loving kindness. According to the multitude of Your tender mercies, blot out my transgressions. Wash me thoroughly from my iniquity. Cleanse me from my sin. For I know my transgressions. My sin is constantly before me. Against You, and You only, have I sinned and done that which is evil in Your sight. (51:1–6)

Evidently, David views his own actions as inappropriate and worthy of contrition.[34]

King David has one other story noted in the Tanakh that relates to his interest in women. Later in life, as David grows old, he cannot stay temperate and is constantly cold. What is his solution? He finds a beautiful young woman to warm him.[35] His entourage arranges a search party to find the most beautiful virgin for this role.[36] Poetic justice seems to be at work in David's life: his greatest mistake involved a beautiful woman with whom he had an inappropriate relationship. At the end of his life, he is forced to rely on a similarly beautiful woman, with whom he has no sexual relationship, to keep warm.[37]

---

way: four sons die (Batsheva's first son, Amnon, Avshalom, and Adoniyahu), thus fulfilling David's statement to Natan the prophet that the rich man in the parable (who represents David) should pay four times the amount he stole from the poor man (who represents Uriah): "He shall restore the lamb fourfold, because he did this thing, and because he had no pity" (II Sam. 12:6). David's statement may be based on the rule in Exodus of the penalty for a man who steals a sheep: "If a man steals an ox or a sheep, and kills it or sells it, he shall pay five oxen for an ox, and four sheep for a sheep" (Ex. 22:2).

34. The Talmud in Shabbat 30a tells a story of David pleading with God, saying, "Master of the Universe, forgive me for that sin." And God declares: "You are forgiven."
35. For an analysis of this story, see Rabbi Alex Israel, *I Kings: Torn in Two* (Jerusalem: Maggid Books 2013), 16–27.
36. This story is reminiscent of Aḥashverosh's search among all the beautiful virgins in his kingdom. However, unlike Aḥashverosh, David does not have sexual relations with any of them, including the chosen woman, Avishag. This is made clear in the verse: "The king did not know her" (I Kings 1:4).
37. The question that remains is why David did not have sexual relations with Avishag. R. Yeshaya di Trani on I Kings 1:4 and Rabbi Yosef Kara on 1:3 explain that only a virgin could warm him, so he felt compelled to restrain himself from being with her.

## David's Sons

### *Amnon*

In II Sam. 13, Amnon, David's oldest son and presumptive heir, tragically submits to the tendency of Yehuda's descendants to misuse male-female relationships by falling in love with his half-sister. His uncle Yonadav (also from the tribe of Yehuda) gives him terrible advice: Pretend to be sick and she will care for you, thus allowing the two of you to be alone in your bedroom (II Samuel 13:5). To the detriment of everyone involved, Amnon heeds this advice. When they are alone, he propositions her, but she refuses. In anger, he rapes her. As revenge for this horrible act, Avshalom (Tamar's full brother) murders him.[38]

### *King Shlomo*

Shlomo, David's son and heir, struggles with the same desire for women. Even though he has an extremely successful reign – he builds the Holy Temple and ensures stability in the land – he has one flaw: "Now King Shlomo loved many foreign women" (I Kings 11:1). He marries 700 women and has an additional 300 concubines! The text emphasizes that his interest is specifically in foreign women from nations God specifically forbade Jews to marry (e.g., those from Egypt, Moab, and Amon) due to their negative impact on their spouses.[39] It is specifically women from these nations about which the verse says "Shlomo joined to these

---

Rabbi Yosef Kaspi on 1:4 writes that he didn't have the physical ability to be with her in that way. These explanations would show that Avishag was part of David's punishment, as she was a temptation he could not act upon.

38. In II Sam. 16:20–22, Avshalom also engages in a forbidden sexual relationship. After being punished for murdering his brother Amnon, Avshalom returns to lead a rebellion against his father. As noted above when discussing the David-Batsheva relationship, when Avshalom removes David from his palace, he (Avshalom) rapes ten of David's concubines on the roof. As also noted above, this episode seems to be one focused on revenge against David and less about the physical desires of Avshalom.

39. The verse states "Now King Shlomo loved many foreign women, together with the daughter of Pharaoh, women of the Moabites, Ammonites, Edomites, Sidonians, and Hittites; of the nations concerning which God said to the children of Israel, 'You shall not go among them, neither shall they come among you; for surely they will turn away your heart after their gods.' Shlomo joined to these in love" (I Kings 11:1–3).

in love" (v. 2). As foreshadowed by the prohibition to marry them, these wives introduce foreign idols into the palace:

> For it happened, when Shlomo was old, that his wives turned away his heart after other gods; and his heart was not perfect with the Lord his God, as was the heart of David his father. For Shlomo went after Ashtoret the goddess of the Sidonians, and after Milcom the abomination of the Amonites. (I Kings 11:4–5)

The text is clear that these wives worshipped foreign deities. However, the text is not clear about Shlomo's role in this – did he worship them as well, or did he not stop them from bringing their gods into his palace?

As should be expected, God does not react favorably to these events: "God was angry with Shlomo and had commanded him concerning this thing, that he should not go after other gods: but he didn't keep that which God commanded" (v. 9–10). Clearly, the impression the reader gets is that Shlomo is responsible and likely involved in the misbehavior in the palace.

Evidently, King Shlomo had allowed his relationship with his wives to intersect the path of his relationship with God. At the onset of his reign, his passion is described with respect to God: "Shlomo loved God" (I Kings 3:3). Later on, his love seems focused on his wives: "Now King Shlomo loved many foreign women. Shlomo joined to these in love" (I Kings 11:1, 2). This transformation leads to the unfortunate description that "his heart was not perfect with God" (I Kings 11:4). When he loved only God, "he sacrificed and burnt incense only in the high places" (I Kings 3:3). However, after he fell for the many foreign women the verse states: "Then did Shlomo build a high place for Khemosh, the abomination of Moab, and for Molekh, the abomination of the children of Amon. So did he for all his foreign wives, who burnt incense and sacrificed to their gods" (I Kings 11:7–8).[40]

Although the text implies that King Shlomo also worshipped these foreign deities, rabbinic tradition posits that he only permitted

40. See Rabbi Alex Israel, *I Kings: Torn in Two* (Jerusalem: Maggid Books 2013), 123–131, for an analysis of Shlomo's sin and, specifically, his love for Pharaoh's daughter.

his wives to do so but didn't worship them himself.[41] Irrespective of this point, Shlomo is punished harshly for this – he is told that his kingdom will become fragmented into two. This split of the kingdom of Israel takes place during the reign of Shlomo's son, Reḥavam. Ten tribes abandon him for a new king, Yorovam from the tribe of Yosef (I Kings 12:16).

The text goes to great lengths to connect the division of the kingdom to Shlomo's misconduct. Immediately after the description of Shlomo's sin, he is told: "You have not kept my covenant and my statutes, which I have commanded you. I will surely tear the kingdom from you" (I Kings 11:11).[42]

Yehuda suffered from a passion for forbidden women. Unfortunately, his descendants suffer from the same passions and missteps. They don't adequately learn to avoid these mistakes, and therefore they must live with the consequences.

---

41. As noted earlier, the Talmud in Shabbat 56b quotes R. Shmuel bar Naḥmani in the name of R. Yonatan that King Shlomo did not err, but his wives did. Then why is there a severe reaction by God? Since God blames him for not stopping them, the text presents the problem as though he had worshipped the idols too. Rashi and Ralbag on I Kings 11:7 both quote this teaching. Ralbag specifically adds that Shlomo's sin was allowing his wives to build altars for their gods and to worship them (see I Kings 11:4–9).
42. The Talmud in Sanhedrin 21b notes that King Shlomo does not follow the unique set of laws assigned to the monarchy, i.e., the commands against the ownership of too many horses, accumulating too much wealth, and having too many wives. These rules are set forth in Deuteronomy 17:16–17: "He should not have too many horses lest this causes the people to return to Egypt; he should not have too many wives lest they sway his heart, and not have too much silver and gold." Unfortunately, Shlomo amasses all three forbidden things:
    (1) He attains horses from Egypt: "The horses that Shlomo had were brought out of Egypt" (I Kings 10:28).
    (2) He marries one thousand wives: "And he had 700 wives and 300 concubines, and his wives swayed his heart" (11:3).
    (3) He amasses incredible wealth: "Now the weight of gold that came to Shlomo in one year was six hundred sixty-six talents of gold" (10:14).

    The central question of the rabbinic tradition is whether it is these three things, and specifically his wives, that led him astray.

**Willingness to Step Back During Challenging Situations**

In Genesis, we witnessed hesitancy in Yehuda's responses to challenges. Taken in context, this may have been part of his strategy – that is, to be patient, waiting for the perfect moment to act. However, this passivity may also signal a disinterest in leading. Yehuda was willing to allow his brothers the opportunity to assert themselves. For instance, he gives the brothers the chance to devise two plans for abandoning Yosef before he suggests selling him. Later, Reuven is the first one to approach Yaakov for permission to bring Binyamin to Egypt. Yehuda is hesitant to establish himself as a leader. On the one hand, it is great to have leaders who do not chase the spotlight. On the other hand, by waiting for others to step up, Yehuda may be risking a less optimal outcome than if he were to lead from the start. This risk becomes apparent in the selling of Yosef. By the time Yehuda inserts himself into the conversation, the brothers have already concluded that they want to get rid of Yosef. At that point, Yehuda's options are limited. Yehuda's descendants will also struggle to find their voices; at times, they will not assert their natural leadership.

After the death of Yehoshua, the Jewish people turn to God and ask, "Who should go up to fight the Canaanites first?" As we saw previously, God answers, "Yehuda should go up" (Judges 1:2). God is selecting Yehuda for leadership; however, the contours of this leadership are ambiguous. What are Yehuda's leadership responsibilities? One option is that Yehuda is charged with the responsibility to "fight for his land first" (see Judges 1:1–2) and be a role model of bravery to all the other tribes.[43] This begs the question of why one tribe should fight first instead of all of the tribes fighting the nations in their land at the same time. Abarbanel on Judges 1:1 explains that the intention of God's command for Yehuda to fight first is to establish a model for battle: God will fight on behalf of the Jewish people. After the death of Yehoshua, there was concern that the nations of the world would think that God was no longer helping His chosen nation, which might lead to other nations attacking the Jewish people. Therefore, the first battle is critical for reestablishing that God is still fighting on behalf of the Jewish nation. In this context, Yehuda's leadership specifically consists of the willingness to be the tribe

43. Rashi on Judges 1:2 writes that God meant for Yehuda to go up to fight first.

that will set a new example for God's role in battle. The descendants of Yehuda, who were members of the tribe Yaakov sent ahead to the land of Goshen, are perfectly suited for this responsibility.

If this is the intent of God's instruction (i.e., for Yehuda to go first in battle), then the opening chapter in the book of Judges records a significant success, as we are told about the tribe of Yehuda's success in destroying the enemies in its land (including the evil Adoni Bezek, who previously conquered seventy kings). Yehuda sets the right tone for the rest of the nation for future battles.

However, there is an alternative understanding of God's leadership instruction to Yehuda. The Hebrew word used in the command is "*yaaleh*" (1:2). "*Yaaleh*" could mean: "will lead from the front," i.e., will stand in the front of the nation.[44] If so, then God is charging Yehuda with the task of leading the nation in each battle against all of the enemies living in Israel. This interpretation would resemble the simplest understanding of a similar phrase. Later in history, the Jewish people ask God again "*Mi yaaleh lanu bateḥila lamilḥama,*" "who should lead us in war [with Binyamin]?" God responds, "*Yehuda bateḥila,*" "Yehuda will lead" (Judges 20:18). In that context, the charge is for the tribe of Yehuda to lead the nation in the war against Binyamin (not to fight first).

If this interpretation is accurate, then the opening chapter in the book of Judges does not represent a success for the tribe of Yehuda; rather, it indicates a failure of mission! How so? The tribe conquers its own territory (including the territory of Shimon that is located inside its land), but does not help any other tribe. The text emphasizes this point by contrasting the successes of the tribe of Yehuda with that of its northern neighbor, Binyamin. That tribe is unable to conquer the land of Jerusalem from the Jebusites. Recall that this land is shared by both tribes (Yehuda and Binyamin). Therefore, the text is telling us that Yehuda conquered its half of the land, but left

44. See Radak and Malbim on Judges 1:2, who interpret this command as part of the replacement of Yehoshua. Specifically, the tribe of Yehuda is being tasked with leading the nation in finishing the work Yehoshua had started, i.e., conquering their entire land and removing all the Canaanites living there.

Binyamin alone to attempt (unsuccessfully) to conquer the rest of that territory. Yehuda does not even help its neighboring tribe conquer a shared piece of land![45] In short, the Jebusites still occupy the land of Binyamin, but not the land of Yehuda, because Yehuda does not help Binyamin in battle.[46]

Similarly, the tribe of Yehuda does not step up to help another geographic neighbor, the tribe of Dan, who is supposed to reside in the southwestern border of Israel. The tribe of Dan proves unable to conquer much of its land, forcing it to seek land elsewhere in northern Israel.[47] The obvious solution to Dan's problem would have been for Yehuda to help them conquer their territory. However, Yehuda does not come to assist Dan, or any of the tribes, to fight for their land.[48]

To summarize, we observe two ways to understand the leadership charge given to Yehuda ("*Yehuda yaaleh*"). Each offers a distinct assessment of the success or lack thereof of Yehuda's leadership during the period of the Judges. One option: He rises to his level of responsibility and leads the Jewish people in fighting the nation of Canaan first.

---

45. Yehuda's failure to help Binyamin drive out the Jebusites is highlighted by the subtle difference between the following two verses. In the book of Joshua the verse states, "As for the Jebusites, the inhabitants of Jerusalem, the children of Yehuda could not drive them out: but the Jebusites dwell with the children of Yehuda at Jerusalem to this day" (Josh. 15:63). In contrast, in the book of Judges it states, "The children of Binyamin did not drive out the Jebusites who inhabited Jerusalem; but the Jebusites dwell with the children of Binyamin in Jerusalem to this day" (Judges 1:21). The textual difference clarifies that during the time of Yehoshua, even Yehuda could not conquer this territory. However, by the period of the Judges, Yehuda was able to remove the Jebusites from its land, but was not involved in helping Binyamin to do the same.
46. See Malbim on Judges 1:8, who explains the difference between the language in the two verses this way.
47. In Judges 1:34, we are told that Dan cannot fight against the Amorites in its land, nor can Dan enter the valley in its territory. In Judges 18:1, we learn that the tribe of Dan seeks a new territory because it does not have enough space to live. The men of Dan ultimately conquer Layish in the north of Israel (18:27) and name the territory "Dan" for their forefather Dan (18:29).
48. Yehuda does help Shimon conquer his land because the territory of Shimon is located inside of Yehuda's territory. The verse states, "The children of Shimon had inheritance in the midst of their [Yehuda's] inheritance" (Josh. 19:9).

The other option: He falls short by not helping those around him to fight the enemies in their territories. However, both approaches reflect a limited scope of leadership because Yehuda focuses on its own battle needs rather than focusing on leading the nation.[49]

**Too Strong**

Yehuda is a man of strength, as are his descendants. While this provides many advantages for Yehuda and his offspring, there are times when it becomes a liability. Specifically, there are situations when a nation needs a merciful and understanding leader rather than a strong or courageous one. We will consider two examples from Yehuda's progeny who express their strength to the point that it becomes a weakness.

***Yoav***

Yoav (from the tribe of Yehuda) is the loyal and fearless general of King David's army. It is his and King David's military leadership that brings about an extended period of peace. Even so, Yoav acts in anger by murdering two men whom he had no permission to kill.

As background, let's consider the time period. After King Shaul's reign, the nation was divided into two. The tribe of Yehuda anointed David as king, whereas the rest of the people were still being led by Shaul's bloodline – namely, his son Ishboshet. Avner, who had served as general under King Shaul, serves a similar role under Ishboshet. After some internal squabbles, Avner decides to change his allegiance to David, bringing the rest of the nation with him. Yoav, who was already serving as David's general, becomes jealous and angry about this decision. Yoav hates Avner for a number of reasons,[50] not the least of which must have been a fear that Avner might usurp his role as general in David's army.

49. Another instance of stepping back from leadership might be Yehuda's allowing Shaul (from the tribe of Binyamin) to occupy the throne. This may explain why a king from Binyamin becomes the first king instead of Yehuda, who is blessed with leadership by Yaakov.

50. Avner had previously killed Yoav's brother, Asa'el (II Sam. 2:23). In addition to this personal reason to hate Avner, Yoav lives with the memories of battling Avner when they each led their sides of the nation in battle against each other (II Sam. 2:14).

In this environment, Yoav wants to get rid of Avner. How does he accomplish this? Yoav pretends that he needs to speak to Avner privately. When they are alone, he stabs him in the stomach, murdering him (II Sam. 3:27). Avner was the first person whom Yoav killed without permission or justification. Yoav feels that David is being too soft and that he is blind to the security risk associated with allowing Ishboshet's general to join their ranks (II Sam. 24–25). He feels his only way to protect David's kingdom (and his role within it) is to defy the command of David and to kill Avner.

Years later, as we previously learned, Avshalom rebels against his father, King David. Avshalom is fairly successful (at least initially) and David is banished from his own palace while Avshalom rapes his concubines. Over time, David attains the upper hand in the battle and sends Yoav to lead his troops to conquer Avshalom and his army. However, David commands them not to kill Avshalom, saying: "Deal gently for my sake with the young man, with Avshalom" (II Sam. 18:5). Yoav is reminded of this charge by someone who spots Avshalom stuck in a tree. Yoav had asked the man why he did not kill Avshalom on sight, to which the man responds by referencing King David's plea not to harm him (v. 11–12). But Yoav ignores the command and the warning, and without hesitation stabs Avshalom in the heart and kills him (v. 14).

For various reasons, King David does not punish Yoav.[51] However, at the end of his life, King David warns Shlomo about Yoav: "Moreover, you know also what Yoav the son of Tzeruya did to me. Do therefore according to your wisdom, and do not let his gray head go down to the grave in peace" (I Kings 2:5–6). Yoav personifies strength and bold action. Usually, this is an asset for David's rulership, leading his army to many victories. However, Yoav does not know how to express pity or softness.[52] He believes that Avner and Avshalom deserve

---

51. After the murder of Avner, David admits, "I am this day weak, though anointed king; and these men the sons of Tzeruya are too hard for me. May God reward the evil-doer according to his wickedness" (II Sam. 3:39).
52. It is not only Yoav who doesn't know when to yield. Both of his brothers, Avishai and Asa'el, display this trait as well. During the Avshalom rebellion while David is running away, Shimi son of Gera leads a group of people to throw stones at David and curse him. Avishai reacts harshly, offering to cut off Shimi's head. David, knowing that

to die for their actions against David. He therefore kills them, even against David's wishes.[53]

### *Reḥavam*

A generation later, after the death of King Shlomo, Reḥavam is approached by the Jewish people, who ask him to lessen the tax burden King Shlomo had placed on them. They feel desperate enough to threaten that if he doesn't reduce taxes, they will revolt against him. Following bad advice from his childhood friends, Reḥavam refuses their request. In this context the verse states: "And the king answered the nation harshly" (I Kings 12:13). Reḥavam not only denies their demand, but intends to increase the tax rates: "My father made your yoke heavy, but I will add to your yoke: my father chastised you with whips, but I will chastise you with scorpions" (I Kings 12:14). His actions seem reminiscent of Pharaoh's, who added more work to the Jewish people's load rather than listening to their complaints to lighten their load (Ex. 5:6–9).[54]

Reḥavam acts harshly towards his subjects, the Jewish people, thereby making them feel unwanted, unheard, and oppressed. "When

---

this would not help unite the Jewish people under his rule and overthrow Avshalom, reprimands Avishai and does not allow him to touch Shimi (II Sam. 16:9–11). So too, his brother Asa'el pursues Avner, not giving up the chase even when Avner warns him that if he does not stop, Avner will be forced to kill him. Asa'el continues to chase him, but is no match for Avner, and he is killed (II Sam. 2:23).

53. For more about the complicated relationship of David and Yoav, see Rabbi Alex Israel, *I Kings: Torn in Two* (Jerusalem: Maggid Books, 2013), 37–46.

54. The Torah describes Pharaoh's command to make the work harder for the Jewish slaves using the term "*tikhbad*" (Ex. 5:9), from the Hebrew root *kaf, beit, dalet*, meaning heavy. Various forms of the same root are used by Reḥavam (I Kings 12:4, 10, 11, and 14). In both stories, we learn that the harsh reactions are part of God's bigger plan. As we know, God hardens Pharaoh's heart and tells Moshe that Pharaoh is not going to listen to him: "And I will harden his heart and he will not send out the nation" (Ex. 4:21). Similarly, God sent the prophet Aḥiya to tell Yorovam that he is going to become king of the ten tribes. The text reminds us of God's hand in this matter: "So the king did not listen to the people; for it was a thing brought about by God, that He might establish His word, which God spoke by Aḥiya the Shilonite to Yorovam the son of Nevat" (I Kings 12:15).

all Israel saw that the king didn't listen to them, the people answered the king, saying, 'What portion have we in David?'" (I Kings 12:16).[55]

Consequently, there is a split in the kingdom when ten of the tribes appoint a new king, Yorovam, from the tribe of Ephraim. Had Reḥavam listened to his advisors who cautioned him to be more understanding, history may have played out very differently.

Reḥavam eventually learns his lesson, however. After losing the ten tribes to Yorovam, Reḥavam's initial reaction is to go to battle. But his plan is interrupted by the prophet Shemaya, who commands him not to fight. Shemaya tells him to go home and accept the new reality (i.e., that there are now two kingdoms) as the will of God. Reḥavam's reaction is remarkable and demonstrates his growth. The verse states: "And they listened to the words of God and they turned and went their way, according to the word of God" (I Kings 12:24).

## CONCLUSION

In many ways it is obvious why Yehuda is chosen to be the leader of the Jewish people. The tribe is courageous, strong, fearless, and intelligent. All the qualities that were seen in Yehuda in Genesis appear over and over again in the stories of his descendants. Not only are his assets repeated throughout history, but his weaknesses are as well. However, the greatest of Yehuda's strengths is his ability to admit to his mistakes and grow from his past errors. Therefore, it is fitting that we are promised the Messiah will come from the tribe of Yehuda.[56]

---

55. This complaint was previously used by the Jewish people in the rebellion of Sheva son of Bikhri against David. When David was running from Avshalom, Sheva led a rebellion, saying, "We have no portion in David, and no inheritance in the son of Yishai! Every man to his tent, O Israel" (II Sam. 20:1). These words are repeated here in the story of Reḥavam, when he says, "What portion do we have in David? We have no inheritance in the son of Yishai! To your tents, O Israel!" (I Kings 12:16). However, the reactions of the two leaders are diametrically opposed: David eventually forgives them and helps end the rebellion of Sheva. (David does not even punish Sheva; he leaves that for Shlomo to do.) In contrast, Reḥavam becomes irate at this outcry. Eventually, this reaction leads to Reḥavam losing his kingdom.
56. This idea is hinted to in the prophecies of Yeshayahu (Is. 11:7, 13) and Yeḥezkel (Ezek. 37:15). The idea of the Messiah being from the tribe of David is quoted in the Talmud in tractate Sukkah 52a–b and Sota 48b.

*Chapter 8*

# Yissakhar and Zevulun in Genesis: The Youngest Sons of Leah

After the birth of Yehuda, a transformation occurs in the home of Leah. Her standing in the home and in Yaakov's eyes has shifted. She no longer feels hated by Yaakov; now, Leah is happy. As noted in Chapter 6, this happiness is evident in the naming of her fourth son, Yehuda. After this high point, the Torah notes that "she stopped bearing children" (Gen. 29:35). Having given birth to four sons, Leah finds herself unable to conceive. Her reaction to this secondary infertility is to follow the example of her sister Raḥel by giving Yaakov her maidservant, Zilpa, as a wife to bear him more children in her stead. Subsequent to that point in the story, we are informed that Raḥel's maid Bilha and Leah's maid Zilpa each have two sons (Bilha – Dan and Naftali; Zilpa – Gad and Asher). Yaakov now has eight sons: four from Leah, two from Bilha, and two from Zilpa. After the births of these eight sons are recorded, the Torah presents the birth of Leah's fifth and sixth sons, Yissakhar and Zevulun.

However, it is not just the birth order that serves as backdrop to the births of Yissakhar and Zevulun. In addition, their backstory includes an event previously introduced in Chapter 2 –Reuven picks mandrakes for his mother, Leah, who exchanges these flowers with Raḥel for a night alone with Yaakov. Immediately after this story, the reader is informed that Leah gives birth to Yissakhar. The Sages[1] presume that the juxtaposition of these stories, combined with the meaning of Yissakhar's name,[2] suggests that Leah conceived Yissakhar on the night of the trade. Given this connection, and how this event restores her fertility, it seems relevant to ask how the changes in her fertility provide significance to the births of Yissakhar and Zevulun and the state of the Yaakov-Leah relationship.

### BIRTH OF YISSAKHAR

> God listened to Leah, and she conceived, and bore Yaakov a fifth son. (Gen. 30:17)

As noted above, after Leah's first four sons are born, the Torah states that "she stopped bearing children" (Gen. 29:35). She offers her maidservant to Yaakov as an additional wife, but only because "she saw that she stopped bearing children" (Gen. 30:9). Amazingly, after she gives the flowers Reuven picked for her to Raḥel, Leah becomes pregnant again!

Surprisingly, there is a Midrash[3] that suggests this was not Leah's first experience of infertility, and that initially she was naturally infertile like her sister Raḥel. However, God "opened her womb" (Gen. 29:31) to help reverse Yaakov's negative feelings for Leah. After the significant improvement in her relationship with Yaakov following the birth of Yehuda, God returns Leah to her default infertile status; accordingly, the verse states: "And she stopped bearing" (Gen. 29:35). Evidently, Leah recognizes the change in her body and now believes that she will remain infertile (like Raḥel). Therefore, she imitates Raḥel's actions when she

1. See Rashi on Gen 30:16.
2. "God has given me my reward" (Gen 30:18).
3. Genesis Rabba 71:1, quoted in Radak on 29:31. Sforno on 29:31 adds that the hatred Yaakov felt for her was fundamentally because he recognized that she was barren.

finds herself in the same situation – she offers her maidservant to Yaakov in order to have more children in her name. If this is true, then the births of Yissakhar and Zevulun are miraculous! What textual evidence might support this idea? Their births are contextualized by God's presence: "And God heard Leah" (Gen. 30:17). Leah becomes pregnant only because God provides her with a miracle. The Torah uses language very similar to that of Reuven's birth, which according to this explanation is also a miracle. There it says: "And God saw that Leah was hated, and [He] opened her womb" (Gen. 29:31) and she gave birth to Reuven. Here the text says: "God heard Leah and she conceived a child" (Gen. 30:17). God reacts to Leah's marital situation by miraculously facilitating her pregnancies.

Alternatively, it could be that Leah may have been able to conceive naturally during the early years of their marriage, but then subsequently suffered from secondary infertility.[4] Regardless of this idea, however, her giving birth to Yissakhar and Zevulun is a direct result of God enabling her to conceive.

So too, with respect to other infertile women, the Torah specifically points out God's involvement when they are finally able to birth a child. In Sarah's case the verse says, "God remembered Sarah, and she conceived and gave birth" (Gen. 21:1–2). In Rivka's story we learn that "God was entreated by him [Yitzḥak], and Rivka his wife conceived" (Gen. 25:21). For Ḥana's situation we're told, "And God remembered her, and she became pregnant and gave birth" (I Sam. 1:19–20).

Another way to understand Leah's story is that she was never infertile at all. She, like every woman, needs God's help to allow her body to work the way it should, to get pregnant naturally. The Talmud in Nidda 31a writes that this verse simply teaches us that God was involved in the birth of Yissakhar, as he is in the birth of every child.[5] The Torah is just highlighting that the timing of her pregnancies was perfectly chosen by God to counter a negative feeling or situation in her complicated

4. This means that even if she had no problems conceiving at the beginning of her marriage, she might have become infertile later and needed God's intervention to allow her to become pregnant again.

5. *Otzar Midrashim* (4:90) writes that there are three partners in the birth of every child: his father, his mother, and God. This idea is quoted in *Iggeret HaRamban* chapter 2, found in the *Kitvei HaRamban*.

marriage to Yaakov. The words "He opened her womb" (Gen. 29:31) could imply something miraculous or just describe God's natural involvement in every woman's pregnancy. So too, "and she stopped bearing" simply means that factually she stopped having children, but this does not imply that anything changed biologically in her body to render her an infertile woman.[6] In this second reading, Leah's ability to have Yissakhar and Zevulun is not a miracle that goes against nature at all. Rather, it simply takes her a while to get pregnant, but she finally conceives after a number of years. The simplest explanation for this long gap between children is because her nights with Yaakov were rare. It seems clear that Yaakov would normally spend his evenings with his wife Raḥel.[7] This helps to explain why Leah would need to trade flowers for a night with Yaakov. It is possible that she was with him so intermittently that she was unable to conceive another child.

There is a second ambiguity in our verse, specifically in the words "and God heard Leah." What did God hear? Does she say something to God that is not written in the text? Did she pray to God at this point to please allow her to become pregnant once again, as she has not had a child in many years since the birth of Yehuda? The first understanding is that she prayed to God. If so, it would be understandable that after she prays to God, He would hear her prayers and grant her a child. This directly parallels the story of Raḥel, where the verse states "And God remembered Raḥel, and God heard her and opened her womb" (Gen. 30:22). Even though it does not tell us that Raḥel prayed to God for a child, it seems obvious that during all the years she was infertile, she would have been turning to God often to beg for a child. Finally, God

---

6. Rav Saadia Gaon on Gen. 29:35 simply translates this verse to mean that she stopped having children.
7. This seems the simplest way to explain the following verse: "Lavan went into Yaakov's tent, into Leah's tent, and into the tent of the two maidservants; but he did not find them" (Gen. 31:33). Why is Raḥel's tent not mentioned until the next verse? It seems that Yaakov's tent and Raḥel's tent are one and the same. Rashi on 31:33 writes that the reason they shared a tent is that Yaakov was always with Raḥel. So too, Rashi on 35:22 explains Reuven's misdeed with Bilha as a reaction to Yaakov moving his permanent bed, which had been in Raḥel's tent, into the tent of Bilha after Raḥel's death. Rashi writes that "the bed of Yaakov was usually put in the tent of Raḥel," implying that Yaakov was with Raḥel most nights, not with Leah.

hears her prayers and grants her a son. Similarly, when Rivka is struggling to have children, Yitzḥak prays to God: "Yitzḥak entreated God for his wife, because she was barren" (Gen. 25:21).[8] So too, Ḥana implores God for a child, as is apparent in the verse: "And she prayed to God and she cried" (I Sam. 1:10). After Eli incorrectly accuses her of being drunk in the Tabernacle, he apologizes, saying, "God should give you whatever you asked from Him" (v. 17). All of these barren women pray for a child, and God hears their cries and grants them a child; in this case as well, God hears Leah's prayers and grants her a son, Yissakhar.[9]

The second possibility is that she did not specifically pray to God: it's not that God heard a prayer (that is not written in the text of the Torah); rather, God heard the words she addressed to Yaakov, words which *are* written in the text: "You must come in to me; for I have surely hired you with my son's mandrakes" (Gen. 30:16). These words are clearly not a prayer, but Leah simply speaking to Yaakov when he comes home with the intention of spending the night with Raḥel. In this verse, Leah invites him into her tent for the night. Immediately following this, the text says, "And God heard Leah." Why would this incident motivate God to give her a child?

Perhaps one could suggest that Leah is being rewarded for her generous and sensitive treatment of her sister. Leah gave Raḥel her precious flowers, which she had received from Reuven. In Chapter 2, we discussed various ways to understand why Raḥel desires these flowers and what they represent. If she wants them for their powers of fertility, then Leah should be rewarded for handing them over since at this

8. Rashi on 25:21 writes that the word "*ye'etar,*" "entreated," implies that Yitzchak is praying to God. Genesis Rabba 63:5 notes that Yitzḥak and Rivka were both praying in different corners. This could explain why the verse says "*lenokhaḥ ishto,*" literally "opposite his wife," since they were both standing on opposite sides of the room. God listens to the prayers of Yitzḥak because the prayers of a righteous man (Yitzḥak) who is also the son of someone righteous (Avraham) have more weight than the prayers of someone who is righteous (Rivka) but the daughter of someone evil (Lavan).

9. Radak on Gen. 30:17 writes that the verse states that he heard her prayers in order to teach us her righteousness, in that her prayers helped to create more tribes of Israel. So too, Sforno on Gen. 30:17 writes that she must have prayed to God for more children, as implied by her naming of Yissakhar: "*yesh sakhar,*" "there is reward," indicating that she is rewarded for an effort.

time both sisters are struggling with fertility issues. Leah's giving them to Raḥel would represent a tremendous sacrifice on her part to help her sister. This might explain why God responds to this great act of kindness by allowing Leah to become pregnant. However, if the flowers are unexceptional flowers that are special only because they signal an expression of love from her son, then giving them over to Raḥel for a night with Yaakov might be an unfair trade. It would seem to imply that Leah took advantage of her extremely vulnerable sister. In fact, this might remind us of Yaakov's own tricking of Esav to acquire the birthright for a bowl of soup (Gen. 25:30–33). (Esav, exhausted and starving from a long day in the field and desperate for food, agrees to the seemingly unfair trade.) If so, why would God reward Leah by giving her another child, after taking advantage of her distressed sister?[10]

To help resolve this problem, the Sages explain that Leah didn't pray to God, and that what God hears are Leah's words to Yaakov to sleep with her that evening, but God responds favorably anyway because He understands that her intentions are favorable, in that she wants to have more children for Yaakov.[11]

## NAMING OF YISSAKHAR

> Leah said, "God has given me my reward, because I gave my handmaid to my husband." She named him Yissakhar. (Gen. 30:18)

The naming of Yissakhar seems to express Leah's appreciation to God for another child, combined with a justification for her meriting this child. Sforno on Gen. 30:17 writes that this shows Leah's extraordinary efforts to provide Yaakov with more children. She is even willing to give him her maidservant, who will become another wife to compete with for Yaakov's time and attention. *Ḥizkuni* on Gen. 30:18 explains that Leah, unlike her

10. In these stories the siblings who are taken advantage of are so desperate that they feel they may die. Esav responds to his brother, "Behold, I am about to die. What good is the birthright to me?" (Gen. 25:32). Raḥel, desperate on account of her childless state, tells her husband, "Give me children, or else I will die" (Gen. 30:1).
11. See Genesis Rabba 62:5. Malbim on Gen. 30:17 expands that Leah's trade had nothing to do with desire or lust, but rather was fully for the sake of God.

barren sister Raḥel, didn't have to give her maid to Yaakov. Rashbam on Gen. 30:18 believes that this alone is insufficient to merit another child. Rather, from the fact that the name Yissakhar is spelled with a doubled letter *sin*, Rashbam derives that Leah did two acts that resulted in her meriting this reward: she gave the flowers to Raḥel and she gave her maidservant to Yaakov to marry. Both actions show Leah's willingness to forego something precious for the sake of someone whom she loves. Rashbam also learns this from the double language found two verses earlier, "*sekhar sekhartikha bedudaei beni*," "This is my reward for giving over the mandrakes of my son" (Gen. 30:16),[12] which is similar to the language Leah uses when naming Yissakhar: "*Natan Elohim sekhari*," "God has given me my reward."

While she is certainly helping Yaakov, her good deed and sacrifice may actually be for her maidservant, Zilpa. In fact, Abarbanel[13] suggests that Leah recognizes that Zilpa, the older sister of Bilha (who is already married and has children), is the only unwed woman of the house.[14] Leah wants to share these same opportunities with Zilpa. Her kindness to Zilpa is the selfless and courageous deed that merits Leah more children.

## NAMING OF ZEVULUN

> Leah conceived again and bore a sixth son to Yaakov. Leah said, "God has endowed me with a good dowry. Now my husband will live with me, because I have borne him six sons." She named him Zevulun. (Gen. 30:19–20)

The naming of Zevulun reminds us that Leah is constantly thinking about her relationship with Yaakov. With the birth of each child, Leah hopes their relationship will improve.[15] Therefore, bearing a sixth son to

---

12. This is also the view of Shadal on Gen. 30:18, who believes that the reason the story of the mandrakes is recorded in the Torah is that it is one of the reasons Leah is given another child. He posits that there are two reasons why she merits another child, but only mentions the greater of the two.
13. Abarbanel on Gen. 30:14 says this in his answer to his eighth question.
14. Much of this will be discussed further in Chapters 10 and 11.
15. Rashi on Gen. 30:20 writes that after bearing a sixth child, Leah hopes that Yaakov will move his permanent residence to her tent.

Yaakov makes her happy and excited. She views her newest son as a present from God. As opposed to Yissakhar, whom she views as a reward that she deserved for her own actions, Zevulun is a "*zeved*" (30:19), meaning gift, i.e., an unexpected present from God.

### PERSONALITIES OF YISSAKHAR AND ZEVULUN

There are no stories about Yissakhar and Zevulun in all of Genesis. However, we know that they are present during numerous key episodes. For example, we have every reason to believe that they are present at the sale of Yosef.[16] They were clearly included among the ten brothers who were sent down to Egypt twice. However, in spite of their physical presence, they are absent in the sense that they are the youngest sons of Leah, who are completely dominated by the presence of their older brothers. They demonstrate no ability to speak up or act on important family issues. Yissakhar and Zevulun are followers who listen and do as they are told. They listen to Yehuda and agree to sell Yosef. They let their father believe that Yosef is dead. They go down to Egypt as part of the group begging Yosef for mercy. They stay quiet as Reuven and then Yehuda plead to Yaakov to allow them to take Binyamin. They fall on their faces in front of Yosef when Binyamin is enslaved for life, leaving Yehuda to attempt to rescue him.

One might suggest that the absence of details about Yissakhar and Zevulun means that there is no way to know anything about them. However, from their silence and apparent ambivalence, they might actually be revealing their personalities! Every family or clan has leaders and followers. Yissakhar and Zevulun, as presented in Genesis, are followers.

---

16. It seems clear that all of the brothers except for Yosef were out in the field that day shepherding their father's sheep (Gen. 37:12). Throughout the chapter, the brothers are referred to as a collective group: "*eḥav*," "his brothers" (37:2, 4, 5, 8, 9, 10, 11, 12, 13, 17, 23, 26). When Yehuda suggests selling Yosef, the verse states, "*Vayishmeu eḥav*," "And his brothers listened" (37:27). Furthermore, Yosef accuses all of them of selling him to Egypt (45:4, 5).

*Chapter 9*

# Yissakhar and Zevulun in Tanakh

In light of the previous chapter, we would expect the progeny of Yissakhar and Zevulun to exhibit only limited instances of leadership throughout history. Furthermore, as the fifth and sixth sons of Leah, born many years after their older brothers and not in their inner circle, these two brothers would bond as a pair. In this chapter, we will highlight the few individuals in Tanakh who are from the tribes of Yissakhar and Zevulun, as well as analyze the partnership between these two tribes. In the end, their descendants are almost always the followers of the nation's leaders.

## LEADERS FROM YISSAKHAR AND ZEVULUN

> "There is no tribe of all of the tribes that did not have from them one judge." (Sukkah 27b)

As noted earlier,[1] the Talmud posits that every tribe has at least one individual to lead among the Jewish people during the eras of judges and kings.[2] Therefore, rabbinic tradition asserts that Yissakhar and Zevulun must beget at least one leader from each of their tribes. Unfortunately, the text of Tanakh offers scant detail about their time as leaders. We hear nothing about an enemy they fight, a battle that they lead, or any significant accomplishment. In fact, the lack of detail makes us question the premise of the rabbinic tradition that they did provide at least one leader apiece. Perhaps their leaders just lead within their own tribes or are limited to a region surrounding their tribal lands. Were there any leaders that led the entire Jewish people? Does anyone from this tribe accomplish anything of note? Are they ever considered heroes?

### *Tola Son of Puah*

> After Avimelekh, there arose to save Israel Tola son of Puah son of Dodo, a man of Yissakhar; and he lived in Shamir in the hill-country of Ephraim. He judged Israel twenty-three years, and died, and was buried in Shamir. (Judges 10:1–2)

These two simple verses are all that is known about the only leader from the tribe of Yissakhar. Tola is the first of the more limited judges,[3] who leads after Gidon and his son Avimelekh. We learn where he leads – in the land of Ephraim (i.e., not in the land of Yissakhar). He leads for a significant period (twenty-three years), but less than the forty-year

1. See Chapter 5.
2. The Talmud infers this principle from II Samuel 7:7, where God states, "In all the places where I have walked with all the children of Israel, I have said one thing to all the tribes of Israel whom I commanded to shepherd my nation Israel." God is speaking about leaders of the Jewish people from all of the tribes.
3. In the book of Judges, there are judges who play significant roles in battle and leadership, about whom we know a great deal – Otniel, Ehud, Devora, Gidon, Yiftaḥ, and Shimshon. Then there are the lesser judges about whom we know very little – Tola, Yair, Ivtzan, Avdon, and Eilon.

generational leadership tenure associated with many other great leaders (i.e., Otniel, Devora, Gidon, Eli, David, and Shlomo).[4]

Interestingly, for all of the lesser judges, there is a template for what we learn about their leadership: location of origin, tenure of leadership, their death, and the location of their burial. Tola's description generally follows this model. However, there are a few additional words: "to save the Jewish people." Evidently, he saved the Jewish people![5] But who was the enemy? Where was the war? We do not know. His experience was apparently not sufficiently relevant for the prophet to record the details of his success.

### *Eilon the Zevulonite*

> After him, Eilon the Zevulonite judged Israel; and he judged Israel ten years. Eilon the Zevulonite died and was buried in Ayalon in the land of Zevulun. (Judges 12:11–12)

Eilon judges the Jewish people after Yiftaḥ and Ivtzan. He judges for only ten years – less than Tola's twenty-three years, but more than Yiftaḥ's six years and Ivtzan's seven years. Unfortunately, the text offers no other details about Eilon.[6]

## A BEAUTIFUL PARTNERSHIP

The Torah highlights numerous elements of the partnership between Yissakhar and Zevulun. Structurally, Yissakhar and Zevulun are

4. Otniel (Judges 3:11), Devora (Judges 5:31), Gidon (Judges 8:28), Eli (I Sam. 4:18), David (I Kings 2:11), and Shlomo (I Kings 11:42) all ruled for forty years. Ehud (Judges 3:30) leads for eighty years (i.e., double the forty-year tenure of other leaders).
5. Radak on Judges 10:1 observes that these words (coupled with his being included among the judges) tell us that he saved the Jewish people from an enemy.
6. Of the five lesser judges, only Tola and Eilon lack any additional identifying information. For the other three – Yair from Menashe, Ivtzan from Yehuda, and Avdon from Ephraim – the text gives information about their numerous children. Evidently, those three appear intent on transferring their leadership to their own progeny. In contrast, Tola and Avdon (the two judges from Yissakhar and Zevulun) show no such ambition. Hence, their children's names are not relevant.

included in the same encampment in the desert (Num. 2:5–8). Geographically, their ancestral lands are right next to each other.[7] Textually, the Torah presents their names next to each other in the list of tribal names.[8] (Typically, they are listed after their older brothers but preceding the names of the maidservants' children).

Further evidence of their bond is seen in the blessing they receive in Moshe's final speech: "Of Zevulun he said, 'Rejoice, Zevulun, in your going out; Yissakhar, in your tents'" (Deut. 33:18). Moshe captures their contrasting essences: Zevulun is out-and-about, whereas Yissakhar is a homebody. And yet, as Rashi comments on this verse, "Zevulun and Yissakhar have a partnership."

Later in Jewish history, the children of Yissakhar are known for their intelligence, while the children of Zevulun are warriors:

> Of the children of Yissakhar, men who had understandings of the times, to know what Israel ought to do, the heads of them were two hundred; and all their brothers were at their commandment. Of Zevulun, such as were able to go out in the host, who could

---

7. The only time they are not together is at Mount Gerizim and Ebal: for the blessings and the curses, they are divided onto different mountains. Yissakhar is on Mount Gerizim for the blessings, along with Shimon, Levi, Yehuda, Yosef, and Binyamin. Zevulun is on Mount Ebal for the curses, along with Reuven, Gad, Asher, Dan, and Naftali. Since they are always together, it is possible that they are purposely divided to have a part of their partnership on each mountain. Or, it could be that Zevulun, as the youngest child of Leah, is placed on Mount Ebal with the lower-status tribes of Reuven (who is cursed for his actions with Bilha), the maidservants' children. Yissakhar is with Raḥel's children and the rest of the children of Leah.
8. The order of Yissakhar and Zevulun's names in the lists throughout Torah are sometimes switched. In Gen. 35:23, 46:13–14, Ex. 1:3, and Num. 1:28–31, 2:5–8, 7:18–19, 26:23–27, Yissakhar precedes Zevulun. In Gen. 49:13–15, Num. 34:25–26, Deut. 33:18–19, and Josh. 19:10–23, Zevulun precedes Yissakhar. Why the changing order? Perhaps the order hints to the interchangeable nature of these two tribes. Accordingly, the message is that the two tribes are equal partners. Alternatively, Rabbenu Baḥya on Deut. 33:18 writes that Zevulun is sometimes listed before Yissakhar (in spite of contradicting the birth order) to praise Zevulun for supporting his brother in the study of Torah. Rabbenu Baḥya cites Pesaḥim 53b, which extrapolates from the Yissakhar-Zevulun relationship the principle that physically supporting an individual's Torah studies merits great rewards.

> set the battle in array, with all manner of instruments of war, fifty thousand, and who could order the battle array, and were not of double heart. (I Chr. 12:32–33)

Based on the collective weight of these references, their constant pairing and their similar status in the family, it is clear why the Sages connect Yissakhar with Zevulun in a more ambitious way: "Yissakhar sits and learns Torah while Zevulun goes out to the sea and brings food and puts it into the mouth of Yissakhar. Zevulun goes out to work and feeds Yissakhar, who is learning Torah" (Genesis Rabba 72).

This fraternal partnership contrasts with another set of brothers where one is also a Torah-studying homebody and the other is a man of physicality, but who lack this special partnership – Yaakov and Esav:[9] "Esav was a cunning hunter, a man of the field, and Yaakov was a plain man, dwelling in tents" (Gen. 25:27). Furthermore, Esav and Zevulun seem to exhibit parallel actions. Gen. 25:28 explains that Yitzḥak loves Esav because "game was in his mouth" (Gen. 25:27) which is explained by the commentators to mean that Esav put food into Yitzḥak's mouth.[10] This is the exact language employed by the Sages to describe Zevulun putting food into the mouth of Yissakhar. However, in contrast to the Yissakhar and Zevulun's bond, Esav and Yaakov fail to form a partnership. In fact, when Yaakov takes Esav's blessing (after Esav exchanges his birthright for a bowl of lentils), irreparable harm is done to their relationship. This is in stark contrast to the Yissakhar-Zevulun bond, leading one to wonder whether the younger pair's relationship was designed as a paradigm to provide a redemptive element to the fraternal bond.

---

9. The Malbim on Gen. 27:5 writes that Yitzḥak intended to give the blessing to Esav because he wanted his two sons to form a partnership, like the one that develops later between Yissakhar and Zevulun. However, Rivka realized that Esav was too evil and would never share the family's inheritance and wealth with his brother.
10. See, for example, Rashi, Ibn Ezra, Ramban, *Kli Yakar*, and *Toldot Yitzḥak* on Gen. 25:28.

## THE FOLLOWERS OF THEIR OLDER BROTHERS

Just as Yissakhar and Zevulun follow the lead of their brothers, silencing their own voices, their descendants follow the leaders from the tribes of Yehuda and Yosef.

During the leadership of the judge Devora, the progeny of Zevulun and Yissakhar join in the fight against General Sisera of Canaan.[11] Similarly, in the time of the judge Gidon, the tribe of Zevulun joins his army.[12] Lastly, in the time of King David, both tribes are noted as being part of his army: the tribe of Yissakhar serves in intelligence, whereas the tribe of Zevulun serves as foot soldiers.[13]

## CONCLUSION

In every nation, there are leaders and there are followers. If everyone endeavored to lead, anarchy would ensue. Among the tribes of Israel, as in all societies, both leaders and followers are necessary for the group to be functional. Yissakhar and Zevulun serve an important function – they are the "nation" being led. They follow, obey, and support their leaders.

11. Zevulun is listed as part of Devora and Barak's army (Judges 4:6, 10). In her victory song, Devora includes both of these tribes in the list of tribes that fought in the war (5:14–15).
12. Judges 6:35.
13. I Chr. 12:32–33.

## *Chapter 10*

# Bilha and Zilpa: The Secondary Wives of Yaakov

Prior to assessing the next four sons of Yaakov, we must consider a key factor that is integral to understanding their collective and individual roles in the family. Specifically, what is the relationship between Yaakov and their mothers, Bilha and Zilpa? What is the status of these two women in the family, and what is their role in the eyes of Raḥel and Leah? Only after reviewing Bilha's and Zilpa's positions in the family structure will we attempt to evaluate the role that their sons play in the house of Yaakov.

### WHO ARE BILHA AND ZILPA?

To understand Bilha and Zilpa, it is helpful to focus on their relationship with Raḥel and Leah. At their respective weddings to Yaakov, Raḥel and Leah are each presented with a handmaid as a gift from their father, Lavan. The Torah tells us that at the marriage of Yaakov and Leah "Lavan gave Zilpa his handmaid to his daughter Leah for a handmaid" (Gen. 29:24), and at the marriage of Yaakov and Raḥel "Lavan gave to Raḥel, his daughter, Bilha, his handmaid, to be her handmaid" (v. 29).

It appears that Lavan is providing each of his daughters' homes with maids from his home.[1] Evidently, this was a typical arrangement, as we know that the first two matriarchs each had a maid – Sarah's was Hagar (Gen. 16:3) and Rivka's was Devora (Gen. 35:8).[2]

The talmudic Sages offer a unique insight into Bilha's and Zilpa's origins: in contrast to the standard situation of a maidservant, these two are Lavan's daughters, born to his concubines.[3] According to this view of the Sages, Leah and Raḥel were born to Lavan from his primary wife, so that all of Yaakov's four wives are sisters. Rashi and other commentators use this background to appreciate the depths of Lavan's reprimand to Yaakov when chasing him, when he says: "Your daughters are my daughters and your sons are my sons" (Gen. 31:43). Lavan is asserting that everything is his, specifically because all the wives of Yaakov are Lavan's daughters. Similarly, Lavan threatens Yaakov, saying: "If you afflict my daughters, and if you take wives besides my daughters" (Gen. 31:50), reinforcing that each of Yaakov's wives is Lavan's daughter.[4]

However, there is another view of the Sages[5] that Bilha and Zilpa are not Lavan's daughters; rather, they are nieces of Devora, Rivka's maid. According to this version, Devora had a brother who was a slave. Lavan frees him from slavery and arranges a marriage for him with one of his maids. This union produces two daughters, Bilha and Zilpa. When their father dies, Lavan presents Bilha and Zilpa to his daughters

1. Radak on 29:24.
2. Devora is described as the "the nursemaid of Rivka" (Gen. 35:8). Evidently, Devora was Rivka's nursemaid from her childhood and later became her maid. It is unlikely that Bilha or Zilpa share a similar trajectory (from nursemaid to maidservant), since we are led to believe that they are having children in roughly the same time period as Leah and Raḥel (or later).
3. See Genesis Rabba 72:14 and Pirkei DeRabbi Eliezer 36, quoted in Rashi on Gen. 31:50 and *Ḥizkuni* on Gen. 29:24.
4. Rashi on this verse quotes the view of the Sages that Bilha and Zilpa are indeed the daughters of Lavan and his concubine, and infers this from the repetitive language in the verse: "If you afflict my daughters, and if you take wives besides my daughters." The double mention of "my daughters" teaches us that he is referring to two sets of daughters.
5. Genesis Rabbati 29:24.

(Raḥel and Leah, respectively) as maids. In this midrash we connect Bilha and Zilpa to another unknown maid, Devora.

Evidently, although Devora is supposed to play a key role in our understanding of the maidservants, the Torah gives very little information about this important woman. Our introduction to Devora is rather indirect. When Rivka leaves her father's house with the servant of Avraham, she takes "her nursemaid" (Gen. 24:29). Presumably this is Devora since later, at the announcement of her death, we learn that Devora was the "nursemaid of Rivka" (Gen. 35:8). Normally, the Torah records the death of only central figures (for example, Sarah[6], Avraham,[7] Raḥel,[8] Yitzḥak,[9] Yaakov,[10] Yosef,[11] Miriam,[12] Aharon,[13] and Moshe[14]). So, given that the Torah reports nothing substantial about Devora's life, why does she warrant being named in death? The Sages offer various answers to this question, two of which we will focus on below.

One possible answer is that her death informs us that Rivka had sent her maid to Yaakov, thus fulfilling her promise when she told him, "I will send for you" (Gen. 27:45).[15]

A second possible answer is that Devora's presence at that time and place, where she subsequently died, was significant because she was there to inform Yaakov about his mother's death. Otherwise, the Torah never tells the reader when Yaakov either interacts with his mother or learns of her death.[16]

---

6. Gen. 23:2.
7. Ibid. 25:8.
8. Ibid. 35:19.
9. Ibid. 35:29.
10. Ibid. 49:33.
11. Ibid. 50:26.
12. Num. 20:1.
13. Ibid. 20:29.
14. Deut. 34:5.
15. This is the opinion of Rabbi Moshe HaDarshan from Genesis Rabbati 113, quoted in Rashi on Genesis 35:8.
16. Genesis Rabba 81:5, also quoted in Rashi on Genesis 35:8, says that this understanding can be derived from the naming of the location where she is buried, "*Alon Bakhut*," literally "tree of crying." Devora tells him about the death of his mother and then she dies, and Yaakov is mourning for both of them.

According to both of these approaches, the rabbinic tradition reflects an enhanced role – more than just a maid – for the maidservants of our matriarchs. In fact, much of what we've seen so far suggests a strong pattern that assumes the servants of our matriarchs had greater significance than a typical maid. They are part of the family, having grown up in our patriarchs' homes, and are not merely random women selected for this role. Simply stated, they are either literal sisters or "almost" sisters. Clearly, according to this approach, Bilha and Zilpa are part of the family.[17]

## FULL WIVES OR CONCUBINES?

> She [Raḥel] gave him Bilha her handmaid as a wife, and Yaakov went in to her. (Gen. 20:4)

> When Leah saw that she had finished bearing, she took Zilpa, her handmaid, and gave her to Yaakov as a wife. (Gen. 30:9)

If we analyze the language surrounding their marriages to Yaakov, Bilha and Zilpa are each presented "as a wife." Evidently, they are full-fledged wives. This implies that they would be considered free women, no longer maids. However, as the story continues, their descriptions constantly change. In Genesis 31:33, they are referred to with the word "*ama*," which implies a maid's position. In Genesis 33:1, they are referred to with the word "*shifḥa*," which means maidservant. So too, in Genesis 35:25, Bilha is "*shifḥat Raḥel*," the maidservant of Raḥel, and Zilpa is "*shifḥat Leah*," the maidservant of Leah. However, in Genesis 37:2, they are called "*neshei aviv*," wives of his father. The Torah's description of these women is very confusing! It seems that the Torah is trying to highlight the ambiguity

17. This contrasts with Sarah's maid Hagar, who is Egyptian and doesn't remain loyal to Sarah, causing fighting and a rift in the family. According to the Midrash, Hagar is someone Avraham and Sarah met when they were in Egypt (Gen. 12), rather than someone who grew up with Sarah (or was given to her by her father on her wedding day). Genesis Rabba 45:3 explains that Hagar is actually the daughter of Pharaoh, and was given to Sarah by Pharaoh after all the miracles that occurred in order to save her.

of their status: They are wives of Yaakov but do not have the same status as Raḥel and Leah.[18] Their standing is lower; they have maid-like responsibilities to their mistresses. Yet these women are not just concubines.[19]

Unfortunately, this conclusion is contradicted by the following verse: "It happened, while Yisrael lived in that land, that Reuven went and lay with Bilha, his father's concubine, and Yisrael heard of it" (Gen. 35:22). For the first and only time, Bilha is explicitly referred to as the concubine of Yaakov! The commentators offer two explanations for the use of the term: Either our above assertion is wrong and both Bilha and Zilpa are indeed concubines,[20] or the intention of the wording of this incident is to emphasize Reuven's mistaken perspective and mistreatment of Bilha.[21]

Let's now consider how Yaakov relates to Bilha and Zilpa. Clearly, he doesn't treat them as equals to Raḥel and Leah. For instance, when Yaakov asks his wives for permission to leave the house of their father, Lavan, and return to Israel, he confers only with Raḥel and Leah (31:4),

---

18. In numerous instances they are called "the maids" and their names are missing from the text. For example, when Yaakov divides his family into three groups before meeting Esav, they are referred to as Leah's group, Raḥel's group, and "the maids'" group. The names of Bilha and Zilpa are not in the text. Likewise, when Lavan searches the tents for his idols, he checks in the tents of Leah, Raḥel, and that of the "*amahot*," "maids," with no mention of Bilha and Zilpa's names.
19. Ramban on 37:2 writes that they were full wives, but when they are being spoken about in comparison to Raḥel and Leah, they are called maids because of their lower status. He gives a second possibility that they were always lower-level wives and only became full wives after Raḥel and Leah both died.
20. See Radak on 35:22 to understand why Reuven engaged with her intimately: He didn't think it was forbidden because she was his father's concubine and not an actual wife. In "Anyone Who Says that Reuven Sinned" (http://etzion.org.il/en/anyone-who-says-Reuven-sinned), Rav Yaakov Medan writes that "it is not clear whether Reuven's misdeed involved real sexual immorality, since Bilha was not his father's wife, but rather only a concubine."
21. *Kli Yakar* on 37:2 writes that Leah's and Raḥel's sons used to refer to Bilha and Zilpa as concubines and maids even though they really were full wives. *HaKetav VeHakabbala* on 35:22 writes that Reuven belittled Bilha by calling her a concubine in public, even though she was really a full wife. He also writes that they must have been full wives because if it were not true, their sons would have been owned by Yaakov and not considered free. And if that were so, their descendants would not have been eligible as tribes to inherit land (30:1).

who grant permission; Bilha and Zilpa are not included in the conversation at all.

Similarly, this two-tiered system is reflected in the layout of the family tents. Raḥel and Leah each have their private tents, as there are references to "the tent of Leah" and "the tent of Raḥel" (31:33). However, the maidservants must share one tent; the text refers to "the tent of the two maidservants" (31:33).

Additionally, Bilha and Zilpa do not name their own children; instead, their children are all named by their respective mistresses, Raḥel or Leah. Furthermore, these children's names have meaning relative only to the lives of Raḥel and Leah rather than relating to their birth mothers, Bilha and Zilpa.

The most obvious disparity between the wives and the maids, however, is the way Yaakov arranges his encampment when meeting his brother Esav. He stations his wives and children in a very specific order for this meeting: Bilha, Zilpa, and their children are in the front, while Leah, Raḥel, and their children are stationed in the back (33:6).[22] Presumably, this arrangement is intended to reduce the safety risk for his main wives and their children.

Similarly, Bilha and Zilpa are not buried in The Cave of Makhpela, the burial caves in Hebron purchased by Avraham after the death of Sarah (Gen. 23). The Torah writes that the following people are buried there: Sarah (23:19), Avraham (25:9), and Yaakov (49:13). We infer that Yitzḥak is also buried there from Yaakov's request to Yosef to be buried at his fathers' gravesite (47:30). On Yaakov's deathbed, he reveals that Avraham and Sarah, Yitzḥak and Rivka, as well as Leah, are buried in the cave, and that he wishes to be buried there also (Gen. 49:31). The Talmud rounds out the list of individuals buried there: Avraham and Sarah, Yitzḥak and Rivka, Yaakov and Leah, and Adam and Ḥava.[23]

22. Amazingly, the basic formula changes within the verse. It is the maidservants followed by their children, Leah followed by her children, but then Yosef precedes his mother, Raḥel. Yosef is placed before Raḥel! By doing this, the contrast between the wives is even stronger. Raḥel, the favorite wife, is all the way in the back, and Bilha and Zilpa are placed at the front, even before their children.

23. The Talmud in Eiruvin 53a writes that this explains the naming of the cave. The word *mahkpela* comes from the Hebrew word *kaful*, which means double or couples. The location of the cave is in Kiryat Arba. Arba means four, symbolizing the four

Raḥel is not buried there because she died on the way into Israel, and was buried near Beit Leḥem.[24] Notably, there is no tradition that Bilha or Zilpa are buried there. Why doesn't Yaakov bury them there (or request to be buried next to them)? Evidently, he does not view them as full-fledged wives.

Finally, and most centrally, in Jewish tradition Bilha and Zilpa never attain the status of Matriarchs of Israel, as there are only four: Sarah, Rivka, Raḥel, and Leah. Bilha and Zilpa are excluded![25]

In summary, there may be evidence to suggest that Bilha and Zilpa are Yaakov's full wives, or concubines, or something in between. Their precise status is unclear. However, one thing is certain: they are not viewed as equals to Yaakov's other two wives, Raḥel and Leah.

But do Bilha and Zilpa have exactly the same status? Why does Yaakov marry each of them? What is the reason behind each of Yaakov's wives electing to give him a maid to marry?

## BILHA

> She said, "Behold, my maid Bilha. Go in to her, [so] that she may bear on my knees, and I also may obtain children by her." (Gen. 30:3)

couples buried in the cave. In addition to the explicit mention of Avraham, Sarah, and Yaakov being buried there, Genesis Rabba 62:3 and *Midrash Aggada* on Gen. 49 add textual evidence that Yitzḥak was buried in the cave as well.

24. Yaakov bears the guilt of not having buried her in the ancestral cave, and on his deathbed, he shares his reasoning with Yosef (Gen. 48:7).
25. Throughout the liturgy of Jewish prayer, Raḥel and Leah are highlighted as matriarchs of the Jewish people. In contrast, there is only one instance where Bilha and Zilpa are included: Rabbi Elazar HaKalir wrote a lamentation (typically numbered as the twenty-sixth lamentation in modern prayer books) that we read on the morning of the Ninth of Av. This lamentation, which begins "When Yirmiyahu went to the graves of the patriarchs," includes the crying of all four wives of Yaakov: "The sounds of Leah weeping, as she pounds on her heart; Raḥel, her sister, weeping for her sons; Zilpa slapping her face; and Bilha lamenting with her two hands."

The story of Yaakov marrying Bilha, Raḥel's maid, is charged with tension and sadness. Whereas Leah gave birth to four sons in succession, "Raḥel was barren" (29:31). After the birth of Yehuda, her fourth son, Leah was much happier but Raḥel felt lacking: "When Raḥel saw that she bore Yaakov no children, Raḥel envied her sister" (Gen. 30:1). Raḥel's feeling of jealousy intensified because her chronic longing for children was sharpened when her sister bore four sons. Unfortunately, this family dynamic might also have created a distance between her and Yaakov. Infertility is always difficult, but Raḥel's situation was doubly challenging because there was the emotional impact of a second wife, who did have children, to contend with. It is in this context that we consider what role Bilha plays in Raḥel's life.

### Competing Wives

In order to truly appreciate Raḥel's difficult situation, let us look at two other situations of two competing wives where one is barren and the other is not.

#### *Sarah and Milka*

Immediately after being told about the marriage of Avraham to Sarah, we are told that "Sarah was barren and had no children" (Gen. 11:30). However, in the preceding verse, Sarah is compared to her sister-in-law, Milka: "And Avraham and Naḥor took for themselves wives; Avraham's wife's name was Sarah and Naḥor's wife's name was Milka. Haran [Avraham and Naḥor's brother] was the father of Milka and Yiska" (Gen. 11:29). In other words, two brothers marry two women; one wife is barren and the other has children (Gen. 22:20). Further, according to the Sages in Megilla 14a, Yiska is the same person as Sarah.[26] If so, then Sarah and Milka are both the daughters of Haran. They are sisters who marry their uncles (who are brothers)!

One can understand how the pain of Sarah's infertility would be compounded by the fertility of her sister.

26. Accordingly, the description of Yiska as beautiful and righteous is really just a description of Sarah. See also Rashi on Gen. 11:29.

### *Ḥana and Penina*

The second relevant story is presented at the outset of I Samuel, regarding the parents of the prophet Shmuel. Like Yaakov, Elkana (Shmuel's father) has two wives, Ḥana and Penina. Similar to Leah and Raḥel, Penina has children and Ḥana does not. In fact, this story utilizes very familiar language: "And he had two wives; the name of the one was Ḥana, and the name of other Penina: and Penina had children, but Ḥana had no children" (I Sam. 1:2). This reminds us of the following verses that compare Raḥel to Leah: "Lavan had two daughters. The name of the elder was Leah, and the name of the younger was Raḥel ... God saw that Leah was hated, and he opened her womb, but Raḥel was barren" (Gen. 29:16, 31).

In fact, these episodes have much more in common than this brief text.[27] In both stories, it is the barren wife who is favored: "But to Ḥana he gave a double portion, for he loved Ḥana" (I Sam. 1:5); "He loved also Raḥel more than Leah" (Gen. 29:30).

In both instances, the favored wife asks her husband to help alleviate her infertility and his response seems insensitive.[28] Unfortunately, the pain of their infertility is exacerbated by the co-wives who provide their husbands with children. This creates a painful rivalry that is explicitly noted in the text: In Ḥana's situation the verse says: "Her rival provoked her sore, to make her fret, because God had shut up her womb" (I Sam 1:6). In Raḥel's case the verse states: "When Raḥel saw that she bore Yaakov no children, Raḥel envied her sister" (Gen. 30:1).

---

27. Interestingly, the endings of the stories also share similarities.
    (1) Each has a son who attains leadership (Shmuel and Yosef, respectively).
    (2) Each one has a son who leaves home at a young age. Shmuel is sent to live with Eli in the Tabernacle and his mother visits him only once a year (I Sam. 1:24). Yosef was sold into slavery at a young age.
    (3) Lastly, in each instance, the son receives a precious coat (I Sam. 2:19; Gen. 37:3).
28. When Ḥana cries and refuses to eat, her husband rhetorically asks her, "Why do you weep, and why don't you eat, and why is your heart grieved? Am I not better to you than ten sons?" (I Sam. 1:8). Similarly, Raḥel exclaims, "Give me children or else I will die" (30:1), Yaakov responds in anger, "Am I in God's place, who has withheld from you the fruit of the womb?" (Gen. 30:2).

It is the comparison to the other wife that drives them to contemplate death. Raḥel says as much explicitly, and Ḥana simply refuses to eat.[29] These parallel episodes bear witness to Raḥel's pain. We can tangibly feel Raḥel's desperation that leads her to give her maid to her husband. Only her craving for children, and the raw pain of observing her sister's reproductive success, would push her to give her husband a third wife to compete for his attention.

### *Bilha as Plan B*

In this context Raḥel recognizes that she is on her own in her plight. Yaakov already has four sons with his wife Leah and therefore does not feel the same lack that Raḥel does. He makes this clear, claiming God "has withheld from you" children, emphasizing that she is alone in her barrenness, as he, Yaakov, has children.[30]

Raḥel recognizes that she needs a new plan to ensure progeny of her own with Yaakov. She decides to replicate the actions of her husband's grandmother Sarah, who was in a similar predicament. Sarah gave her maidservant, Hagar, to her husband to marry in order to bear children through her: "Perhaps I will be built from her" (Gen. 16:2). Each woman gives her husband her maid to marry, with the hope that any child born of the new union will be considered her own.[31] Hence, after Bilha's sons are born, it is Raḥel who names them.

29. While one might be tempted to compare Rivka to these two women, there are differences, especially that Rivka does not have a co-wife to deal with. Rivka and Yitzḥak marry when he is forty years old (Gen. 25:10), and they have the twins Yaakov and Esav twenty years later (Gen. 25:26). Evidently, the couple struggled to conceive for twenty years. However, their situation is very different because they struggled together. The story continues with Yitzḥak praying on behalf of himself and his wife, and God answers them and gives them twins, Esav and Yaakov.
30. Ramban on 30:1 writes that as Yaakov's favorite wife, Raḥel was expecting him to put on sackcloth and fast, mourn, and pray until she gave birth. She was therefore devastated that he seemed content about just having children with Leah.
31. Ironically, this plan failed for Sarah because Hagar refused to allow Sarah to be the mother of her baby. This caused fighting between the women, and ultimately Hagar was thrown out of the home.

### ZILPA

> When Leah saw that she had finished bearing, she took Zilpa, her handmaid, and gave her to Yaakov as a wife. (30:9).

What motivates Leah to offer Zilpa to Yaakov as a wife – and possible competition for her husband's attention? Leah already has children and therefore has no reason to give her maidservant to Yaakov!

### The More the Merrier

Leah's motivation may simply be a desire for even more children. Although she already has four sons of her own, she may aspire for even more because she realizes that her relationship with Yaakov improves with each new child. Unfortunately, after Yehuda's birth, she experiences trouble conceiving. The Torah alludes to this, revealing that she has been struggling with fertility issues since the birth of Yehuda: "Then she stopped bearing" (Gen. 29:35). These words are repeated and emphasized when she offers Yaakov her maid: "When Leah saw that she had finished bearing…" (30:9). Radak on Genesis 30:9 writes that although her predicament is not nearly as challenging as her sister's struggle, Leah also wants more children and therefore copies her sister in giving her maid to Yaakov.

From Leah's perspective, her situation has improved because of her ability to have children. After Yehuda's birth, and once she began to experience trouble conceiving, she may have been worried that Bilha would provide children for Raḥel, thus encroaching on her newfound attention from Yaakov. To ensure she would "stay ahead" and continue to have babies, she enlisted Zilpa in her plan.

### Chosen Nation

Alternatively, she may have felt a sense of competition with her sister, but for a national, not personal, reason. Until now, only one son has been selected from each generation to continue the line of the Jewish people. Avraham chose Yitzḥak and rejected his seven other sons.[32] Yitzḥak gave

---

32. "Avraham gave all that he had to Yitzḥak, but to the sons of the concubines Avraham had, Avraham gave gifts" (Gen. 25:5–6).

the blessing to Yaakov, thereby rejecting Esav as the progenitor of the chosen nation (Gen. 27). Therefore, Yaakov's wives might have assumed that only one of his sons was to be part of this chain. Therefore, the more sons each one had, the greater likelihood that she would be the mother of the chosen one. The Sages observe that the matriarchs knew there would be twelve sons born to Yaakov.[33] Ramban on 30:9 writes that as a result, the wives were competing to have as many of the twelve sons as possible. Leah wanted more children to ensure a larger share of the twelve "spots" available for national destiny.

### Zilpa's Welfare

However, Abarbanel[34] believes that Leah's actions were focused on Zilpa's best interests.[35] She felt that Zilpa, as Bilha's older sister, would have been shamed if she were the only non-wife. Therefore, Leah acted against her own self-interest by offering Zilpa to Yaakov.

## CONCLUSION

When considering all of the evidence, it is clear that Bilha and Zilpa are neither mere maidservants nor equal co-wives to Raḥel and Leah. Rather, they had a middle status. This tension affects their sons too, which becomes apparent at the start of their lives, when they are named as directed by Leah and Raḥel instead of by their birth mothers. Amazingly, as we will see in the next chapter, these four boys are similarly neither fully servants nor perceived as equals to the sons of Leah and Raḥel.

33. See Genesis Rabba 72:6.
34. See Abarbanel on Genesis 29 in his answer to question 7.
35. Upon Yissakhar's birth a few years later, Leah exclaims: "'God has given me my reward, because I gave my handmaid to my husband.' She named him Yissakhar" (Gen. 30:18). Apparently, she feels entitled to a reward as a result of her considerate treatment of her maidservant.

*Chapter 11*

# Dan, Naftali, Gad, and Asher: The Children of the Maidservants

In the previous chapter, we discussed the ambiguous marital relationship between Yaakov and his maidservants, Bilha and Zilpa, especially relative to his relationships with Raḥel and Leah. In this chapter, we will consider the status of the sons of the maidservants. Are they viewed and do they behave as equals to the sons of Raḥel and Leah? What is the collective role of these men in the family structure? Do they each have individual roles in the family?

## THE NAMING OF EACH CHILD

Bilha, Raḥel's maid, is the first maidservant to marry Yaakov. She gives birth to two sons, who are named by Raḥel.

**Dan**

> Raḥel said, "God has judged me, and has also heard my voice, and has given me a son." Therefore, she called his name Dan. (Gen. 30:6)

What is Raḥel suggesting by selecting this name? Let us consider two approaches to the meaning behind the name.

Think about the context of Dan's birth. He is Raḥel's first surrogate child after suffering so many years of infertility and isolation. Why choose a name that seems harsh, or at least distant, as is indicated by Raḥel saying "God has judged me"? This is not a name that suggests she is finally happy, or even satisfied, by the recent course of events. She doesn't name him Simḥa (meaning "happiness") or any other name that would capture her excitement. Why not? Perhaps she is not consoled because, after all, he is not her biological child. Therefore, deep down, she is still hoping and praying for a son of her own. This first possibility might show the relevance of his naming.[1]

Alternatively, one might sense excitement and a pouring forth of emotion that has been building up for many years. She is exclaiming, "Finally, God has given me what I have been asking for all these years. God has judged me and given me what I deserve!" She recognizes that God is behind the decision of who can have children and when those children are born. Hence, she is thanking Him for having listened to her cries and allowing her to have one who feels like her own (since she gave Bilha, her servant, to Yaakov so that she might bear children in her stead).

---

1. Rabbi S. R. Hirsch on 30:6 explains Raḥel's thoughts as follows: "God has dealt very strictly with me and has denied me the ability to have children myself, but He has nevertheless now heard my prayer; inasmuch as He has granted me a child [for] whom I can at least be a spiritual mother; and although I did not actually bear him, I can look after him and bring him up as my contribution to the house of Yaakov."

**Naftali**

> Raḥel said, "With mighty wrestlings have I wrestled with my sister and have prevailed." She named him Naftali. (Gen. 30:8)

With the name of her second surrogate son, Raḥel is focused on the competition with Leah. After the birth of Bilha's two children, she feels back in the race (either for Yaakov's affection or for an increased chance of being mother to a chosen son).[2] She declares: "I have prevailed!" She feels that this second son has not only enabled her to compete, but also to win.[3]

For Raḥel, Bilha's two sons reflect directly on her standing with Yaakov and her status within the family. We will now turn to the two sons born to Zilpa, Leah's maid. Just as Bilha's sons are named by Raḥel, Zilpa's two sons are named by Leah.

**Gad**

> Leah said, "How fortunate [*bagad*]!" She named him Gad. (Gen. 30:11)

On this verse, Rashi writes that "*bagad*" is a combination of two words: *ba gad,* meaning "wonderful." This son is another notch on Leah's belt.

---

2. Her newfound excitement might stem from an expectation that her maid would now have more children, so that she will soon have additional sons, just like her sister. Alternatively, Raḥel realizes that because she is the favored wife, she doesn't need to compete with Leah; two sons are enough to maintain Yaakov's primary affection.
3. Rashi on 30:8 writes that her goal is not to beat her sister; rather, she is praying to God for equality with her sister. God accepts her prayer and lets her be equal. Ibn Ezra on 30:8 disagrees. He writes that Naftali's name implies the triumph of someone fighting or struggling with someone else. In context, this means Raḥel feels she has beaten her sister (i.e., not just achieved equality with her sister's motherhood). Rabbi S. R. Hirsch on 30:8 suggests this struggle against Leah is spiritual in nature. He describes Raḥel's mindset as follows: "A sacred wrestling competition did I wage with my sister, not a match that struggles for something low or common, of which one would be ashamed, but for a sacred end did I compete against my sister, to do my part, too, for the spiritual building up of our home."

Her naming him is just an exclamation of happiness. Hurray, another one![4]

Rashi offers a second explanation for this name, saying that the name can be understood as originating from the Hebrew root *beit, gimmel, dalet,* which means to betray. Leah is reflecting her feelings of betrayal due to her husband's agreeing to marry her maid. In fact, *Ḥizkuni* on 30:11 explains that her offer of Zilpa as a wife was a test she devised for Yaakov. Leah hoped he would refuse. This name represents Leah's wish that Yaakov would finally prove that he loves her (by refusing the offer of another wife), but she is only disappointed and rejected again.

**Asher**

> Leah said, "Happy am I, for the daughters will call me happy." She named him Asher. (Gen. 30:13)

The birth of Asher, the sixth son in Leah's clan, is met with rejoicing and excitement. Having six sons means she has been blessed with a very large share of Yaakov's family. She feels blessed by her situation and her ability to continue to have children, even through Zilpa, her maid. Interestingly, her excitement is focused on the other women who will praise her for her progeny.[5] *Ḥizkuni* adds that she is also praising herself for the courage to offer her maid to her husband. Leah acknowledges that she sacrificed something by providing Yaakov with another wife to ensure an even larger family.

Even if these names reflect the dynamic between Yaakov, Leah, and Raḥel, they offer limited information about the children of Bilha and Zilpa. We therefore now turn to other episodes to learn about them.

---

4. This is also the understanding of Ibn Ezra. The word "*bagad*" is broken into two words, "*ba gad*." These two words either mean 'good fortune' or imply praising God for giving her more children.
5. See Rav Saadia Gaon and Radak on 30:13.

### RELATIONSHIP WITH YAAKOV

> Yaakov lifted up his eyes and looked, and beheld that Esav was coming, and with him four hundred men. He divided the children between Leah, Raḥel, and to the two handmaids. He put the handmaids and their children in the front, Leah and her children after, and Raḥel and Yosef at the rear. (Gen. 33:1–2)

There is very little known about the children of the maidservants; they never play a focal role in any of the stories in Genesis. Therefore, our best source of information will be in the subtle details that are shared about their lives within narratives where they play minor roles. Thus, when meeting with Esav, Yaakov puts these sons at the front of the family's encampment. Evidently, Yaakov is worried about a negative encounter with his brother and he appears willing to risk their lives in order to save the lives of his other sons. Shockingly, this story is the only direct interaction between Yaakov and these four sons that is recorded in Genesis.

They are silent throughout the various family events. They seem to have no voice at all, especially as pertains to their father and brothers.

### RELATIONSHIP WITH THEIR BROTHERS

The nature of the relationship between these brothers and the sons of Leah and Raḥel is ambiguous. The sons of Bilha and Zilpa are silent during the entire episode surrounding the sale of Yosef, going down to Egypt, and the potential loss of Binyamin over the allegedly stolen goblet. Does this silence teach us anything? Why were they quiet?

At its simplest level, they are quiet because they are the younger, less influential brothers in the presence of their older, more established brothers. They take their social cues from their older brothers, those born to the "real" wives of Yaakov. When their older brothers step up, they step back.

However, since Raḥel's sons are not older than they are, one could wonder whether the above synopsis is equally applicable to her sons as it is for Leah's. Does it apply here too?

Our question might be addressed in the following verse: "This is the history of the generations of Yaakov. Yosef, being seventeen years old, was feeding the flock with his brothers. He was a boy with the sons of Bilha and Zilpa, his father's wives. Yosef brought an evil report of them to their father" (Gen. 37:2). What does it mean that "he was a boy with [*vehu na'ar et*] the children of Bilha and Zilpa"? The word "*na'ar*" is apparently used here as a verb, though it is more typically used as a noun. This unusual usage could suggest three distinct ways to interpret this verse, each with implications for understanding the dynamic between the children of Yaakov.

Rashi on 37:2 offers the first option. He splits this phrase into two parts, explaining that the statement in the first clause – "Yosef acted like a boy" – describes Yosef's focus on his appearance, tending to his hair and eyes. The second clause – "With the children of Bilha and Zilpa" – means that Yosef would specifically spend time with the children of Bilha and Zilpa, not the sons of Leah. Rashi writes that this detail is crucial to understanding a difference between Yosef and Leah's sons. The Torah is revealing inner squabbles among the brothers. The children of Leah mistreat the maidservants' children, whereas Yosef, son of Raḥel, treats them pleasantly.[6]

Rashbam on 37:2 offers an alternate explanation by painting a slightly different picture of the family dynamic. According to Rashbam, the verse is to be read, "Yosef would spend time with the children of Bilha and Zilpa because he was a boy." Yosef is significantly younger than the sons of Leah. Therefore, he stays in the company of the sons of Bilha and Zilpa because they are his contemporaries. Similar to Rashi's view, this explanation assumes that Yosef feels more closely connected to the sons of Bilha and Zilpa.

Ramban ad loc. reads the words of this verse in the same way as the Rashbam, but understands the situation differently. He writes that because Yosef was so young, he needed to be watched and guarded by his brothers. Therefore, Yaakov commanded the children of the maidservants to embrace Yosef and to babysit him. Ramban writes that Yosef

6. See also *Kli Yakar* on 37:2, who explains the evolution of how Bilha and Zilpa are described. Here they are "the wives of Yaakov," whereas when Reuven engages with Bilha, she is called a concubine. He explains that Bilha and Zilpa were full wives, making their sons full-fledged sons of Yaakov. However, the brothers would tease them by calling their mothers concubines and calling the sons servants. Genesis Rabba 84:4 explains that one of the items that Yosef told his father in his "evil report" about his older brothers is that Leah's sons called the other brothers "servants."

was with the maidservants' children "because their father commanded them to watch him and to serve him." In this view, even Yosef doesn't necessarily have a healthy fraternal bond with them. Perhaps he is their master! When he runs home to his father to "bring an evil report" about his brothers, Ramban believes that it is about the maidservants' sons. Ramban's support for this understanding is that the maidservants' children don't protect Yosef at the time of his sale. Evidently, they also hate him and therefore want him to be sold. Unlike Leah's sons, they do not wish to be rid of him because they believe he is stealing their rights within the family or because he dominates their father's attention; rather, they'd like to remove him from the family because he mistreats them!

Apparently, Ramban's vision of Yaakov's home includes the children of Bilha and Zilpa with no friends at home. The older sons don't speak to them. Even Yosef, whom they are forced to be around, informs on them. They are friendly only among themselves.

Interestingly, rabbinic tradition presents one more interaction between Yosef and the maidservants' children. When Yosef finally reveals himself to his brothers, he introduces them to Pharaoh. But he only introduces five of his brothers (Gen. 47:2). The Torah does not reveal which brothers are included among the five. However, the Sages write that the chosen five are Reuven, Levi, Binyamin, Shimon, and Yissakhar.[7] None of Bilha's or Zilpa's sons are selected! It seems that even years later, Yosef treats them differently than Leah's and Raḥel's sons.

However, there is a second rabbinic tradition regarding the identity of the five brothers. The Talmud (Bava Kama 92a) quotes in the name of Rava the opinion that the five brothers introduced to Pharaoh are the same ones that in the future would receive additional strength in Moshe's final blessing (by doubling their names): Dan, Zevulun, Gad, Asher, and Naftali. Rashi on Gen. 47:2 explains that Yosef intentionally introduces Pharaoh to these tribes because of their weakness.[8] In this

7. Genesis Rabba 95.
8. Yosef does not want Pharaoh to desire any of his brothers. He wants to ensure that Pharaoh does not take any of his brothers to work for him and recruit them into his army. Therefore, Yosef purposely chooses the weakest brothers, so Pharaoh would assume they were all weak and leave his family alone.

view of the Sages, all four sons of Bilha and Zilpa are viewed as weak (including their descendants during the time of Moshe).

### LOWER IN STATUS

In addition to the ambiguity of how Yaakov and the other brothers view the sons of Bilha and Zilpa, the Torah reflects an ambivalent stance regarding their status in the family.

Dan, Naftali, Gad, and Asher are presented last on almost every list of the names of the tribes. Even though Yissakhar, Zevulun, Yosef, and Binyamin are born after them, these names usually precede the maidservants' children's names.[9] Furthermore, in the division of the encampments in the desert, the encampments of the maidservants' children are not only listed last but are positioned behind the rest of the Jewish people throughout their journey in the desert. Also, when the tribes are distributed between the mountains of Gerizim for the blessings and Ebal for the curses, all four tribes of the maidservants are situated on Mount Ebal (Deut. 27:13). Lastly, when Moshe blesses all the tribes before he dies, these are the last four tribes to receive blessings. Abarbanel[10] writes that Moshe had to bless them last because it would have been a "disgrace and embarrassment and would infuriate the other tribes" if Moshe had blessed a child of a maidservant before

9. Consider these instances:
   (1) In Genesis 35 when the Torah lists the children born to Yaakov, they are last.
   (2) In Genesis 49, when Yaakov blesses his sons, Yissakhar and Zevulun are noted prior to the children of Bilha and Zilpa.
   (3) In Exodus 1, in the list of people going down to Egypt, they are noted last.
   (4) In Numbers 1, in the census of the Jewish nation, they are counted last.
   (5) In Numbers 7, when the Tabernacle is dedicated, they are last to give their sacrifices (except for Gad).
   (6) In Numbers 13, the spies from these four tribes are listed last.
   (7) In Numbers 26, in the second census of the Jewish people, three of them are listed last.
   (8) In Numbers 34, in the explanation of who will inherit land, Asher and Naftali are last.
   (9) In Joshua 19, Asher, Naftali, and Dan receive their land last. (Gad lives with Reuven on the other side of the Jordan river.)
10. See Abarbanel in his introduction to Deut. 33, where he compares the blessings given by Moshe and Yaakov.

them.[11] Even at the end of Moshe's life, the descendants of Dan, Naftali, Gad, and Asher are treated differently.

In spite of this portrayal of the sons of Bilha and Zilpa, they are unquestionably part of the nation of Israel. They are called "sons of Yaakov" on numerous occasions.[12] Further, they are listed and counted as part of the twelve tribes. They receive a blessing by Yaakov and later Moshe, just like the other brothers.

With all of this in mind, it is not surprising that Dan, Naftali, Gad, and Asher play an ambiguous role with no major leadership positions in our history. The children of Leah and Raḥel never look to them for leadership or control.

Until now, our portrayal of these four sons has been as a singular unit. Of course, in reality, each of them has a slightly different path and role in history. Therefore, our next focus will be to discover what differences might exist among these four brothers.

## OLDEST VERSUS YOUNGEST

One way to discern differences among them is to consider their placement within the family. In spite of the limited information in the Torah about them, we can try to focus on the differences between the firstborn sons of Bilha and Zilpa – Dan and Gad, respectively, versus the second ones, Naftali and Asher.

### Dan and Gad

The oldest son in every family is treated differently than the other brothers and has a special status as the firstborn. In Yaakov's family, Reuven is the oldest son, but Dan is Bilha's oldest, and Gad is Zilpa's oldest, and later Yosef is Raḥel's oldest. In some way, there may be more of an expectation of leadership or responsibility from these four sons because of their firstborn status. However, Dan and Gad are given no special

11. Abarbanel specifically asks why Gad's name isn't after Reuven's, since the rest of the list resembles the order in which the tribes were given land. Gad, who inherits land with Reuven, should be listed second on the list. The maidservants' other tribes are given land last, so they are blessed last anyway. Abarbanel writes that if Moshe had moved up the blessing of Gad, it would be viewed as an insult to the other tribes.
12. For example, consider Gen. 35:22: "And Yaakov had twelve sons."

treatment and don't appear to rise above their brothers. Ibn Ezra on Genesis 48:16 points out that when Reuven loses his status as firstborn, the birthright can't pass to Dan or Gad because they were the children of the maids; therefore, it is passed to Yosef. This lowered status, as well as the loss of a right they would have received had they been born to a different mother, plagues Dan and Gad and will have a lasting impact on their descendants.

**Naftali and Asher**

The opposite is true for the younger sons of Bilha and Zilpa. They have no rights to any leadership position or special treatment, as they are both the younger children of the maids. They seem fine with this position, for we don't find any instances of their complaining about their lowered status.

In the ensuing chapters, we will examine each of these four sons for differentiating factors between them. A number of factors will be taken into account in our analysis: Which family are they born into (that of Raḥel or Leah)? Are they the older or younger son of each of the maidservants? Do they bear resentment about their status in the family or are they complacent and content? We will analyze these differences and how they affect the personalities of their descendants.

*Chapter 12*

# Dan: The Oldest Son of Bilha

The four maidservants' children don't have distinct stories and personalities. Yet even a casual perusal makes it clear that Dan is different. What is it about Dan that sets the stage for his tribe to influence Jewish history and produce more distinguished individuals than the rest of the maidservants' sons?

Dan, the first child born to one of the maidservants, has a special story surrounding his birth. After years of infertility, Raḥel presents her maidservant Bilha to Yaakov to bear a child, saying, "Go in to her that she may bear on my knees" (Gen. 30:3). A close look at these words reveals that Raḥel's true intention is that this will be *her* child. In fact, it would be easy to confuse the identity of Dan's actual mother when Raḥel states, "God has given me a son" (30:6). She is obviously unaware that one day she will conceive a child of her own; she ostensibly believes that this is as close as she can come to motherhood. She, not Bilha, names the child. He is her baby!

If so, then from the time he is born until the birth of Yosef, Dan might bear an element of personifying the special oldest child of Raḥel. Furthermore, it is not only plausible that Raḥel would treat him this way, but Yaakov might do so as well. Years later, Yaakov shows clear favoritism to Yosef, his preferred wife's child, giving him a special coat to represent his elevated status in the family. It is therefore conceivable that before Yosef's birth, Dan might have received somewhat similar distinguishing treatment from his father. This less extreme favoritism probably exists[1] (along with the brothers' reactions to it), but since Dan is not Raḥel's biological child, it is not recorded in the text.[2]

Once Yosef is born, however, any special treatment for Dan ends abruptly.[3] He would certainly be removed from Raḥel's tent, downgraded to live among the other maidservants' children in their tents. In one instant, his ranking is upended. He is demoted from "favored son" to son of Bilha, the maidservant. Yaakov's view is evident when he places Dan with Bilha's and Zilpa's children on the frontlines when approaching Esav. Similarly, Yehuda captures this sentiment in a speech to Yosef years later, repeating his father's words: "My wife gave me only two sons" (Gen 44:27), not four.

Dan's demotion is dramatic and destructive, leaving permanent scars on him and his descendants, manifested by anger and loneliness. Dan finds it hard to fit in. He doesn't necessarily connect with the older brothers, as he is the child of a maidservant. However, he doesn't fit in with the maidservants' children either, since he likely experienced a privileged status during his early years in Raḥel's tent.

---

1. There are clear differences between Yosef's and Dan's births. Dan wasn't a "miracle" child, born after years of infertility, nor was he the natural child of Raḥel. However, during the time he was being treated as Raḥel's baby, it seems reasonable to assume he received special treatment.
2. The favoritism shown to Binyamin is also not recorded in the Torah until it becomes relevant to the storyline, when the brothers want to take him down to Egypt. In both cases (Dan and Binyamin), not only is their favored status not the focus of the Torah's account of them, but neither are any possible attempts on their part to instigate friction with the other brothers reported (unlike in Yosef's case).
3. Yosef's naming demonstrates that Raḥel no longer views Dan as her child: "God has removed my shame... and should give me another child" (Gen. 30:23–24). Raḥel now views Yosef as her first child, who removes her shame of being unable to conceive. She asks for another son in order to have a pair from the same parentage. She ignores the fact that according to her intention, she already has two children from Bilha.

At the same time, his exposure to an elevated lifestyle affects him positively as well. He will naturally be chosen to be the leader of the maidservants' children.[4] In short, Dan will live a life of tension, reflecting his dual experiences.

### YAAKOV'S BLESSING

In fact, Yaakov's deathbed blessing to Dan reflects this dualism:

> Dan will judge his people, as one of the tribes of Israel. Dan will be a serpent in the way, an adder in the path that bites the horse's heels, so that his rider falls backward. I have waited for your salvation, Lord. (Gen. 49:16–18)

"Dan will judge his people" indicates that he will serve in leadership positions. Most traditional commentaries on this verse (including Rashi, Radak, and Ramban) connect this to prediction to Shimshon, a judge in the book of Judges who acts as God's agent against the Philistines (Judges 14–16). In contrast, Ibn Ezra on 49:16 links this prediction to Dan's leadership of an encampment in the desert that includes most of the maidservants' children (Num. 10:25). *Ḥizkuni* on 49:16 adds that Dan is a strong tribe of warriors, placed at the back of the camp to rebuff anyone who attacks the Jewish people from behind. In this way, the tribe of Dan is judging and avenging those who try to hurt the Jewish people.

Yet, "Dan will be a serpent": Dan is likened to an animal that bites its enemies by silently attacking from below. This form of attack, sneaking up silently, is the behavior of a species that operates alone or in small groups. Someone who acts like a snake would be a loner.

Even more so, the biblical representation of the snake is not just as a lonely creature but as an evil one. Beginning with the early days of creation, when the snake tricks Ḥava into eating from the Tree of Life, the Torah describes the snake as "the trickiest of all the animals of the field" (Gen. 3:1). After the sin God tells the snake, "Cursed are you above all cattle, and above

4. He does not become the leader only because he is the oldest of the four children of the maidservants. Birth order is insufficient for leadership, as evidenced by Reuven's case (see Chapter 2). Dan can be chosen only if he exhibits leadership qualities.

every animal of the field. I will put enmity between you and the woman, and between your offspring and her offspring. He will bruise your head, and you will bruise his heel" (3:14–15). God decrees that the snake will be detested and loathed by humankind. The ending of this curse – that snakes bite the heels of humankind – resembles the symbolic description in Yaakov's deathbed blessing to Dan of his tribe biting a horse's heel.

Yaakov's blessing captures both the positive and negative aspects of the tribe of Dan. He will lead and be successful against his enemies; yet concurrently, he will be isolated, angry, and disliked by those around him.

### MOSHE'S BLESSING

Moshe's blessing to Dan is extremely short and cryptic: Of Dan he said, "Dan is strong like a lion's cub that leaps forth from Bashan" (Deut. 33:22). The key phrase here – "strong like a lion" – is borrowed from the blessing of Yaakov to Yehuda,[5] thus drawing a comparison between Yehuda and Dan. This parallel foreshadows both tribes' future leadership qualities of strength and fearlessness. So too, the choice of a lion to characterize Dan highlights another aspect of Dan's nature. A lioness stalks her prey before she attacks, which reminds us of the description of the snake in Yaakov's blessing to Dan, since a snake would attack a horse by biting its heel, sneaking up on its prey from behind.

The second half of the verse, according to most commentators,[6] reflects the tribe's discontent with its territory, and thus their choosing to conquer two portions of land, one in the north and one in the south.[7] The tribe of Dan is unhappy with its situation,[8] its land, as well as its lack of support from the other tribes to help conquer its territory.

5. Yehuda's blessing in Genesis 49:9 is: "Yehuda is strong like a lion." As we will see, there are many times that descendants of Yehuda and Dan are compared or contrasted.
6. See Rashi and Malbim on Deuteronomy 33:22.
7. Rabbi S. R. Hirsch on Deuteronomy 33:22 writes, "The picture could then show Dan as a lion with his claws spread out in two different directions; Bashan is just a mountainous district in the northeast in the neighborhood of Leshem, which Dan conquered. Dan at the same time took possession of provinces in the southwest and northeast."
8. Rabbi S. R. Hirsch on Deut. 33:24 writes, "Naftali, in contrast to Dan and probably on that account placed together with him without any division or paragraph, is completely and fully satisfied with the province allotted to him."

**DAN IN TANAKH**

The tribe of Dan's drastic change of role from "child of Raḥel" to "child of Bilha" is reflected in the way that the Torah lists the twelve tribes. Typically, Dan is listed along with the maidservants' children, befitting his place in the family. However, in two particular lists, Dan is counted along with the children of Raḥel.

Numbers 34, when discussing ancestral inheritance of land, presents the order of tribes as follows: Yehuda, Shimon, Binyamin, Dan, Yosef, Zevulun, Yissakhar, Asher, and Naftali. In I Chronicles 2, the tribes are listed as follows: Reuven, Shimon, Levi, Yehuda, Yissakhar, Zevulun (the children of Leah), Dan, Yosef, Binyamin (where Dan is included with the biological sons of Raḥel), Naftali, Gad and Asher (the other children of the maidservants). These lists reflect Dan's mixed status as a half-brother to Yosef and Binyamin.

Even when Dan is listed among the maidservants' children, he is usually listed first,[9] reflecting his leadership. In the division of the tribes into encampments, Dan is the leader of the encampment of the maidservants' children. His encampment is called "the encampment of Dan," in which the tribe of Dan leads the tribes of Asher and Naftali as the Jewish nation travels for forty years in the desert. This encampment is placed at the rear position and is responsible for any stragglers and for protecting the Jewish people from those who may attack from behind (Num. 10:25).[10]

Transitioning from the forty years in the desert to living in the land of Israel, Dan is not allocated any territory near the other maidservants' children. The others live in the north, but Dan is given land in the south, neighboring Yehuda and Binyamin (Josh. 19:40–48). This apportionment implies a higher status, as it is among the children of Leah and Raḥel. However, being a loner, the tribe of Dan is given no aid in conquering its land and is unable to take control over its territory (Judges 1:34). Leah's and Raḥel's children offer no assistance, and the tribes of the other maidservants' children are too far north to come to Dan's aid. Eventually, the tribe of Dan feels forced to seek a new territory

---

9. See Gen. 35:25, 49:16; Ex. 1:4; Num. 2:25–31, 7:66–71, 10:25, 13:12, 26:42–43, 34:22.
10. See Ibn Ezra on Genesis 49:16.

in the north, near the tribes of Naftali, Gad, and Asher, the other sons of the maidservants (Judges 18). Unfortunately, however, Dan gets no assistance from them either.

The tribe of Dan never feels a sense of belonging among the rest of the tribes. It ends up geographically alone. Dan's encampment is the *last* encampment to travel. It is also the *last* tribe to receive its land in the time of Yehoshua, and the *last* tribe to conquer its land. Its land is *furthest* to the southwest, and later its new land is *furthest* to the north. The most famous character from the tribe of Dan, Shimshon, is the *last* judge in the book of Judges.[11]

These attributes of being last, not fitting in, and loneliness – juxtaposed with leadership, strength, and fearlessness – are found within the prominent individuals from the tribe of Dan.

## PERSONALITIES FROM THE TRIBE OF DAN

### Oholiav

> Behold, I have appointed with him Oholiav, the son of Aḥisamakh, of the tribe of Dan; and in the heart of all who are wise-hearted I have put wisdom, that they may make all that I have commanded you. (Ex. 31:6)

Just as there is a comparison between the personalities of Yehuda and Dan ("strong like a lion"), there is parallel description of the wisdom of Oholiav from the tribe of Dan and Betzalel from the tribe of Yehuda.[12]

---

11. So too, the tribe of Dan is listed last in the list of King David's soldiers (I Chr. 27).
12. The wisdom of Betzalel of the tribe of Yehuda is compared to the wisdom and expertise of Oholiav from the tribe of Dan. "He has filled him [Betzalel] with the spirit of God, in wisdom, in understanding, in knowledge, and in all manner of workmanship; and to make skillful works, to work in gold, in silver, in brass, in cutting of stones for setting, and in carving of wood, to work in all kinds of skillful workmanship. He has put in his heart that he may teach, both he and Oholiav, the son of Aḥisamakh, of the tribe of Dan. He has filled them with wisdom of heart, to work all manner of workmanship, of the engraver, of the skillful workman, and of the embroiderer, in blue, in purple, in scarlet, and in fine linen, and of the weaver, even of those who do any workmanship, and of those who make skillful works" (Ex. 35:31–35).

Oholiav is selected to assist Betzalel in the building of the Tabernacle, thus creating a partnership between Yehuda and Dan.

At first glance, the collaboration of Yehuda and Dan may seem strange. They are born to different mothers and live in different households. (Dan is the son of Raḥel's maid, not Leah's.) Upon further inspection, however, we recognize the link between them. First, they are likely very similar in age. Dan is born right after Yehuda. During their early years, Reuven was off on his own (see Chapter 2), while Shimon and Levi were a twosome (see Chapter 4). Yehuda is left to spend time with the next brother, Dan. Furthermore, during this early period Dan may actually have been treated more like a child of Raḥel than of Bilha, his biological mother; therefore, he would have been in a position to befriend the sons of Leah, especially the one closest in age to him.

This connection between Yehuda and Dan continues when the land in Israel is allocated and Dan's territory is located right next to Yehuda's. Interestingly, they pair up again in the building of the Holy Temple. King Shlomo (from the tribe of Yehuda) selects an assistant from the tribe of Dan.[13]

The description of "strong as a lion," associated with Yehuda and Dan, accurately portrays the strongest individuals in the history of each tribe – David and Shimshon, respectively. The story and personality of Shimshon remind us in so many ways of King David.[14] Both men kill a lion with their bare hands.[15] Both fight the Philistines alone, without the support of an army, and over the course of their careers they each

13. In II Chr. 2:13–14 Shlomo receives a man described as a "skillful man, endowed with understanding, the son of a woman of the daughters of Dan; and his father was a man of Tyre." Since he has a Jewish mother, he is Jewish, and because his father is not Jewish, he becomes a member of her tribe as well. The description of his wisdom reminds us of Oholiav, also from the tribe of Dan, and of Shlomo and Betzalel from Yehuda.

14. Both have their wives taken from them by their fathers-in-law and married off to another man. Specifically, Shimshon's father-in-law marries Shimshon's wife off to another man (Judges 15:2). Shaul, David's father-in-law, takes away David's wife Michal and gives her to Palti son of Layish (I Sam. 25:44).

15. Shimshon kills a lion on his way home to tell his parents that he wants to marry (Judges 14:6). So too, David tells a story about how he killed a lion and a bear (I Sam. 17:35).

kill thousands of enemies. Both men are passionate and desire women who are forbidden to them.[16] It seems fitting that Numbers Rabba 10:5 identifies Shimshon's mother as a member of the tribe of Yehuda.

Furthermore, *Yalkut Shimoni* on Gen. 49:16 adds, based on Yehuda and Dan both being described as "strong as a lion," that in the future the Messiah will come from a combination of both of them. A man from Yehuda will marry a woman from Dan, and they will be the parents of the Messiah.

How is one to understand this connection between Yehuda and Dan? Let's consider two opposite possibilities with regard to the nature of this relationship.

One option: The pairing is designed to elevate Dan. The comparison of Dan to Yehuda shows that Dan evidently deserves to be associated with Yehuda's. Therefore, Dan and Yehuda must have similar attributes (e.g., their leadership qualities of strength and wisdom).

The other option: The pairing is designed to contrast Dan to Yehuda. In contrast to Yehuda, Dan's flaws become more readily apparent. The good in Dan is so limited that it is visible only when paired with Yehuda, as Dan needs Yehuda to bring out the good in him. Exodus Rabba 40:4 states the following: "There is no tribe greater [*gadol*] than Yehuda and no tribe worse [*katan*] than the tribe of Dan. God said, 'Let us pair them, so no one will degrade him, to teach that good and bad are equal before God.' This is referring to Betzalel from Yehuda and Oholiav from Dan, who is paired with him." This second understanding provides a more negative perspective on the tribe of Dan, considering Dan as the opposite of Yehuda in every way, including righteousness, thereby needing Yehuda to bring out the good that is inherent within the tribe.

Furthermore, there are other episodes in Tanakh that reflect this contrast between the two tribes. For instance, the book of Judges begins with the tribe of Yehuda conquering its apportionment and concludes

16. David takes a married woman (Batsheva), and Shimshon has three stories about being with non-Jewish women, including a prostitute. Both men are influenced by beauty. Shimshon tells his parents that he wants to marry a non-Jewish woman because "she finds favor in my eyes" (Judges. 14:3). David's wife Batsheva is described as extremely beautiful (II Sam. 11:2).

with Dan's inability to conquer much of its land. Otniel (from the tribe of Yehuda) is the first judge. He leads the entire nation and successfully defeats Aram, resulting in forty years of peace (Judges 3:10–11). In contrast, Shimshon (from Dan) is the final judge recorded in the book of Judges. He lacks military support and is unsuccessful in removing the enemy from the land, resulting in instability.[17] In fact, within the details of Shimshon's story, his only interaction with other Jews is when the tribe of Yehuda ties him up and hands him over to the enemy (Judges 15:12–13).

Relatedly, as noted above, Numbers Rabba identifies Shimshon's mother as a member of the tribe of Yehuda (and the text tells us that Shimshon's father, Manoaḥ, is from Dan). As we'll see, his mother is clearly more virtuous than his father, deserving of God's intervention. For instance, the angel who reveals that they will have a child appears only to his mother.[18] When Manoaḥ prays to God for the angel to appear

---

17. See Judges 15:20, where the verse states: "And he judged the Jewish people during the time of Philistines for twenty years." However, we are also told, "And God gave us into the hands of the Philistines for forty years!" (Judges 13:1), teaching us that he judged during the Philistines' forty-year rule over the Jewish people. In other words, Otniel's forty years of peace are in direct contrast to the forty years of the Philistines' rule, during which Shimshon was a judge and there was no peace.
18. The verse states that the angel appeared "to the woman" (Judges 13:2).

    Also, and significantly, her description reminds us of the matriarchs: "And she was a barren [*akara*] woman and didn't have children" (13:3). This biblical language resembles these instances:

    (1) Sarah: "And she was barren [*akara*] and had no children" (Gen. 11:30).
    (2) Rivka: "She was a barren [*akara*] woman" (Gen. 25:21).
    (3) Raḥel: "And Raḥel was barren [*akara*]" (Gen. 29:31).

    The wife of Manoaḥ, like the matriarchs, suffered years of infertility followed by the miraculous birth of a son who is vital to the history of the Jewish people. As in the case of Sarah, an angel comes to reveal that a son will be born. However, unlike Sarah's experience, in which the angel speaks to Avraham and Sarah overhears the discussion, the angel speaks directly to the wife of Manoaḥ.

    Interestingly, unlike in the case of his wife, there is no verse that compares Manoaḥ to the patriarchs. In fact, the opposite is true. In reaction to the angel disappearing and fire descending onto the food that Manoaḥ serves him, Manoaḥ cries out, "We will surely die because we saw God!" (Judges 13:22). This seems like the antithesis of Yaakov's reaction to a similar encounter, when he calmly stated, "I saw God face to face and survived" (Gen. 32:31). They react so differently to the experience of a visit from an angel (a "man of God"): Manoaḥ panics and screams out in

to him, it revisits only his wife. Manoaḥ doubts that the visitor is an angel; his wife realizes it from the start.[19] Only after the angel disappears into the fire does Manoaḥ believe that he was a figure sent by God, and he screams, "We shall surely die, because we have seen God" (Judges 13:22). It is his wife who comforts him and reminds him that they cannot die, as they have been given the task of parenting the next leader of the Jewish people (13:23). In this episode, the descendant of Yehuda is righteous[20] and Dan's descendant is less so.[21] This mixture of Yehuda and Dan provides one element of the complicated nature of Shimshon, an amalgam of conflicting attributes.

Even though Yehuda and Dan together build the Tabernacle and the Temple of God, Dan separates from Yehuda when the kingdom splits. Dan, along with nine other tribes of Israel, abandons Yehuda. These other tribes, including Dan, are led by numerous corrupt kings who lead them into exile years prior to the exile of the kingdom of Yehuda.

### The *Mekalel*: The Man who Curses God

> The son of an Israelite woman, whose father was an Egyptian, went out among the children of Israel; and the son of the Israelite woman and a man of Israel strove together in the camp. The son of the Israelite woman blasphemed the Name, and cursed; and they brought him to Moshe. His mother's name was Shlomit, the daughter of Divri, of the tribe of Dan. They put him in custody, until the will of God should be declared to them.... Moshe

fear of death, whereas Yaakov celebrates his experience by renaming the location of his encounter with God to remind him of the location where he saw God's face.

19. She states to her husband: "A man of God came to me, and his face was like the face of the angel of God" (Judges 13:6).
20. *Pesikta DeRav Kahana* 20:1 includes her on the list of seven righteous barren women. The others on the list are Sarah, Rivka, Raḥel, Leah, Ḥana and Tzion, i.e., Jerusalem. So too, *Otzar Midrashim* 474:21 includes her in the list of twenty-four righteous Jewish women of Tanakh.
21. The Talmud in Eiruvin 18b and Berakhot 61a describes Manoaḥ as "a simple, unintelligent man." Berakhot 61a stresses that "he follows his wife's lead."

> spoke to the children of Israel; and they brought forth him who had cursed out of the camp and stoned him with stones. The children of Israel did as God commanded Moshe. (Lev. 24:10–12, 23)

Presented as an isolated narrative within a book of laws, this story is one of only two narratives found in the entire book of Leviticus. The text and the context are vague, leaving us unsure about many of the relevant details. However, one detail we do know: the man in question is from the tribe of Dan!

Furthermore, in this short episode, we are exposed to elements of Dan's negative characteristics. The man is a loner, out of place among the Jewish people; his father is not Jewish, which exacerbates his feeling of displacement. Unlike other rebellions in the desert, this man is not trying to rile up a crowd nor cause a revolt. He is frustrated by his own predicament and lashes out at God.[22] This story is about a man who is isolated and feels completely out of place. Rabbi S. R. Hirsch on Leviticus 24:10 writes, "He went out of the bounds within which he belonged, into the midst of the children of Israel, where he did not belong."[23]

Not only is there an element of loneliness in this story, but also one of anger. This man exhibits fury when cursing God. How much resentment and wrath he must have felt to be able to utter such words!

---

22. The background story to this event is captured by *Midrash Tanḥuma* 34, quoted by Rashi on Lev. 24:10, and many commentators. This man went out to pitch his tent among the tribe of Dan. A fellow Jew came out to question why he thought he could live there, as his father was not from the tribe of Dan. He argued that since his mother was from Dan and his father wasn't Jewish, he should be included in the tribe of Dan. This controversy leads to his feelings of abandonment and isolation. The midrash goes one step further by making an inference from the name of his mother, Shlomit daughter of Divri, that she is talkative by nature. Shlomit is impregnated by an Egyptian, who is later killed by Moshe. Rabbenu Baḥya believes that perhaps this is the source of the disagreement between the man and the members of the tribe of Dan. The Jewish man tells the man from Dan what happened to his father. When he finds out that Moshe killed him using God's name, the man reacts by cursing the name of God. Either way, this story is about an extremely secluded man who is unassociated with Jewish society, who reacts with anger against God and the Jewish people.
23. He further explains that because he doesn't have a Jewish father, it is unclear whether he is considered Jewish (and whether he is from the tribe of Dan) because before the giving of the Torah, the standards for determining one's status as a Jew might have been different.

This incident is a representation of Dan's feelings of displacement and resentment.

**Shimshon**

Shimshon is the full representation of Dan's persona. He displays anger and seeks revenge. He acts alone, without the nation's support or even his parents' approval,[24] and he is alienated by the three women in his life.[25] He seeks no authority's permission before acting. In spite of these negative elements, he is a leader of the Jewish people for twenty years (Judges 16:31).

Shimshon's anger is obvious throughout his life. When his wife reveals the solution to his riddle and the men are able to declare the answer,[26] he reacts violently. Instead of laughing at their ability to fool him, he sees this as an act of betrayal. He banishes his wife from his home, back to her father's house, within the first week of their marriage. He then kills thirty Philistines as revenge for cheating and gives their clothing to the men who solved the riddle as their reward (Judges 14:12–19). Later, when his father-in-law arranges a marriage for his daughter (Shimshon's ex-wife), Shimshon collects three hundred foxes, ties their tails together with a burning torch, and sets them lose to burn the fields of the Philistines (15:3–5). In retaliation, the Philistines burn his ex-wife and ex-father-in-law. Shimshon avenges their deaths by killing a large number of Philistines (15:8). When the tribe of Yehuda hands him over to the Philistines, he breaks through the rope and kills another thousand Philistines (15:15). After he is captured and tortured, he uses his last ounce of strength to bring down the entire building where many thousands of Philistines were celebrating his capture, killing all of them (16:28–30).

---

24. His parents warn him against marrying a non-Jewish woman and he ignores their request (Judges 14:2–4).
25. His wife shares the answer to his riddle. The second woman is a prostitute. The third woman, Delila, seeks to aid his enemies by learning the secret behind his strength. She cuts off his hair, allowing him to be captured and beaten.
26. During their wedding, Shimshon challenges his guests with a riddle: "Out of the eater came forth food, out of the strong came forth sweetness" (Judges 14:14). After the men threaten his new wife so she will reveal the answer, they tell Shimshon, "What is sweeter than honey? And what is stronger than a lion?" (14:18).

At the same time, ironically, Shimshon is a leader: "He judged Israel in the days of the Philistines, twenty years" (Judges 15:20). This is repeated after his death: "He judged Israel for twenty years" (16:31). Superficially, these verses are challenging, as Shimshon spends a considerable amount of time living among the enemy and not among the Jewish people. In fact, we have no evidence in the book of Judges of his interacting with the Jewish people in a leadership fashion. But the most befuddling question is how Shimshon could judge the Jewish people according to Jewish law if he regularly violates the law. He has intimate relations with non-Jewish women, he seeks revenge, commits suicide, and, in spite of being a Nazirite, he exposes himself to impurities by coming into contact with dead bodies.[27]

In spite of our question, we are reminded that God supports and helps him. In fact, each time he acts aggressively, the Torah writes, "The spirit of God came mightily on him." These words are written when he kills the lion (14:6), when he kills thirty Philistines (14:19), and when he breaks the rope and kills another thousand Philistines after they capture him (15:14–15). Why, we may wonder, does God lend support to a man who commits so many sins?

Our question is strengthened by the two times that God immediately responds to Shimshon's prayer. When Shimshon is tired and thirsty after killing the thousand Philistines, he requests water. God enables water to stream out of the cheekbone that Shimshon used as a weapon. Of course, this miracle reminds us of the water pouring out of a rock in the time of Moshe. So too, once Shimshon's hair was cut, thus minimizing his strength, he prays to God to return his strength just one more time; instantly, he is able to pull down an entire building. God's

27. See Judges 15:20. The commentators debate the meaning of this verse and its implications for his leadership. Abarbanel on Judges 15 writes that he actually leads the Jewish people, like every other judge of Israel. Radak on 15:20 writes that he does not judge the Jewish people but does fight on their behalf, so he is considered a leader. Ralbag on I Sam. 4:9 writes that Shimshon's leadership years overlap with those of Eli, the next judge found in I Samuel, and the reason for this is that for most of Shimshon's period of leadership, he is in the land of the enemy and therefore cannot judge or lead the Jewish people.

immediate response to Shimshon's requests is simply puzzling![28] Perhaps God is with him because he is the only one helping the Jewish people fight against their enemy. Or perhaps there is good within Shimshon that God recognizes despite all of his evil actions and sins.

The confusion over the character of Shimshon – whether he is a hero or villain or something in between – mimics our confusion over the personality of the tribe of Dan. In the tribe, as well as within Shimshon, there is both good and bad.

**The Idol of Mikha: Descendants of Dan who Steal the Idol**

Near the very beginning of the book of Judges, we learn that the people of Dan are unable to fully conquer their land. No one comes to their aid; by the end of the book of Judges, they are compelled to look for a new portion of land. They send a team of five men to scout out alternative plots of land (Judges 18). During their journey, these men reach Mikha's home, which hosts an idol. Mikha, from the tribe of Ephraim, had appointed a man from the tribe of Levi to act as the priest for his local house of worship. When the men from Dan enter the home, they turn to the Levite for spiritual guidance and ask if their mission will be successful. He tells them to go in peace and that God will help them on their path. After successfully finding a new homeland for their tribe, they return home to gather their tribe to join them. On their way back north with the tribe, they follow the same route via the home of Mikha. The five men enter his home and steal his idol and religious articles. When the Levite approaches them to question their actions, they offer him the opportunity to join them and run their house of worship in their new territory. He agrees. Then, the tribe of Dan leaves with the Levite, the idol, and the various religious items (against Mikha's will).

---

28. Further evidence of his leadership being from God is described in the story of how he is selected. Judges 13 presents the story of Shimshon's parents, which is reminiscent of the birth of Yitzḥak. His then-infertile mother is told by a visiting angel that she will give birth to a son. He is given the special role of being a Nazirite, thus forbidden from drinking wine and cutting his hair, similar to the prophet Shmuel (I Sam. 1:11). The angel explains, "He shall begin to save Israel out of the hand of the Philistines" (13:5). He is destined for greatness and leadership.

At this point, the tribe of Dan travels to Layish, where a quiet nation resides, and murders them, burns the city to the ground, and claims the land as its own. The members of the tribe rename the city "Dan," erect the idol, and appoint the Levite to be their priest. The story ends by noting that this idol remains there throughout the entire time that there is a Tabernacle in Shiloh.[29]

In many ways, this story appears to be a reaction to Dan's solitude. The tribe doesn't feel connected to the rest of the nation. Its members are left without land because no one helps them, so they don't feel the need to be considerate or helpful to others. They don't hesitate before stealing the idol from a man from the tribe of Ephraim. Evidently, they don't see him as family.[30]

Similarly, they don't feel connected to the national religious center (the Tabernacle). During the time of the judges, the entire nation is commanded to worship God in the Tabernacle in Shiloh.[31] However, the men from Dan seek guidance from a local house of worship and set up a permanent house of worship outside of the Tabernacle. In fact, in the future the territory of the tribe of Dan is one of the locations chosen by Yorovam for his altars to avoid having to travel to the lands of Yehuda and worship in Jerusalem (I Kings 12:29). The tribe of Dan is comfortable serving God outside of the standard central venue.

## CONCLUSION

The tribe of Dan has a pattern of unusual episodes reflecting irregular leadership. Dan's descendants embody leadership skills but at the same time are self-indulgent and self-focused. They display strength but also anger. At times these traits are used to aid the Jewish people; at other times they are used for their own greed. Dan partners with Yehuda to build the central locations of worship for the Jewish people, while the

29. In Deut. 12:13–14, Moshe tells the Jewish people that external altars are forbidden. In Zevaḥim 112b it is written that this law pertains to certain times in history, and that specifically during the time of Shiloh, this rule applied.
30. There is an irony to Dan stealing from Yosef's son. It evokes a clear connection to the original Dan, who lost his place in the family upon the birth of Yosef.
31. Shmuel's father, Elkana, travels to Shiloh every year to worship God and give Him sacrifices (I Sam. 1:3).

tribe of Dan itself worships God in other formats. At times, they lead the Jewish people, but other times they exhibit dissociation from the nation. Dan's personal experiences reflect clearly on the lives, decisions, and experiences of his descendants.

*Chapter 13*

# Gad: The Oldest Son of Zilpa

Gad is the oldest child of Zilpa, the fifth (surrogate) child of Leah, and the eighth child of Yaakov. This places him in a strange position within the family. He is the firstborn of his biological mother's two sons, yet he is nowhere near the age of the oldest of Leah's progeny (Reuven) or the oldest of the maidservants' children (Dan, son of Bilha).

We know nothing about his personality or character from the stories in Genesis. Next to his older brothers, Gad has no voice. Our only hint to his persona is his father's deathbed description of this son: "Gad, a troop will press on him; but he will press on their heel" (Gen. 49:19). Yaakov's description of Gad is of someone who is strong and able to be victorious against his enemies. This blessing implies that Gad will lead (at least) in battle and presents the possibility that he may establish his own voice in the future.

Various commentators connect this blessing to specific military events in the future. For instance, Rashbam on Genesis 49:19 suggests that this foreshadows Gad's military leadership in the campaign against Canaan. Ramban on 49:19 writes that it is hinting to the future battle of

Yiftaḥ and the men of the land of Gilad (a city in the land of Gad on the other side of the Jordan River) against the Ammonites. Rabbenu Baḥya on 49:19 writes that this description insinuates that Gad will engage in many battles with the enemy. These interpretations share the commonality that Gad is the tribe that provides military leadership in support of the political leadership of the time (whether it is under Yehoshua, the judges, or the kings).

## REUVEN AND GAD'S PARTNERSHIP

The eldest child of Zilpa is stripped of his firstborn-related privileges because of his place in the larger family structure. In spite of being Zilpa's eldest, he is Yaakov's eighth son. Furthermore, his mother is "only" a maidservant. At least to some, this picture suggests that we might expect a similarity to Reuven, the rejected firstborn of Leah. Both men are resentful and feel defrauded of their firstborn rights. Why are they rejected for the role of firstborn? Reuven is rejected because he is the son of Leah (not born to the favorite wife, Raḥel) and because of his misbehavior with Bilha.[1] Gad is rejected because he is the son of Zilpa, the maidservant of Leah. Both brothers feel scorned because of their father's preference for Raḥel. These shared feelings create a bond between Reuven and Gad, which is reflected on numerous occasions.

### Reuven and Gad as a Pair

The tribes of Reuven and Gad share an encampment in the desert, which is led by Reuven. Included in Reuven's encampment are the tribes of Shimon and Gad (Num. 2). So too, they stand together on Mount Ebal, as destined by Moshe, to hear Yeshoshua's rendition of the blessings and the curses (Deut. 27:13, Josh. 8). The list of tribes on Mount Ebal juxtaposes Reuven's and Gad's tribes, even though the rest of the maidservants' children's names are at the end.[2]

1. See Chapter 2 for more on the context of Reuven losing the birthright.
2. As presented there, the list of tribes on Mount Ebal is in the following order: Reuven, Gad, Asher, Zevulun, Dan and Naftali. One might have expected Reuven and Zevulun (both sons of Leah) to be mentioned first, followed by the four maidservant children.

Beyond naming conventions and tribal lists, their partnership is most profoundly expressed in Numbers 32. The leaders of the tribes of Reuven and Gad approach Moshe for permission to reside on the eastern bank of the Jordan River.

Why would the descendants of Reuven and of Gad want to separate themselves geographically from the rest of the Jewish people? The Torah tells us: "Now the children of Reuven and the children of Gad had a very great multitude of cattle" (Num. 32:1). But this explanation seems incomplete. How can they know that this land is better for their cattle than the land of Israel, where they have never been? Why would they want to live outside of the land promised to them by God? Do they really have so much material wealth (i.e., cattle) to require living alone? If so, why does Moshe become enraged by their request?

Rabbenu Baḥya (Num. 32:2) writes that this story highlights certain negative aspects of these two groups: they are greedy people who love their money and possessions. They value their belongings so much that they are willing to separate from the rest of the Jewish people and forego the blessings of living in the land of Israel. This perspective lands them in trouble later in history, when they are two of the first tribes to be expelled (I Chr. 5:26).

However, a completely different perspective emerges within our story when comparing it to two similar episodes in the Torah. In fact, there are two other stories in Torah where too much material wealth creates a distance between brothers (and one brother leaves the land of Israel). They are the stories of Avraham and Lot and of Yaakov and Esav. In the story of Avraham and his nephew Lot,[3] the reason for their split is that "the land was not able to bear them, that they might live together: for their substance was great, so that they could not live together" (Gen. 13:6). Avraham remains inside Israel and Lot relocates to Sodom, outside the borders of the land of Israel. Similarly, Yaakov and Esav separate from each other "for their substance was too great for them to dwell together, and the land of their travels couldn't bear them because of their cattle" (Gen. 36:7). Esav moves out of Israel to the land of Seir,

3. According to the Talmud in Sanhedrin 69b and Megilla 14a, Yiska is Sarah. Accordingly, Lot would be Avraham's brother-in-law.

and Yaakov stays behind, thus inheriting the land. Both episodes include a separation of kin due to apparent affluence; one relative remains in Israel and the other family member leaves the land.

In both situations, however, it is clear that it is not only material wealth that precipitates the familial division. Rather, a more fundamental issue underlies the family split. Ideologically, there is no way that Yaakov can live with Esav, or that Lot can live with Avraham. Their value systems and moral senses are mutually exclusive. Esav doesn't want to live under the rules and values of Yaakov.[4] Lot doesn't want to be held hostage by the ethics of Avraham; rather, he prefers the anarchy of Sodom; with regard to Sodom the text states: "Now the men of Sodom were exceedingly wicked and sinners against God" (13:13).[5]

Similarly, it is plausible that the two rejected oldest sons intend to live in their own lands, away from the watchful eye of the other tribes. Rabbi S. R. Hirsch on Num. 32:1 writes that "settling by themselves within special boundaries outside those of the general nation appealed to them." They want to live apart from the rest of the nation of Israel!

Rabbi Mordechai Breuer suggests[6] that Moshe immediately recognizes the underlying motivation for their request – to separate themselves from the nation. As rejected eldest children, they feel compelled to follow the path of prior firstborn cast-offs (e.g., Esav and Yishmael), who leave the Jewish people. This accounts for Moshe's harsh reaction to their request. He understands that it has nothing to do with the size of their flocks, but rather with their perceived destiny which they see as requiring them to abandon their brothers.

To counter their lack of belonging within the Jewish people, Moshe strikes a deal with them – they can live on the other side of the Jordan River but only after leading the rest of the Jewish people in battle against the Canaanites inside of Israel (Num. 32:29–30). Moshe

4. *Sifrei* Num. 69 writes "[It is] a known fact [that] Esav hates Yaakov." The Maharam on Gen. 36:7 writes that Esav values idolatry and therefore couldn't live in Israel with Yaakov in the presence of God.
5. See Rabbenu Baḥya on Genesis 13:12–14, who writes that Lot chooses to reside in Sodom because he identifies with the Sodomites, and thus chooses to live among people whose values are evil. See also Rabbi S. R. Hirsch on 13:6.
6. Rabbi Mordechai Breuer, *Pirkei Bereshit* Vol. 1, (Alon Shevut: Tevunot, 1999), 251.

is acknowledging the validity of their request, but conditions his acceptance on their willingness to show loyalty and connection to the Jewish people. They can't just separate and live in the land that is already conquered, effectively removing themselves from the Jewish people.

Years later, after most of the land has been conquered, Yehoshua permits them to return to the eastern bank of the Jordan River. What is their first public act upon returning to their lands? They build a "great altar to look at" (Josh. 22:10). Yehoshua immediately assumes rebellious motives. The nation gathers an army, foreshadowing the possibility of a civil war. However, before initiating the battle, Yehoshua sends Pinḥas (Aharon's grandson) to ascertain the true intent of their actions. What is their response? That they are not rebelling against the Jewish people! On the contrary, they reveal that they built the altar to remind future generations that they are part of the nation of Israel.

How are we to understand this story? At face value, its conclusion provides a happy ending, showing that the tribes of Reuven and Gad are connected to the people. On the other hand, it reveals that Yehoshua assumes they could be breaking away from the Jewish people. In short, Reuven and Gad's sense of rejection will always cause suspicion that they might dissociate from the rest of the Jewish people.

In each of these instances, we might wonder if Reuven and Gad are equal in their partnership, or perhaps one is the leader and the other the follower.

It is important to note that in every verse other than the introductory one, Gad's name precedes Reuven's.[7] Typically in Tanakh, the elder sons and the children of the matriarchs are listed before the younger sons or the maidservants' children. Therefore, listing the tribe of Gad before Reuven is intentional.[8] Ibn Ezra, Ramban, and *Ḥizkuni* on 32:1 all explain that Gad is listed first because the tribe of Gad is the instigator. It is Gad's idea to live on the other side of the Jordan River. In fact,

---

7. See Num. 32:2, 6, and 25. Moshe even gives Gad their land before Reuven (v. 31). Gad builds their cities before Reuven (v. 34).
8. Rabbenu Baḥya on 32:1 adds that not only is Reuven older, but he is a child of a full wife, whereas Gad is the son of a maidservant. For both these reasons, Reuven's name precedes Gad's name in the first verse of this story.

Ramban and Rabbenu Baḥya add that it is the tribe of Gad who leads the initiative to negotiate with Moshe. The tribe of Reuven follows suit only after the process has commenced. Ramban writes explicitly about the tribe of Gad that "they are stronger than the children of Reuven."

### MOSHE'S BLESSING

> Of Gad he said: "Blessed be he who enlarges Gad: He dwells as a lioness, tears the arm, yes, the crown of the head. He provided the first part for himself, for there was the lawgiver's portion reserved; he came with the heads of the people. He executed the righteousness of God, His ordinances with Israel." (Deut. 33:20–21)

Moshe's final words regarding the tribe of Gad are further proof of the tribe's strength. This blessing furthers our understanding that Gad is the leader on the other side of the Jordan River. Rashi on Deut. 33:20 writes that Gad's comparison to a lion is a blessing focused on the strength he will need to live on the opposite side of the river. Similarly, Rabbenu Baḥya on 33:20 adds that the blessing is necessary due to the tribe's closer proximity to the threat of other nations, away from the protection of the rest of the Jewish people. Ramban on 33:20 summarizes this school of thought by adding that this specific blessing is given to Gad instead of Reuven because the tribe of Gad is mightier and more capable of protecting both itself and the tribe of Reuven.

### CONCLUSION

The tribe of Gad experiences incongruence between its secondary role among the Jewish people and its steadfast desire to lead. Gad pairs up with Reuven, Leah's rejected firstborn, to establish its own sense of independence. Sadly, this leads to their demise at the hands of Pul and Tilgat Pilneser, kings of Ashur. When they attack Gad, the other tribes do not attempt to enter the battle to save them (I Chr. 5:26).

*Chapter 14*

# Naftali and Asher: The Younger Sons of Bilha and Zilpa

Naftali and Asher are the younger sons of the two maidservants. They know their place in the family. Neither one possesses much of a voice; they follow the directions of the leaders of the family. Throughout history, they are happy to follow; they never rebel or assume leadership positions.

## NAFTALI

Genesis Rabba 14:11 describes Naftali as the obedient messenger of his father; he is someone who swiftly fulfills every mission. Because of his dependability and amicable personality, his father and brothers speak nicely of him. *Midrash HaGadol* 49:21 adds that he is also the dutiful messenger of his brothers; he happily does whatever they ask of him.[1]

1. What is the origin of the assumption that Naftali was a quick messenger? Yaakov compares him to a deer (Gen. 49:21). Rabbi S. R. Hirsch on Gen. 49:21 writes, "If

### Barak

The only known descendant of Naftali is Barak, a general in the Jewish nation's army who shares Naftali's personality. Like his ancestor, Barak shows no interest in leading; he would rather follow someone else. Although he serves as general in Devora's army, Barak prefers that Devora lead, thus allowing him to follow. When Devora requests that he lead the battle against General Sisera of Canaan, he responds, "If you go with me, then I will go; but if you do not go with me, I will not go" (Judges 4:8). As opposed to other military leaders who anticipate the opportunity to lead men into battle, this general is unwilling to go into battle without his civil leader! In fact, he even refuses to meet her at the battlefield. Rather, he waits until she meets with him in the land of Naftali. She must figuratively hold his hand the entire way, as he needs her to accompany him to the battlefield and guide him in the battle. He never becomes the hero; that is a role destined for Devora.[2]

Throughout the battle, General Barak exhibits Naftali's characteristic: he follows rather than leads. So too, the tribe of Naftali follows leaders in their battles against the enemy. The tribe joins Barak to fight against General Sisera and Canaan (Judges 4:10) and is praised by Devora for its involvement in the battle (5:18). So too, they join the army of the judge Gidon to fight against the nation of Midian (6:35, 7:23).

## ASHER

As noted above, Naftali is not the only tribe to eschew leadership. His half-brother Asher is remarkably similar. Asher and his progeny never play an active or engaged role in the Jewish people's history. Asher's descendants are mentioned only as soldiers in the army, not as military

---

one could use deer as messengers, one would be sure of obtaining the speediest delivery. Accordingly, whatever one entrusts Naftali to do will be speedily carried out. Naftali does not act on his own initiative and is not productive on his own, but he quickly adopts and carries out what others have decided for the benefit of the community."

2. Devora unequivocally declares this: "I will surely go with you; notwithstanding, the journey that you take shall not be for your honor, for God will sell Sisera into the hand of a woman" (Judges 4:9). Sisera escapes from Barak and is murdered by a woman named Yael.

officers. In the book of Judges they struggle to conquer their own land, with many Canaanites remaining in their territory (Judges 1:31–32). They don't receive any help from the other tribes in extricating the Canaanites from their land, nor do they offer to help Devora's army against Canaan. At the end of the war, Devora rebukes them for not coming to help their brothers (5:17). Sometime later, during the leadership of Gidon, the tribe of Asher does join his army to fight against Midian. Interestingly, the text informs us that Gidon specifically gathers an army from Menashe (his own tribe), as well as Asher, Zevulun, and Naftali – all tribes who follow others' leads (6:35 and 7:23). A few generations later, the tribe of Asher is vindicated, as it is listed as part of David's army. We are told that there are 26,000 warriors that come from the tribe of Asher (I Chr. 7:40). The tribe is taking on more of a role, but still just as soldiers, not as officers.

### Seraḥ Daughter of Asher

Other than the standard identifying of the *nesiim,* princes, the only descendant of Asher identified by name is his daughter Seraḥ. The Torah mentions her in various lists (whereas most women's names are excluded from the lists). First, she is one of the seventy family members joining Yaakov in going down to Egypt.[3] Additionally, Seraḥ is included in the list of potential soldiers for the army (Num. 26:46). In that counting, the only other women included are Miriam (26:59) and the daughters of Tzelofḥad (26:33). Similarly, she is the only woman listed among members of the tribe of Asher (I Chr. 7:30). In fact, in this list, which includes fifty-three grandsons of Yaakov, she is the only granddaughter to be included. Clearly, she is a uniquely important person![4]

To explain the focus on Seraḥ, the Sages attribute various virtuous acts to her. For example, they say that Yosef's brothers were worried that the shock of the news of him being alive might overwhelm

3. Gen. 46:17. The only other woman listed is Dina (Gen. 46:15). It is very hard to believe that she is the only granddaughter of Yaakov. Note that the wives of Yaakov are not listed as part of the seventy family members.
4. Abarbanel on Num. 26 says explicitly that Seraḥ is an important woman deserving to be listed along with Miriam, the sister of Moshe and Aharon.

Yaakov. Therefore, they requested that Seraḥ gently convey the news to her grandfather Yaakov, which she did successfully.[5] Similarly, the Sages credit her as the bearer of the verbal tradition connected with the future redeemer of the Jewish people, according to which the redeemer would announce himself by using the root *peh, kuf, dalet,* meaning "remember" – a tradition that she received from her father, Asher.[6] He (along with the other brothers) received it from Yosef, who heard it directly from Yaakov. Later, Seraḥ confirms this code when Moshe utters those words to the Jewish people: "God remembered the children of Israel" (Ex. 4:31). She is also credited with being the one who informs Moshe as to where the bones of Yosef are buried.[7] More remarkably, the Sages associate her with the wise woman who transfers the head of Sheva son of Bikhri to David's general Yoav, to prevent Yoav from destroying her city.[8] This story occurs hundreds of years after her generation! In fact, there is even a view according to the Sages that Seraḥ never died.[9]

---

5. There are varying descriptions of how Seraḥ told Yaakov the news. Midrash HaGadol 26 contends that she told him in a low whisper. *Sefer HaYashar* (*Vayigash* 9) offers the well-known explanation that she played the harp and sang, repeating the words "Yosef my uncle is living, and he rules throughout the land of Egypt, and is not dead."
6. Exodus Rabba 5:13.
7. See Sota 13a, *Mekhilta DeRabbi Shimon Bar Yoḥai* 13:18. This may be based on the similar wording "to remember" (from the Hebrew root *peh, kuf, dalet*) used in the story of Moshe taking Yosef's bones (Ex. 13:19). Further, while the Torah states that all the men of that generation are dead, it never says that the women are dead (Ex. 1:6), hence the inference that she could be the only living individual who might know this tradition.
8. See Genesis Rabba 94:9, Ecclesiastes Rabba 7:11, quoted by Radak on II Sam. 20:16. Midrash Mishlei 31:26 writes that the words "*Piha patḥa beḥokhma,*" "She opens her mouth with wisdom," are referring to the "wise woman" ("*isha ḥakhama*"), who is Seraḥ bat Asher. According to this source, she saves her city with her wisdom.
9. *Masekhet Kallah Rabbati* 3 writes that she is included among the people who ascended alive to the Garden of Eden. *Sefer HaYashar, Vayigash* 9 and *Otzar HaMidrashim* on Gen. 46:17 write that Yaakov blessed her with eternal life as a reward for the compassionate way that she revealed that Yosef was still alive. *Pesikta DeRav Kahana* 11:13 writes that she even appears during the time of the Talmud to help R. Yoḥanan explain Exodus 14:22 (as she was present at the time of the splitting of the sea).

## CONCLUSION

The congenial and respectful personalities of the tribes of Naftali and Asher are captured in the beautiful blessings which they receive from Yaakov and from Moshe.[10] In the blessings, there is no mention of violence or rebellion. They are happy with their lot[11] and respected by their brothers. They are the followers of the leaders of *Am Yisrael.* Every leader needs a follower; thus, the role of Naftali and Asher is extremely significant. They are the "nation" of the "nation of Israel." They are the soldiers in the army who dutifully follow the instructions of the leaders. Their names may not be mentioned or highlighted, but that does not detract from their significant role in Jewish history.

10. Naftali's blessings:
    From Yaakov: "Naftali is a doe set free who bears beautiful fawns" (Gen. 49:21).
    From Moshe: "Of Naftali he said, 'But Naftali is fully satisfied with what he wished for and is full of God's blessings, west and south he inherits'" (Deut. 33:23).
    Asher's blessings:
    From Yaakov: "Out of Asher his bread will be rich. He will yield royal dainties" (Gen. 49:20).
    From Moshe: "Of Asher he said, 'May Asher be blessed with children. He will be desired by his brothers and dip his foot in oil. Your closure is iron and copper and weakness corresponds to your days'" (Deut. 33:25).
11. Rabbi S. R. Hirsch on Deut. 33:24 writes, "Naftali, just in contrast to Dan and probably on that account placed together with him, without any division or paragraph, is completely and fully satisfied with the province allotted to him."

*Chapter 15*

# Yosef in Genesis: Yaakov's Favorite Son

It seems difficult to fathom the perspective of a child who is born with almost every one of life's advantages – especially the love and adoring treatment from his father – but is nevertheless forced into slavery. Yosef's life story is almost overwhelmed by the vacillations of his experiences. In spite (or, perhaps, specifically because) of the vicissitudes that transpire, Yosef's personality and, ultimately, his growth, become apparent.

Yosef is born with undeveloped qualities of leadership which mature throughout his life's experiences. In his early years, his youthful dreams that apparently show a desire to lead the family coupled with his father's partiality towards him cause tension with his brothers. Therefore, the first significant dynamic to consider is the degree to which Yosef is culpable both for this discord with his brothers and for the events that transpire in his early years.

Yosef must learn to correct his flaws through his trials and tribulations before he can earn the respect and loyalty of his family. Therefore, the second key factor in understanding Yosef is how this evolution occurs. Are there foundational events during which Yosef expresses a newly found maturity?

To begin addressing these central questions about Yosef, let us start with his formative years in the house of Yaakov.

### YOSEF'S EARLY YEARS

> Now Yisrael loved Yosef more than all his children, because he was the son of his old age, and he made him a coat of many colors. (Gen 37:3)

This verse encapsulates so many of the central themes of Yosef's childhood. He is the favorite son of Yaakov,[1] born to his preferred wife, Raḥel,[2] after many years of her suffering infertility.[3] Yosef and Yaakov share many experiences in their lives, which strengthen their bond.[4] Additionally, Yosef's personality is very charming,[5] adding to his father's feelings

---

1. Gen. 37:2 states, "These are the generations of Yaakov: Yosef." Instead of listing all of Yaakov's children, the verse contains only the name of Yosef. Typically, after the phrase "These are the generations," the subject's entire progeny is listed. See for example Noaḥ (Gen. 6:9–10), Yishmael (Gen. 25:12–15), Aharon (Num. 3:1–2), and Peretz (Ruth 4:18–22). *Kli Yakar* on 37:2 writes that the omission highlights that Yosef is the most important of Yaakov's children.
2. The word "love" is used to describe Yaakov's feelings towards both Raḥel and Yosef – "Yaakov loved Raḥel" (Gen. 29:18) and "Yisrael loved Yosef" (37:3). Rashi on 37:2 writes that Yaakov loved Yosef because of his connection to Raḥel, the woman for whom Yaakov elected to work hard for seven years, and then to labor another seven years to earn the right to marry her.
3. Yosef is not the only miracle baby who grows into a leader of the Jewish people. Consider Yitzḥak (Gen. 21:2), Shimshon (Judges 13:24), and Shmuel (I Sam. 1:20).
4. See Genesis Rabba (84:6), cited by Rashi and Rabbenu Baḥya on Gen. 37:2, which says that Yaakov bonds with Yosef because they share similar life experiences. For instance, both men have mothers who struggled with fertility, experienced difficult labor, and bear two sons. Both men are subject to sibling hatred and are forced to flee from their homes. Interestingly, both men marry women from outside of Israel and have children outside of Israel.
5. When Yosef is away from his brothers, his charming personality surfaces, as we see in later stories. For example: "And Yosef found favor in his [Potiphar's] eyes" (Gen. 39:4); "And he found favor in the eyes of the officer of the jail" (39:21). Potiphar and the officer in jail find Yosef charming. Therefore, they favor him and elevate his status above the rest of the prisoners. Similarly, Yaakov elevates Yosef above the rest of his brothers, clearly recognizing his charm and leadership abilities.

of partiality towards him. This special love (expressed by the Hebrew word "*ahav*") between this father and son reminds us of the unique love that Avraham had for Yitzḥak[6] and that Yitzḥak had for Esav.[7] The Torah is demonstrating who Yaakov believes most deserves the blessing of being the next link in the chain leading to the chosen nation.[8]

Yaakov does not hide his feelings for Yosef and makes him a special coat, a gesture charged with symbolism and significance. He wants his favorite child to be wrapped in the warmth of the coat, reminding him of the warm and loving embrace of his father.[9] Yaakov endows Yosef's coat with a second symbolic message – leadership. Leaders of all types – kings,[10] prophets,[11] princes,[12] and other members of the monarchy[13] – wear special coats indicating their prestige. Yaakov foreshadows the eventuality that Yosef will become a leader, a bearer of fine garments. Additionally, by giving a special coat to Yosef, Yaakov is suggesting that he will transfer his own leadership to him in the future.[14] Yaakov's demonstration of favoritism towards Yosef is reflected in other

6. God tells Avraham to take the child "that [he] loves, Yitzḥak," and sacrifice him (Gen. 22:2).
7. "And Yitzḥak loved Esav" (Gen. 25:28).
8. The Hebrew word "*ahav*" is also used to describe Yaakov's love for Raḥel: "And Yaakov loved Raḥel" (29:18), as well as for her second son, Binyamin, in the words of Yehuda: "And his father loves him" (Gen. 44:20).
9. This symbolism reminds the reader of a similar coat in the story of Shmuel. Like Raḥel, Ḥana (Shmuel's mother) struggles with infertility. In her prayers for a child, Ḥana promises to dedicate her son to God. She fulfills her promise by consecrating Shmuel's life to God and the Tabernacle. Each year she visits her precious and miraculous son. With each visit, she brings him a new coat (I Sam. 2:19). Imagine the love that Ḥana invests in the coat that her son will wear for the upcoming year. This coat serves as Shmuel's reminder of his mother's constant love.
10. For example, Shaul wears a coat as part of his royal garb, which David rips when the king pursues him (I Sam 24:4).
11. For example, Shmuel has a special coat (I Sam. 28:14).
12. For example, Yonatan, the son of Shaul, transfers his special coat to David to indicate that David will be the next king (I Sam. 18:4).
13. For example, Tamar (David's daughter) wears "a striped coat," described in the same words as Yosef's coat, to symbolize her status as a virgin princess (II Sam. 13:18).
14. Aharon's clothes are put onto his son Elazar, when Elazar assumes his role as high priest (Num. 20:26). Eliyahu leaves his cloak for Elisha when transferring to him the role of head of the prophets (II Kings 2:14).

episodes too. For example, Yaakov places Yosef in the most secure area when the family faces a confrontational meeting with Esav (Gen. 33:7).[15]

Unlike his relationship with his father – which is fairly straightforward – the answers to many of the central questions surrounding Yosef's relationship with his brothers are unclear. What role does he play among his brothers? Does he attain a status of authority over his older brothers? What type of relationship does he have with the maidservants' children? Providing a context for these questions will help us understand Yosef's character. We will consider these questions in light of the following text:

> These are the generations of Yaakov. Yosef, being seventeen years old, was feeding the flock with his brothers. He was a boy with the sons of Bilha and Zilpa, his father's wives. Yosef brought an evil report of them to their father. (Gen. 37:2)

Each of these clauses contains an ambiguous statement!

"Yosef, being seventeen years old, was feeding the flock with his brothers." What does it mean that he is feeding the flock with his brothers? Does he work with them as an equal, or is he assigned to be their boss, or alternatively, their underling?

"He was a boy with the sons of Bilha and Zilpa, his father's wives." Does this imply that he plays with them as an equal, or perhaps that he bosses them around?

"Yosef brought an evil report of them to their father." Regarding which brothers is Yosef snitching to his father? Does this allude to the sons of Leah, the maidservants' children, or all of his brothers?

The traditional commentators present three options to understand the context of these statements. The first approach – presented by Rashi, Rashbam, and *Kli Yakar* on 37:2 – suggests that, due to the similarity in age, Yosef is closest to the maidservants' children. He is their friend; textual evidence for this can be found in the words "he played with them."

15. It is interesting that for the rest of the children, the mothers are placed in front of them; in contrast, Yosef is in front of Raḥel. Radak on 33:7 writes that Raḥel is holding Yosef in her arms as they walk in unison to meet Esav.

In contrast, the sons of Leah tease and mock the maidservants' children on account of their status in the family, calling them slaves.[16] As a result, Yosef, confident in his relationship with Yaakov, feels emboldened to tattle on Leah's children about their mistreatment of the others.[17] Not surprisingly, enmity grows in the hearts of Leah's sons, whereas an alliance develops between Yosef and the maidservants' children.

Ibn Ezra and Ramban on 37:2 offer a different approach to understand Yosef's role in their home life. Yaakov assigns the maidservants' children the job of watching and caring for Yosef. Instead of being appreciative, Yosef snitches on the maidservants' children to his father. Ramban and Rabbenu Baḥya on 37:2 explain that this behavior is what motivates them to join in selling Yosef.

A third approach, found in Malbim on 37:2, is that Yosef is selected as the overseer of all of the brothers. He supervises their shepherding. He snitches on all of them to his father about how the different cohorts of brothers speak meanly about each other. What motivates Yosef's behavior? He longs for peace and camaraderie between Leah's sons and their half-brothers. Yosef naively believes that by reporting the misbehavior to their father, he can intercede to resolve the tensions.

Collectively, Yaakov's favoritism[18] of Yosef and Yosef's elevated position in the family as boss of (some or all of) his brothers make his brothers' reaction predictable and almost expected: "His brothers saw that their father loved him more than all his brothers, and they hated him, and couldn't speak[19] peaceably to him" (Gen. 37:4).

---

16. For example, Rashbam on 37:2 suggests he befriends Yaakov's younger children (i.e., the maidservants' children), as evidenced by the words, "He acted like a young boy".
17. Rashi on 37:2 adds that Yosef also tattles about other faults he (mistakenly) believes to be true about his brothers. For example, he tells their father that he saw them engaging in forbidden activities such as eating the flesh of live animals and committing adulterous acts.
18. Rabbi S. R. Hirsch on 37:4 places the blame with Yaakov. In his words: "Love is prefixed with the individualizing of giving oneself completely up to another and wishing to have that person in the closest proximity. The opposite is hatred, where one is regarded as a thorn to reject, to keep as far away from as possible. The extremes engender a cause-effect situation. In this case, the love of the father for one of his sons begot the hatred of the other sons to their brother."
19. *Kli Yakar* on 37:4 notes that they do not speak with him because they do not want him to take their words and bring them back to their father.

Amazingly, Yosef seems naively unaware of this hatred. Hence, when he has dreams of dominion over his family, he shares the details of the dreams with his brothers without concern about the envy or indignation this might elicit within them. Predictably, this increases their antipathy towards Yosef. The verse states: "They continued to hate him" (37:5), and again, "They hated him all the more for his dreams and for his words" (37:8).[20]

Their negative reaction to his first dream does nothing to stop Yosef from continuing to share the visions in his subsequent dream with his brothers.[21] Yosef's youthful naiveté and undying confidence in his leadership are blinding. These factors prevent him from considering the impact of his behavior on his brothers.

Interestingly, his brothers' reaction changes after Yosef's second dream. In the context of the first dream, the language of hatred is used three times (37:4, 5, 8). Such intense negative feelings may induce the hater to desire physical distance between the parties.[22] In contrast, this time the verse states, "And they were jealous of him" (v. 11). Their emotions evolve from hatred to jealousy. Jealousy implies that one desires what the other person has, or desires to be like that person.[23] The brothers' reaction to

---

20. Precisely which of Yosef's words motivate their hatred? The commentators offer at least three options:
    (1) Rashi and Radak on 37:8 suggest this refers to Yosef's snitching in an earlier verse.
    (2) Ramban and Sforno on 37:8 suggest this refers to his bragging about his dreams and asking them to listen to him discuss the dreams.
    (3) Malbim and Rabbenu Baḥya suggest this refers to Yosef's choice to voice aloud his visions to his family. *Kli Yakar* on 37:8 adds that their hatred stems from his audacity to share his dreams with them even as they attempted to avoid speaking with him (v. 4).
21. It is possible that Yosef is oblivious to his brothers' feelings. Alternatively, Yosef is simply indifferent due to the certainty of his convictions.
22. Hatred is also the language used by Yitzḥak to explain why Avimelekh expels him from the land of Philistines: "You hate me and sent me away" (Gen. 26:27). Similarly, Yiftaḥ accuses the elders of Gilad of hating him: "Don't you hate me that you kicked me out of my father's house?" (Judges 11:7). Shimshon's father in-law announces that he thought Shimshon hated his daughter, and that is why he arranges her marriage to another man (Judges 15:2). Amnon, David's son, "hates [Tamar] with a tremendous hatred" and therefore expels Tamar from the room and locks the door (II Sam 12:15).
23. For example, jealousy describes the feelings of the Philistines with regard to Yitzḥak and his wealth (26:14), motivating them to steal his wells. Similarly, Raḥel is jealous

the second dream differs from their initial reaction. What changes from the first to the second dream that causes the change in their reaction?

In the first dream, the brothers' sheaves bow to Yosef's sheaf, symbolizing that Yosef's brothers would one day bow to Yosef as their leader. However, in the second dream, eleven stars, the sun, and the moon (symbolizing Yosef's brothers and parents) bow to him. His father is in the second dream! Moreover, this time Yosef reveals his dream to his brothers but also to his father.

How does Yaakov react? "He told it to his father and to his brothers. His father rebuked him, and said to him, 'What is this dream that you have dreamed? Will I and your mother and your brothers indeed come to bow ourselves down to you to the earth?'" (Gen 37:10). Yaakov chooses to rebuke Yosef! Immediately after this, we are told that the brothers are jealous. Why does Yaakov's rebuke directly precede the brothers' jealousy? To understand their transition from hatred to jealousy, we need to take a closer look at Yaakov's rebuke.

Let's begin by assessing Yaakov's behavior in this episode in the context of his reaction to his children's prior missteps. Specifically, when Reuven sins with Bilha, Yaakov is silent (35:22),[24] with no immediate reaction (until his deathbed). Similarly, when Dina is kidnapped and raped, Yaakov is silent (34:5).[25] After Shimon and Levi murder an entire city, Yaakov screams at them (34:30). When they challenge him, he is silent once again (34:31). Remarkably, Yaakov's reaction to Yosef's second dream is the first time he asserts his parental role! When it comes to Yosef, Yaakov always acts differently. The bond between Yaakov and Yosef enables him to voice his disapproval.[26] In short, by comparing Yaakov's response to Yosef versus his prior responses to his other children, we observe his capacity to react in a way that he does not with his other children. Perhaps it is this openness between Yaakov and Yosef that makes the other brothers jealous.

---

of her sister's ability to bear children. She doesn't want Leah's children, but children of her own (30:1).

24. See Chapter 2 describing the sin of Reuven with Bilha and Yaakov's lack of reaction.
25. See Chapter 4 describing the actions of Shimon and Levi and Yaakov's reaction.
26. Ironically, Yaakov observes the jealousy of his sons, but is silent (v. 11).

Additionally, their jealousy derives not just from the fact that Yaakov responds, but in the exact nature of his response. The brothers inferred something from his tone and diction. The words "and his father scolded him" (37:10) draw attention to his tone. Rashi on 37:10 observes the lack of substantive criticism. Yaakov offers no details in his rebuke because he does not genuinely think the dream warrants criticism. Rather, Yaakov scolds Yosef as a ploy to help avoid the brothers' irritation. By pretending to be upset, Yaakov hopes to dodge another tense moment among his children.[27] But the brothers see right through this façade; hence, they are jealous![28]

Sforno on 37:11 offers a slightly less dramatic version of this approach. He suggests that Yaakov is hoping the dreams will come true. Hence, his response is really an expression of hope, instead of anger or jealousy. Ramban on 37:10 thinks that Yaakov is merely dismissing Yosef's dreams. His rebuke is the scolding of a parent to a child who tells a silly story; he doesn't offer the severe scolding that the brothers are hoping for. Yaakov's casual reaction causes the brothers to lose any hope that Yaakov would ever recognize the truth about Yosef (as they perceive it). Their reaction concretizes their sense of jealousy.

**Summary of Yosef's Childhood**

When reflecting on Yosef's childhood in his father's home, we find a boy with the ambition to rule over his brothers and whose father sees within him potential for leadership. However, at this stage, Yosef is still immature and naïve to the vantage point of his brothers, and therefore he attempts to assert power over them. He tattles on them to their father and reveals his dreams of leadership. Their reaction is hatred and jealousy, attempting to impede his visions of grandeur. It is not surprising that at this point they reject his leadership and even turn violently against him.

---

27. With regard to the words of the next verse, "And his father observed the matter" (v. 11), Rashi notes that this refers to the dreams. Yaakov silently awaits the fulfillment of Yosef's dreams.
28. Malbim on 37:11 summarizes this view. Yaakov rebukes Yosef to prevent the brothers from becoming angry and jealous. The brothers realize (due to the insincerity of his tone) that he believes Yosef will indeed rule the family. This is the cause of their jealousy.

## THE SALE OF YOSEF

With this as background, we encounter that pivotal day when the brothers almost kill Yosef, throw him into a pit, and then end up selling him into slavery.

Could these events have been avoided? Should Yaakov and Yosef have anticipated that their behavior leading up to this day might escalate to this extent?[29] Do they bear any responsibility for transparently acknowledging their special bond and feelings? We can reflect on these questions from the varied perspectives of Yaakov and Yosef.

### Yaakov's Perspective

Raḥel – Yaakov's favorite wife – tragically dies during Binyamin's birth (Gen. 35:19). Consequently, Yosef is the only child whom Yaakov enjoys alongside Raḥel. For six years, Yaakov experiences his fantasy, living with his beloved wife and their miracle child. After her unexpected death, the Torah uses language to describe Yosef that resembles Yaakov's description of Raḥel.[30] This parallel language suggests that each time Yaakov sees Yosef, he most likely envisions the face of his beautiful wife. How could Yaakov avoid feeling and expressing a special attachment to Yosef?

Concurrently, the sons of Leah rebel against Yaakov and question his family leadership. Reuven sins with Bilha (see Chapter 2). Shimon and Levi, without the approval of their father, kill an entire city (see Chapter 4). Yehuda leaves his family, possibly forsaking his father's moral compass, and ends up conceiving twin sons with his daughter in-law when she is in disguise (see Chapter 6). In contrast, Yosef stands by his side. Yosef is loyal, reporting to his father the happenings of the day (37:2). He follows the directives of his father, even if that puts him in danger.[31]

---

29. It is clear that the brothers are reacting to both of them: The brothers remove the coat that Yaakov gave Yosef and that Yosef proudly wore. Then they say, "Now we will see of what will be of his dreams" (37:20). They are speaking about the dreams that Yosef dreamt and repeated, which Yaakov hardly denounced.
30. The language utilized is actually identical (ignoring gender). Compare 29:17 to 39:6.
31. Ramban on 37:13 notes that when Yaakov asked Yosef to check on his brothers in the field, Yosef could have refused because of the inherent danger involved in the trip. However, out of respect for his father, Yosef did not hesitate. Rashbam on 37:13 observes that the Torah offers additional details, i.e., that Yosef cannot initially

**Yosef's Perspective**

For six years, Yosef lives in a loving home, adored by his mother and father. But Raḥel dies when Binyamin is born, and Yosef's life changes in an instant. Rabbi S.R. Hirsch on Gen. 37:2 writes, "So the picture presented to us is of a motherless and [essentially] brotherless youth. All the others grew up in company with brothers and under the wing and influence of mother-love. Yosef stood alone. He had lost his mother early in life, and Binyamin was still a child and no companion for the youth."

With this as background, it is possible to understand the special bond between Yosef and Yaakov. Yaakov clings to Yosef as a reminder of his beloved deceased wife; Yosef clings to Yaakov because he is basically alone in the world with only his father to lean on. Their shared tragedy creates a special connection. They need each other in a way that none of the children of Leah, Bilha, or Zilpa could understand.

What does all of this reveal to us about Yosef during his early years? Yaakov sees in Yosef the potential for leadership, strength, persistence, charm, dedication, and loyalty. Yosef clearly envisions his role and life's mission to be the leader of the family and the leader of the future Jewish nation. However, Yosef does not yet know how to earn the respect of his brothers. All the ambitions of leadership are useless if no one follows his lead. In the eyes of his brothers, Yosef is immature and haughty. To them, he is insensitive: Why else would he choose to wear his special coat from Yaakov in their presence?[32] Even on the day he goes out to the field to check on his brothers, away from his father's protection, Yosef does not remove the coat that is so objectionable to them. The brothers feel the need to actively reject his leadership.

Yosef naively thinks he is untouchable. Yet, when alone with his brothers, he is completely powerless. They grab him, remove his coat,

---

find the brothers so he asks a man, who leads him to a second location, in order to highlight the extent to which Yosef would travel to fulfill his father's requests. At any point he could have returned home. Yosef goes through great effort to honor his father's wishes.

32. According to Malbim on 37:3 this was a housecoat, made for Yosef to wear when taking care of his father in the home. If so, it would seem even more inappropriate for Yosef to wear the coat when going out to fields to check on his brothers.

and throw him into a pit. Later, he is sold into slavery. While this is transpiring, Yosef is crying and begging for mercy but the brothers just ignore him (Gen. 42:21). At this point in his life, Yosef is the source of anger and jealousy for his brothers. He does not earn their admiration, nor does he learn how to properly engage with them or inspire them towards positive behavior. He has much to learn about these qualities later in life.

Yosef's childhood is punctuated by the contrast between his perspective and that of his brothers. He seems to relish a role as an influencer based on his likeability and innate skills. The brothers hate him and are jealous of him precisely because they perceive his misuse of these attributes.

**Summary**

Yosef is sold as a slave by his own brothers, with no hope of emancipation. Yaakov loses his most treasured son, the miracle-child of Raḥel. The reader clearly feels pangs of pain for both the father and son. And, yet, upon closer inspection, neither Yaakov nor Yosef emerge innocent. How could Yaakov expect that favoring Yosef so blatantly would have no consequences for the broader family dynamic? How could Yosef not contemplate his brothers' perspective when tattling on them, wearing the special coat in their midst, and bragging about his future as their leader? Yosef seems to behave as though he is in a bubble, unaware of the damage and hurt caused by his actions. He believes he is invulnerable and destined to lead the family. How wrong were these assumptions, as he is absolutely powerless when the brothers gang up against him.

## YOSEF IN EGYPT

In Egypt, the positive attributes of Yosef's personality continue to be highlighted, and destiny raises him from the misery of slavery and imprisonment to the top of the political universe.

Furthermore, the Torah emphasizes Yosef's charm in various situations as a source of his triumph (Gen. 39:4, 21, and 41:37). At this point, Yosef is able to express the charisma that Yaakov anticipated but the brothers never recognized. Potiphar, the head of the prison, and later on even Pharaoh are taken in by his leadership attributes. He is eventually promoted all the way up to the position of viceroy to Pharaoh.[33]

Clearly, Yosef learns how to implement these important characteristics of leadership. When he was a lad at home, these raw attributes led to family dissent. When and how does Yosef learn to channel these talents in a uniquely productive manner? What is the pivotal experience where Yosef learns self-restraint – the discipline to limit voicing his personal aspirations?

The simplest approach is that Yosef learned these lessons during the trauma of being sold by his brothers into slavery. Seeing the severity of their feelings towards him, Yosef learns his lesson quickly: A leader must be humble, respected, and kind. Accordingly, his transformation is first noticeable when Yosef invests time and energy into hearing about the challenges of the other prisoners. He uses his skills to help them (not himself) and allay their fears.[34]

However, there may be signs that Yosef's growth is still incomplete, as reflected in the episode between Yosef and the wife of Potiphar, as recounted in Genesis 39:7–13:

> It happened about this time that he went into the house to do his work, and there were none of the men of the house inside. She [Potiphar's wife] caught him by his garment, saying, 'Lie with me!' He left his garment in her hand and ran outside. (Gen. 39:11–12)

There are two opposing approaches for understanding that story.

**Virtuous Yosef**

Rabbinic tradition labels Yosef as righteous (he is called "*Yosef HaTzaddik*"),[35] an appellation he earns because he never sins or wavers

---

33. Interestingly, the only other person (besides his mother) to share a similar description of beauty also shares the same description of charm. Esther is described as beautiful (Esther 2:7) using the same language as the description of Yosef (Gen. 39:6). She also gains favor in the eyes of everyone around her (Esther 2:16–17), resulting in being appointed queen of the most powerful empire at the time. Eventually, Yosef and Esther use their powerful positions on behalf of the Jewish people.
34. The Torah writes that after dreaming their dreams, the baker and butler are "forlorn" (40:6). Yosef approaches them and asks, "Why do you look so sad today?" (40:7).
35. See *Sifrei* Deut. 334 and Rashi on Ex. 1:5.

in his beliefs and values while in Egypt, even in his encounter with Potiphar's wife. Therefore, according to tradition, Yosef refuses her advances. On that specific day, he expects other people to be in Potiphar's home, hence he is caught off guard by her approach. In an instant, she begins to undress him. Desperate to escape the situation, Yosef removes his outer garment and runs from the room. In this understanding of the story, Yosef demonstrates his faith and maturity even at this early stage.

**Flirting-with-Power Yosef**

However, there is an alternative approach to the encounter (and past encounters) between Yosef and the wife of Potiphar. Yosef may refuse her advances, but in a manner that encourages her to continue her attempts at a relationship (see Gen. 39:10). Hence, he is fine being alone in the house with her on that specific day. The Talmud (Sota 36b) states that he refrains from sinning with her only because he envisions the image of his father. Evidently, it took this vision to force him to cease being there with her. He hastily runs (instead of walking) out of the room to prevent the evil inclination from overwhelming him.[36] According to this approach, his subsequent fall from Potiphar's home reflects his second significant lapse in judgment. Perhaps now, he will finally mature! God places him in jail now to allow him the time to learn what he should have already known from his experience with his brothers, after being thrown into a pit and sold as a slave.

---

36. See *Haketav VeHakabbala* on 39:10. Nehama Leibowitz (*Parashat Vayeshev* 6) also alludes to this interpretation when she asks why the Torah precedes this story with a description of the outer beauty of Yosef (39:6). She cites Rashi on 37:2 who observes that Yosef would pamper himself with physical and aesthetic pleasures. Based on this interpretation, she observes, "Yosef was attracted by the charms of Egyptian high society life, its wealth, culture, and, above all, the power granted him by his master. He forgot his slavery and alien origin, the gulf separating a son of Yaakov, bearer of the Abrahamic mission, slave only of the Supreme Master, from the Egyptians. He began to fraternize with them and curry favor with them until the inevitable happened." Elsewhere, in *Parashat Vayeshev* 3, she adds that "his disgust for idols and the Egyptian regime of slavery, and his sense of repulsion for their sexual malpractices began to pall. Yosef then found himself on the brink of spiritual disaster."

As Yosef's narrative progresses, the reader is left wondering whether he has finally learned his lesson.

## YOSEF AS VICEROY OF EGYPT

Not long after this episode, Yosef attains the leadership opportunity that coincides with his dreams when he is appointed viceroy over all of Egypt. He lives with the trappings of royalty, wearing royal garb, riding Pharaoh's horses, and receiving his ring (Gen. 41:42–43). Only Pharaoh is more powerful (v. 40) than he! In this role, Yosef is entrusted with enormous responsibility, including the burden of ensuring that Egypt avoids the pains of an extended famine. His role includes designing the famine survival plan and making sure it is implemented correctly. He collects food for the seven years of plenty he predicted from Pharaoh's dream (47:14–15). He executes this stage of the plan flawlessly. Then, when the famine occurs, Yosef oversees the distribution of food.[37] Yosef is empowered by Pharaoh to determine who gets food, how much they receive, and at what cost. In fact, there seems to be no check on his authority, as evidenced by the lack of reaction to Yosef's mistreatment of his brothers (by imprisoning them). In spite of this, Yosef successfully oversees the process he initiated and effectively handles the power it offers him, with no evidence of complaints or uprising by the Egyptian people. Clearly, at this stage in his development Yosef is an able leader who has the wisdom and intelligence to balance the competing needs of the people and the monarch.[38]

Is this evidence that Yosef has now learned his life's lessons about leadership and humility? Consider this question from the vantage point of the two perspectives about Yosef – namely, is he virtuous or flirting with power?

---

37. When the Egyptians cry to Pharaoh for food, he tells them to speak with Yosef and do whatever he orders them to do (Gen. 41:55). The Torah informs us that people came from all over the entire land to Yosef for food (41:57).
38. His exceptional intelligence is acknowledged by Pharaoh when selecting Yosef for this responsibility. Pharaoh declares, "There is no one as intelligent and wise as he [Yosef]" (Gen. 41:39).

**Virtuous Yosef**

This approach maintains that Yosef has matured and is poised to stay within the boundaries of his new role. In Genesis 47, which describes the process by which Yosef distributes the food, "to Pharaoh" appears nine times, and the word "Pharaoh" appears eleven times. This redundancy seems to be emphasizing Yosef's mindset: this whole process is on behalf of Pharaoh. It is not about himself, but his leader.[39] Ramban on 47:10 observes Yosef's wisdom and trustworthiness in this episode, which might explain why the Egyptians respect Yosef and never rebel against him.[40] The people notice that Yosef's food program is for their and Pharaoh's benefit. In fact, during the height of the famine, when the people are poor and desperate for food, they offer themselves as slaves to Pharaoh in return for provisions (47:25). But Yosef rejects their offer! He now knows when to unilaterally constrain his authority. For this, he gains the respect and the loyalty of the people.

**Flirting-with-Power Yosef**

Alternatively, the food distribution program may reflect another expression of Yosef's unchecked desire for power.

During the first seven years – a period of surplus food production – Egyptians donate food towards Yosef's program. During the subsequent seven years, Yosef insists that the monarchy should charge everyone (even the donors!) for any food distribution. Where is the equitability

---

39. Yosef's deference for Pharaoh is reflected in other stories as well. Consider these two examples:
    (1) Yosef waits for Pharaoh's permission to move his family to Egypt (45:17–18) and to reside in Goshen (47:5–6).
    (2) Years later, Yosef seeks Pharaoh's blessing before leaving Egypt to bury his father in Israel (50:5–6).
40. There are many parallels between Yosef and Mordekhai in this story. Both rise to power quickly, receive royal clothing, and receive the king's ring (Gen. 41:42, Esther 8:2, 15). Both are escorted on the royal horse through the streets of the city (Gen. 41:43, Esther 6:11). Both go out "from in front of the king" ("*milifnei hamelekh*") (Gen. 41:46, Esther 8:15). Both are senior advisors to the king when a major tax is imposed on the people (Gen. 47, Esther 10:1). Just like Yosef, Mordekhai is "accepted by the multitude of his brothers, seeking the good of his people, and speaking peace to all his children" (Esther 10:3).

in charging exorbitant prices during the famine to the Egyptians who provided the food during the earlier period? They are expected to relinquish their money, animals, and land in order to survive! After only one year, the impoverished people of Egypt come to Yosef and say: "We will not hide from my lord how our money is all spent, and the herds of cattle are my lord's. There is nothing left in the sight of my lord but our bodies and our lands!" (Gen. 47:18). When this episode is over, there is still little evidence that Yosef has learned the lesson of humility.[41]

Not surprisingly, only one generation after Yosef enacts these policies, the Egyptian people are willing to treat Yosef's family as outsiders and enslave them. Why? Do the Egyptians blame Yosef for their predicament? At the end of the famine, the Egyptians are completely destitute and no longer own their own land. In contrast, the Jewish people are flourishing; they have plenty of food (47:12) and possess the land of Goshen, the choicest territory in Egypt (47:11). The contrast is striking and could be a motivating factor in the Egyptians' loathing of the Jewish people.

### Yosef the Puppet

In addition to considering Yosef as a mature and virtuous leader or as someone who has yet to grow past the trappings of power, there is another angle to assess Yosef's leadership in Egypt. This perspective begins by exploring why Pharaoh would promote Yosef to viceroy. Specifically, why would a king elevate a complete stranger, with an alleged criminal background, to the second most powerful role in the land? More specifically, why would Pharaoh select *him* to oversee the project that

41. Evidently, Yosef feels confident that he has the authority to implement such an impactful policy. He does not fear the pushback from the people or Pharaoh. Yosef acts on principle first, and then seeks Pharaoh's approval because he feels sure that he will obtain it (based on their relationship up to this point). This is consistent with Yosef's general reaction to Pharaoh's authority as expressed in other episodes. For example, Yosef instructs his brothers to bring their father to Egypt (45:9) prior to requesting Pharaoh's consent to move his family there (45:17–18). Similarly, he offers Goshen as their location (45:10) before asking for Pharaoh's permission (47:5–6). Later, he promises to bury Yaakov in Israel (48:21) before gaining Pharaoh's approval to leave Egypt (50:6).

determines the future of his kingdom? Clearly, Pharaoh sees wisdom and intellect in Yosef, as he says, "There is no one as intelligent and wise as Yosef" (Gen. 41:39). However, does that sufficiently explain why he gave Yosef so much power? Before addressing this question, consider the utter lack of originality in Yosef's fourteen-year plan. Just how creative is it? Given that he believes in Pharaoh's dreams and the anticipation of an extended famine, isn't the plan entirely predictable? Wouldn't everyone suggest collecting and storing food before a famine?

Conceivably, Pharaoh is really the wise one: He observes Yosef's desire for power. He knows that Yosef would happily accept a position of authority, without seeing the potential associated risks. Pharaoh finds himself in a predicament based on Yosef's interpretation of his dream. The simplest solution is to gather food during the years of plenty and use that food for the years of famine. As a responsible steward of the country's future, Pharaoh needs to implement this plan. On the other hand, he recognizes that Yosef's interpretation of the dreams may be wrong. If so, after collecting food from his people for seven years, they might rebel if there is no famine. Pharaoh is in a terrible predicament with no easy resolution.

Therefore, Pharaoh devises a plan that balances the possibility of either outcome. He elevates Yosef to the position of "point person" of the program, thus creating separation between himself and the food operation. If the famine never materializes, he can blame Yosef for collecting the food during the first seven years. He cleverly doesn't promote someone to that role whom he fears could depose his leadership. Rather, he promotes Yosef, a foreigner who can never become the ruler of Egypt. Therefore, even if the plan is successful, Pharaoh has no fear of losing his monarchy, plus he is entitled to receive all of the money that Yosef collects in return for the food (and the people would blame Yosef, not Pharaoh, for having to pay for it).[42] By the end of the narrative, Pharaoh owns all of the land in Egypt, without having had to lift a finger. Yosef has done it all, "for Pharaoh"!

After the urgency of surviving the famine, the Egyptians start to distress over their destitution. Eventually, this evolves into

42. This could explain why Pharaoh insists that the Egyptians who are requesting food must go to Yosef (Gen. 41:55).

resentment toward Yosef. Years later, they take out their wrath on the descendants of Yosef, the Jewish people.[43] They never show anger towards Pharaoh.

In summary, Yosef's rise to leadership in Egypt validates his strengths and exposes his weaknesses. Amazingly, his drive to lead enables him to always elevate himself. Under conditions in which most people would give up, i.e., as a slave in jail, Yosef catapults his way to the top. Simultaneously, this same drive limits his ability to perceive the risky implications of his actions. He seems to struggle with the fine line between a healthy desire for power and a destructive passion for leadership that causes him to overstep his bounds.

We return to our earlier question: Does Yosef learn his lesson? In particular, do these leadership episodes teach Yosef how to act appropriately towards his brothers? So far, the evidence has been mixed. Let's now turn to the story of his reunion with his family.

## REUNITING WITH HIS FAMILY

Considering Yosef's trajectory to leadership, why does he not send a message to his father informing him that he is alive? Why does he not reveal himself to his brothers the moment they arrive in Egypt?[44] Why does he put them through a series of challenges (calling them spies, jailing them, and locking up Shimon) before revealing his identity?

---

43. Yehoshua Bachrach offers a similar interpretation for the relationship between Haman and Aḥashverosh. Contrary to conventional wisdom, he suggests that Haman is manipulated by Aḥashverosh. After assuming the kingship and surviving an assassination attempt, Aḥashverosh protects himself by hiding in his palace. He elevates Haman into a very public and powerful role to serve as the face of the kingdom. In so doing, he creates the perception that any royal decree is connected to Haman. Bachrach offers the insight that only someone with a great desire for power and greatness could fall for such a scheme. See Yehoshua Bachrach, *Kitvuni LeDorot* (Israel: Or Etzion 1989), 65. Going beyond Bachrach's application to Haman and Aḥashverosh, one can apply this human insight into understanding the relationship between Yosef and Pharaoh. Just as the evil Haman has a sudden rise to power (Esther 3:1) and, in an instant, is elevated above the rest of the officers of the king (41:40–42), the righteous Yosef has a similar experience. There are numerous other similarities between these two stories.

44. Yosef recognizes them immediately but hides his identity from them (Gen. 42:7).

There may be multiple ways to view Yosef's perspective – and his own inner turmoil – when he unexpectedly encounters his brothers in Egypt.

**Indignant Yosef**

Given his history, one could understand if Yosef simply wants to move on with his life and leave his past behind.[45] He is now a new man, with an Egyptian identity. He is Tzofnat Pane'aḥ, an Egyptian name (see Ibn Ezra and Rashbam on 41:45). He marries an Egyptian woman, Osnat, the daughter of Potiphera. Twice we are told that she is the daughter of a priest, emphasizing that marrying her gives Yosef pedigree (Gen. 41:45, 50). He has two sons whom he names for his life experiences. His first son is named Menashe, as a tribute to God for allowing him to forget his pain associated with his father's house (41:41). He is celebrating his ability to forget his troubled past and his ability to create a new and better life in Egypt. He names his second son Ephraim to thank God for all of the success he now has in Egypt (v. 42). Perhaps Yosef does not contact his family simply because he chooses to keep that part of his identity in the past. He is a new man with a new family and new aspirations. He has replaced his old parochial dream of leading his family for a much more ambitious one – leading Egypt and saving the world from starvation.[46]

When his brothers arrive in Egypt, they unknowingly upend his new reality. In some ways, their presence threatens to shatter his new dream and new life. How does he react? Yosef hides his new identity from them: "He acted like a stranger to them" (42:7). He then implements a three-part scheme to convince them to leave Egypt and

45. Clearly, Yosef remains God fearing, even if he cuts himself off from his family. Yosef speaks about God when interpreting the dreams of the baker, the butler (40:8), and Pharaoh (51:16, 28), as well as when naming his sons (41:51, 52). Furthermore, the Torah acknowledges that God is with Yosef, thus showering blessing on those around him (39:5, 21). Pharaoh even refers to him as a "man with the spirit of God" (41:38).

46. "And Yosef remembered his dreams that he dreamed about them" (Gen. 42:9). Why does the Torah inform us about Yosef now recollecting his old dreams after he sees his brothers for the first time? The Torah might be hinting that Yosef had forgotten his old dreams and replaced them with new dreams.

deters their eventual return. First, he unreasonably jails them under the false accusation of spying (42:9, 16). Punishing them so harshly when they know they are innocent concretizes in their minds that they should fear the repercussion of committing a crime. Hence, later on, when they find their money returned into their bags, they ought to conclude that returning to Egypt is not a viable option. Second, Yosef demands that they may only return if they come with their younger brother, Binyamin. Yosef is certain that Yaakov would never allow them to bring Binyamin.[47] By making this demand, he provides another reason that they would not return to Egypt. To be absolutely certain they would never reappear, Yosef jails Shimon (42:24). This reinforces the message that going to Egypt implies the risk of being imprisoned unfairly. Yosef surmises there is no way that Yaakov would permit Binyamin to be introduced into this environment.

Yosef's entire scheme seems designed to ensure that his brothers do not return, leaving him alone in Egypt with his new life, his new nuclear family, and his new role as the viceroy of Egypt. However, this interpretation presupposes a specific motivation (i.e., that of wanting to escape his old home and establish his new one) for Yosef's behavior towards his brothers.

**Virtuous Yosef**

There is an alternative perspective on Yosef's interactions with his brothers when they come down to Egypt. Potentially, Yosef really does want to reconnect with his family. He really does believe in the veracity of the original dreams and his implied leadership within the family. If so, how do we understand his behavior towards them, which appears to undermine a healthy reconnection with his family? Further, what do we make of his seemingly new identity? Let's begin with the latter question.

---

47. Yaakov refuses to send Binyamin in order to protect his precious son. "But Yaakov didn't send Binyamin, Yosef's brother, with his brothers; for he said, 'Lest harm happen to him'" (42:4). Later, when the entire family is starving, Yaakov still refuses to let them take Binyamin to Egypt: "He said, 'My son shall not go down with you; for his brother is dead, and he only is left. If harm happens to him by the way in which you go, then you will bring down my gray hairs with sorrow to the grave'" (42:38).

Contrary to our assertion above, Yosef's new name, identity, and family may not be evidence of Yosef's mindset. His new name is given to him by Pharaoh. To ascend to a senior role in the government in Egypt, Yosef needs an official title including an Egyptian name; therefore, Pharaoh names him Tzofnat Pane'aḥ. Similarly, Pharaoh presents him with an Egyptian wife, offering him little choice but to marry her.[48] In contrast to these external identifiers, Yosef always sees himself as "Yosef." (He is called Yosef throughout the Torah.)

Taking a slightly different approach, some suggest that Tzofnat Pane'aḥ is actually a Hebrew name, meaning "the one who reveals visions" (see Rav Saadia Gaon and Ramban on 41:45), highlighting Yosef's enduring Jewish identity. Similarly, the Sages resolve the issue of his marrying an Egyptian woman by assuming she converted[49] or is not even Egyptian. According to this latter view, she is assumed to be the daughter of Dina, and the granddaughter of Yaakov, who was born to Dina and Shekhem (conceived when he raped her).[50] Yosef marries her specifically because of her connection to the house of Yaakov and Yosef's desire to be associated with his family (see *Ḥizkuni* on 41:45).

Regarding his sons' names, Menashe and Ephraim, Menashe's name – thanking God for letting Yosef forget his father's home – shows the extent to which his family has been on his mind. Clearly, he has not forgotten them, sine he names his son in reaction to their memory. Ephraim's name, which thanks God for his success in Egypt, is appropriate for a second,

48. "Pharaoh called Yosef's name Tzofnat Pane'aḥ; and he gave him Osnat, the daughter of Potiphera, priest of On, as a wife. Yosef went out over the land of Egypt" (41:45). For Yosef to rule in Egypt, Pharaoh first had to change his identity as evidence of his loyalty and commitment to Egypt.

49. *Yalkut Shimoni* Josh. 9 includes her in the list of righteous converts, along with Hagar, Tzippora, Shifra, Puah, Batya the daughter of Pharaoh, Raḥav, Ruth, and Yael. (According to this view, Shifra and Puah are not believed to be Yokheved and Miriam but rather righteous Egyptians).

50. *Yalkut Shimoni Vayishlaḥ* 134 explains that she arrived in Egypt via the angel Michael. The angel protects her from Yaakov's family, who mistreat her, by removing her from the house of Yaakov and bringing her to the house of Potiphera, to be cared for by his infertile wife. Hence, she is in Egypt – and specifically Potiphera's home – ready to marry Yosef and reconnect each of them back to their ancestral roots.

not first, child specifically because his Egyptian identity is secondary to his Jewish identity.

Upon Yosef's brothers' arrival in Egypt, the Torah states twice, "And he recognized them" (42:7–8). This repetition highlights how quickly he recognizes them. It as if Yosef is looking for them each time someone appears before him requesting food. He looks closely into the face of each person that comes before him to ascertain if he is his brother. Until this point, he has been unsuccessful, but now they have arrived; they are finally here! This is the moment he has been waiting for; he can reunite with them. "Yosef remembered the dreams that he dreamed about them" (42:9): Yosef recognizes that his dreams are finally coming to fruition.[51]

This does not yet address why Yosef does not actively seek contact with his family once he is in Egypt or why he doesn't reveal himself to his brothers immediately when they come to Egypt.

Many commentators address these questions. Ramban on 42:9 contends that Yosef delays the full reunion until he fulfills his original dreams. First, his eleven brothers come and bow to him (i.e., the first dream), and only then all eleven brothers and his father come and bow (i.e., the second dream). Yosef needs to keep up his charade until all the brothers, including Binyamin but excluding Yaakov, bow down to him. Abarbanel on 42:7 explains that Yosef does all of this to determine if his brothers have changed their ways since the days when they sold him.[52]

---

51. The word "*vayizkor*," "and he remembered," may mean that he is actively recalling something he had previously forgotten. Alternatively, as implied in this instance, it might be indicating that, while Yosef had never forgotten the dreams, this is the moment at which their significance is fully realized. Other instances where this latter approach to memory is relevant include these examples: "And God remembered Noaḥ" (Gen. 8:1), "And God remembered Raḥel" (Gen. 30:22), and "And God remembered his covenant with Avraham, Yitzḥak, and Yaakov" (Ex. 2:24).

52. Nehama Leibowitz (*Parashat Miketz* 4) develops this approach, including Yosef's test to see if they would treat Binyamin the same way they treated him. Only after they defend Binyamin at the risk of their own lives does Yosef reveal himself to them. This is consistent with the passage in Yoma 86b, which explains that full repentance includes avoiding a past transgression when faced with the opportunity to commit the same sin.

Abarbanel also offers a second explanation for Yosef's behavior – revenge. Each of Yosef's actions against the brothers resembles something they had previously done to him. Yosef accuses them of being spies in retaliation for their accusations against him for tattling on them to his father. He imprisons them as punishment for their throwing him into a pit.[53] He puts their money back into their bags so they feel the burden of being controlled by someone else manipulating money, just as they had received money for Yosef's sale into slavery.[54] He coerces them into bringing Binyamin, their father's (now) favorite son, in order that they treat him well and protect him – all this to punish them for their horrible actions towards him, when he was their father's favorite son.

Taken at face value, if this is all an elaborate plot to exact revenge, then it would suggest that he is not really interested in reuniting with them. Ironically, coordinating this very detailed scheme takes time and planning. Moreover, it indicates that Yosef remembers every detail of how the brothers abused him years earlier. When he is ruling in Egypt during the seven years of plenty, it occurs to him that during the famine when all mankind will come to him to beg for food, his family may also arrive. He meticulously plans every detail of his retribution for when they arrive. If so, it would seem that Yosef still has some maturing to do.

However, the motivation for Yosef's actions may not be as extreme as vindictive revenge. Rather, he might be aiming for his brothers to understand what extraordinary suffering they put him through. By experiencing somewhat similar hardships, they might better identify with his feelings and realize the implications of their actions. Yosef knows that for him to rejoin the family, the other brothers need to both understand him and regret their involvement in his most difficult experiences. In other words, his perceived revenge is not about him, but about creating the environment where the family can heal and reunite in an honest way.

53. Rabbinic tradition suggests that Yosef keeps Shimon in jail to punish him for his harsh treatment of Yosef when they were children. Rashi on 37:24 writes that Shimon leads the plotters of Yosef's murder and then later throws him into the pit. (See Chapter 4 for more about this.)

54. Whether they actually sold him is not relevant here; Yosef certainly believes they are the sellers. In fact, he mentions it twice (45:4, 5).

### Confused Yosef

In spite of all of these reasons for not contacting his brothers, it is still puzzling that Yosef never contacts his father. Why doesn't he?

Perhaps it is because he is so full of questions and confusion about why he was sold. Yosef may even wonder whether his father was part of the plan.[55] Perhaps he isn't sure if he wants to rejoin the family after the way they treated him. Perhaps he does not even know if he should be more Egyptian or continue to identify himself as Jewish. Paralyzed by all of this uncertainty, he waits until his brothers come to Egypt; only then does he learn that they are truly sorry for their prior mistake. Now he knows it is time to rejoin his family.

## LESSON LEARNED

The following two stories illustrate the extent to which Yosef has learned the lessons required for a cohesive family.

### Story 1: Blessing of Ephraim and Menashe

> Yosef said to his father, "Not so, my father, for this is the firstborn, [so] put your right hand on his head." (Gen. 48:18)

Yaakov is about to bless Yosef's sons when Yosef observes that his father is putting his dominant (right) hand on the head of his younger son. Immediately, Yosef objects! After years of living with the fallout from his father's favoritism, Yosef wants a different future for his own children. He begs his father not to repeat the pattern of favoring the younger son over the older one.

55. Rabbi Yoel Bin-Nun addresses Yosef's uncertainty about his father's possible involvement in his sale. His father sent him to the field that day even though that exposed Yosef to possible danger. After years of waiting for his father to find him, his confusion increases to the point where he may have become convinced that his father must been involved in the sale. Yosef might have surmised that he is being rejected, much like Avraham rejected Yishmael and Yitzḥak rejected Esav. Once he convinces himself of this, he decides not to contact his family. See Rav Yoel Bin-Nun, *Pirkei HaAvot* (Alon Shveut: Tevunot, 2013), 174–176.

But Yaakov refuses to listen to Yosef, as his blessing predicts the future: "I know, my son, I know. He also will become a people, and he also will be great. However, his younger brother will be greater than he, and his seed will become a multitude of nations" (Gen. 48:18–19).

Yaakov knows that Ephraim's children will be greater and more influential than the children of Menashe. While this is how the episode concludes, Yosef's perspective clearly differs; he now recognizes the tragic effect of his exclusive relationship with Yaakov and the detrimental impact this had on his brothers.[56]

### Story 2: After the Death of Yaakov

> "God sent me before you to preserve you a remnant in the earth, and to save you alive by a great deliverance. So now it was not you who sent me here, but God, and He has made me a father to Pharaoh, lord of all his house, and ruler over all the land of Egypt." (Gen. 45:7–8)

After Yosef reveals his identity to his brothers, the reader is introduced to a very different facet of his. He places no blame nor holds any grudge against them. Yosef instantly recognizes God's role in the dramatic events that occurred to him.

He treats his family remarkably well. Yosef feeds them, offers them the best real estate in Egypt (47:11–12), and creates the opportunity for them to flourish and grow into a nation (47:27).

After Yaakov's death, the brothers fear Yosef's retribution. They beg Yosef for forgiveness, even offering themselves to him as slaves

---

56. In truth, Yaakov and Yosef are correct about the impact of this blessing on Yosef's descendants. On the one hand, Yaakov is right that the children of Ephraim will be greater than Menashe's. For instance, Yehoshua, Devora, Avdon, and Yorovam emerge from Ephraim. Furthermore, the head of the encampment of Yosef is Ephraim, and Menashe follows behind. In contrast, weaker leaders like Gidon, Avimelekh, Yair, and Yiftaḥ come from Menashe. In spite of this, Yosef's concern is also correct. Favoring a younger child over an older one leads to jealousy and conflict. In fact, a struggle transpires between the children of Ephraim and Menashe, as we will discuss in Chapter 16.

(50:18). The "old Yosef" would have cherished this moment. He might have relished the power imbalance. Earlier, in Gen. 42, the brothers bowed to him, but that was when they didn't know who he was. They thought they were bowing to a powerful Egyptian ruler. Now, they are choosing to bow to him, their brother Yosef. How does Yosef react in this instance? Yosef cries! He reiterates that this was all God's plan and then calms them by promising that he will happily continue to care for them and feed them (50:19–21). He no longer dreams of ruling over them, but rather wants to be accepted by them. This change in Yosef is astonishing.

This episode reveals a heretofore undeveloped aspect of Yosef's personality. He cares about emotional connections with his family and is at times overwhelmed by his feelings. Of course, this isn't the first time that Yosef has emoted. Recall that when the brothers come to Egypt, the Torah reports four instances when Yosef breaks down in tears. The first time is when his brothers initially come to Egypt and acknowledge, amongst themselves, their guilt for selling Yosef (Gen. 42:24). After that, Yosef sheds tears upon seeing Binyamin (43:30). The next time he cries is when Yehuda defends Binyamin and offers himself in his place (45:2). Finally, Yosef cannot hold back his tears after the brothers tell him that their father's dying wish was for Yosef to forgive them (50:17). How should these emotional expressions be understood? They may be a sign of weakness, showing that he can't maintain composure during critical moments; or, on the contrary, they could be a sign of emotional strength, reflecting his capacity to experience the full gamut of emotions.[57]

---

57. Yaakov blesses Yosef twice. In Gen. 48 Yaakov blesses Yosef's two sons. Then in chapter 49, he blesses all twelve of his sons. Why does Yosef receive two blessings? What is the purpose of the special blessing in chapter 48?

There are two distinct ways to understand the extra blessing that Yaakov gives to Yosef:

(1) Acceptance within the family: chapter 48 contains Yaakov's blessings to Yosef's sons, which serve as notification that Yosef and his sons are welcomed back into the chosen nation. Chapter 49 has Yosef being blessed alongside his brothers as an accepted member of the family. What is the need for the first blessing? In a sense, Yosef had disassociated himself from his family, creating a new life as an Egyptian with an Egyptian family. Yosef is likely worried that he can no longer be accepted into the family as part of the Jewish nation. This fear is captured

## CONCLUSION

There are more stories about Yosef than about any other tribe. The Torah narrates Yosef's life from adolescence through his experiences as a slave, a prisoner in jail, and then as viceroy in Egypt. We learn about his leadership in Egypt and his re-assimilation into the family of Yaakov. Throughout these episodes, the same fundamental elements of Yosef's personality are stressed. Yosef dreams of leadership with such passion that he risks being corrupted by it.[58] He doesn't always have the ability

---

in a midrash (*Pesikta Rabbati* 683), which says Yosef feared that his children, born in Egypt to an Egyptian woman, would not be accepted and blessed by his father. Yosef pleads with his father to bless his sons, promising that their mother is virtuous and deserving. However, Yaakov cannot bless them because the *ruaḥ Hashem,* Godly spirit, required to bless them is not present. Finally, after Yosef leaves the room to cry and beseech God for help, God commands the *ruaḥ Hashem* to allow Yaakov to bless Yosef's sons and accept them as part of the nation of Israel.

(2) Limited leadership blessing: chapter 48 has Yaakov's notification that Yosef's sons are tribes, just like Reuven and Shimon. They will be like all the other tribes, but not necessarily leaders. Chapter 49 records Yosef being blessed, but not with kingship. What is the significance of the second blessing? As we've seen, Yosef may still hold onto the dream of leading his family. Accordingly, Yosef is still expecting to receive the blessing of leadership and kingship over his brothers. However, during the years that Yosef has been absent from the home of Yaakov, Yehuda has proven to be the true leader. Therefore, before Yaakov blesses Yehuda with the role of the future king of Israel, he needs to inform Yosef of the changed reality. In chapter 48, Yaakov informs Yosef that his sons will be like the tribes of Reuven and Shimon. They will be like all the other tribes, but not the leaders. Then in chapter 49, Yosef is given a blessing that does not include kingship. However, Yosef *is* blessed with the birthright. Therefore, the comparison to Reuven and Shimon could simply imply that each of Yosef's sons earns the status of a separate tribe, like Reuven and Shimon (see Ibn Ezra on 48:4). Hence, each one receives a separate portion of land in Israel (Josh. 16–17). In short, even though Yosef is passed over for leadership, he is once again the favorite son, with an elevated role: "The sons of Reuven the firstborn of Yisrael, for he was the firstborn; but, because he defiled his father's couch, his birthright was given to the sons of Yosef the son of Yisrael; and the genealogy is not to be reckoned after the birthright. For Yehuda prevailed above his brothers, and of him came the prince; but the birthright was Yosef's" (I Chr. 5:1–2). See Radak, Ralbag, and *Daat Mikra* on I Chr. 5:2.

58. Berakhot 55a offers the view of Rav Hama bar Ḥanina, who states that Yosef dies before the other brothers as punishment for flaunting his authority over them. In

to see the negative outcomes of his actions. On the other hand, he is uniquely successful as a leader; he is strong[59] as well as charming. All the while, he shows an emotional aspect to him that, at times, is overwhelming. Interestingly, throughout his life, he is always second in command, never the ultimate leader.[60] Therefore, it is not surprising that his descendants will have many leadership positions, but will trail behind the leadership of Yehuda.

explaining this view, Rashi provides textual evidence from the verse: "And Yosef died and all of his brothers" (Ex. 1:6), which places Yosef's death before that of his brothers.

59. Yaakov emphasizes the strength of Yosef in his blessing: "But his bow abode in strength, the arms of his hands were made strong" (Gen. 49:24).
60. Consider his authority figures in Egypt: Potiphar, head officer of the jail, and Pharaoh.

*Chapter 16*

# Yosef in Tanakh

The book of Genesis concludes with an emphasis on Yosef. In fact, the final fourteen chapters (chapters 37–50) focus almost exclusively on the stories of Yosef – from his youth in the house of Yaakov through tumultuous events in his life and his eventual ascendance in Egypt, culminating in his moving the house of Yaakov to Egypt. Within these stories, Yosef's personality and personal growth emerge. Throughout these ups-and-downs, the reader encounters Yosef's leadership, interest in authority, emotional sensitivity, and naiveté. Looking at Yosef's descendants throughout Tanakh, we see many of these same attributes and patterns of behavior.

## ROLLER COASTER OF EXPERIENCES

The vacillations of Yosef's life in the book of Genesis are replicated in the experiences of his descendants throughout Tanakh. Yosef is the favorite child in his father's home, but then sold as a slave. Next, he becomes the chief of staff in Potiphar's home, but is thrown into jail after Potiphar's wife's false accusation. Upon his release from jail, Yosef is promoted to viceroy of Egypt. Clearly, the story of Yosef is a roller coaster. In fact, these fluctuations continue after his death. The details of Yosef's death and deathbed wishes are noted (Gen. 50:24–26); in contrast, we hear nothing about the final days of any other brother until the beginning of the book of Exodus. There, the death of Yosef is repeated and the deaths of the other brothers are generalized together: "Yosef died, as did all his brothers, and all that generation" (Ex. 1:6). The star of the show and the focus of the text is Yosef. However, this changes two verses later when we are told, "Now there arose a new king over Egypt, who did not know Yosef" (1:8). Not only does the new king not remember Yosef, it seems that Yosef's legacy is forgotten. However, Yosef's message that life contains highs and lows is not forgotten, as it is evident in the leadership of Yosef's descendants.

After Yosef's death, during the period of slavery and redemption, Yosef's family's role in leadership is limited to just Yehoshua. (We will discuss him in later sections of this chapter.) Yosef's descendants play no other role for a few generations. At this stage in history, Levi's family dominates (Moshe, Aharon, Elazar, and Pinḥas), supported by Yehuda's progeny (Kalev, Ḥur, and Naḥshon). This period of history is a downturn for the tribe of Yosef as their leadership is on hiatus. However, after Moshe's death, Yosef's descendants experience resurgence as they assume multiple mantles of leadership for the next few hundred years. Following Moshe's death, Yehoshua is appointed as leader of the Jewish people for twenty-eight years.[1] Yehoshua is followed by the period of judicial leadership, which includes numerous descendants of Yosef (Devora, Gidon, Avimelekh, Yair, Yiftaḥ, and Avdon). After Avdon there is another downturn in Yosef's lead, as Levi's family resumes its leadership (Eli and Shmuel), followed by Binyamin's rule (King Shaul), and then Yehuda (Kings David, Shlomo, and Reḥavam). However, Yosef's leadership rises again with the reign of Yorovam, who appropriates ten tribes from King Reḥavam's monarchy (I Kings 12:20).

This cycle of ups-and-downs in leadership is consistent with Yosef's own fluctuations in the book of Genesis. In fact, in Genesis Yosef always *wants* to lead, even if the opportunity does not permit it. Therefore, it may not be surprising if his descendants share that passion and volunteer for leadership positions. During the time of the judges

1. See *Seder Olam*, chapter 12.

and when Yehuda's monarchy is faltering, Yosef's progeny happily step into the leadership roles. However, consistent with Yosef's own experiences, his progeny are not blessed with continual leadership. Hence, when the tribes of Yehuda and Levi assert themselves, Yosef is forced to take a step back.

## LEADERSHIP

The passion and ability to lead is bequeathed to the descendants of Yosef. In the desert, Yosef's son Ephraim is the head of an encampment of Raḥel's children, which includes the tribes of Ephraim, Menashe, and Binyamin (Num. 2:18). Not only is the tribe given a leadership position at this time, but many of Yosef's descendants have vital leadership roles.

### Yehoshua

The strongest and most famous leader from the tribe of Yosef is Yehoshua, who leads the Jewish people after the death of Moshe. During Yehoshua's reign, the Jewish nation conquers the land of Israel; they then divide and settle the land. The strength and success of his leadership is captured by the repeated refrain: "The people served God all the days of Yehoshua, and all the days of the elders who outlived Yehoshua, who had seen all the great work of God that He had performed for Israel" (Josh. 24:31, Judges 2:7). Under the leadership of Yehoshua, the Jewish people prevail in their battles against thirty-one Canaanite kings (Josh. 12)![2] Yehoshua orchestrates the distribution of land to each of the tribes, and then rallies the tribes to finish conquering all the Canaanites who remain in the land. He is also responsible for transmitting the Jewish tradition as well as the Torah and the ceremony of the blessings and the curses to the next generation (Josh. 8). The culmination of his leadership, after winning all the battles, is an era of peace from enemies: "God had given rest to Israel from all their enemies around them"

2. There is only one battle with casualties in the time of Yehoshua, which is the first battle against the city of Ai (Josh. 7). God explains to Yehoshua that the deaths of thirty-six men in that battle are a punishment for the sin of Akhan (from the tribe of Yehuda) for taking forbidden booty from Jericho. After Akhan is executed, Yehoshua leads the nation in a successful second battle against Ai.

(Josh. 23:1). Yehoshua proves to be one of the great leaders of the Jewish people, displaying a trait passed down to him from Yosef in Genesis.

### The Daughters of Tzelofḥad

The brotherless daughters of Tzelofḥad from the tribe of Menashe boldly request their father's inheritance (Num. 27:1–11). Without hesitation, they approach Moshe, Elazar, and all the princes, asking to inherit their father's land. Because of their request, Moshe proclaims that daughters can inherit land from their father if there are no sons. Later, their tribe complains that this may result is the loss of land from one tribe to another – i.e., if a woman who inherits land marries into another tribe, the land goes to her husband's tribe. The daughters of Tzelofḥad righteously marry their cousins to avoid dispute (Num. 36:11). They teach the lesson of standing up for one's rights while minimizing conflict. For their tremendous impact on Jewish history, they are practically the only women listed in the second counting of the Jewish people (Num. 26:33).[3] Their intelligence and piety are captured by the statement in Bava Batra 119b: "The daughters of Tzelofḥad are wise; they are interpreters of the law, and they are righteous."

### Judges from the Tribe of Yosef

After the death of Yehoshua, the people ask God for a new leader. God replies, "Yehuda will lead" (Judges 1:2). Regrettably, Yehuda's descendants do not assume this role. During the entire period of the judges, only two are from the tribe of Yehuda, who rule for a total of just forty-seven years.[4] In contrast, six judges descend from Yosef and lead for 119 years.[5]

One of those judges from the tribe of Yosef is Devora, who completes Yehoshua's mission to fully conquer the land of Canaan (Judges 4:23–24). Devora fights against Yavin, king of Canaan, and his general,

3. Two other women are included in this list. They are Seraḥ daughter of Asher (26:46) and Miriam, the sister of Moshe and Aharon (26:59). Abarbanel on Num. 26 notes that this list includes only the most important women.
4. Otniel leads for forty years (Judges 3:11); Ivtzan leads for seven years (12:9).
5. Devora leads for forty years (Judges 5:31), as does Gidon (8:28); Avimelekh leads for three years (9:22); Yair leads for twenty-two years (10:3); Yiftaḥ leads for six years (12:7); Avdon leads for eight years (12:14).

Sisera. When Barak, Devora's general, is petrified to enter the battlefield without her, she accompanies him and orchestrates the military strategy that culminates in their victory. Under her guidance, they overcome an enemy that has a strong army, horses, and chariots (thus reminding us of Moshe's victory over Pharaoh[6]). She sings a song of praise and thanksgiving to God, marking the conclusion of a series of battles against Canaan.[7]

Another judge from Yosef's family is Gidon, who leads a military action against Midian and successfully removes them from Canaan. He is so effective in battle and at rallying the nation that the Jewish people request he be promoted to the role of king. "Rule you over us, both you, and your son, and your son's son also; for you have saved us out of the hand of Midian" (Judges 8:22).

A third judge is Yiftaḥ, who shares commonalities with Yosef. Yiftaḥ is born to a different mother than the rest of his brothers, and they exile him from his father's home (Judges 11:1–4). He is forced to live in the desert, where he gathers support from other rejects of society. Amazingly, when his family and tribe is under attack by the nation of Amon, Yiftaḥ is called upon to lead them. In every detail, this story mimics the story of Yosef: Both men are born to a different mother from

6. There are numerous similarities between these stories and their textual presentations. In both instances there is an emphasis on the strength and size of the enemy (Ex. 14:6, 9, 15:4; Judges 4:3, 13). Ironically, in both instances, the enemy's chariots, which are clear expressions of strength, become a liability when they get stuck in the mud; this causes the enemy soldiers to abandon their chariots, thus leading to their downfall. In fact, the unusual word "*vayaham*," "and He confused [the enemy]," describes God's intervention in both stories (Ex. 14:24, Judges 4:15). Similarly, the same sentence is used in both stories to portray the loss to the enemy: "And there was not a man left" (Ex. 14:28; Judges 4:16). Both stories conclude with the Jewish leader (first Moshe, then Devora) singing "*shira*," a song of praise to God, after the victories (Ex. 15, Judges 5).
7. Songs are sung by our leaders to mark a major victory or event.
   (1) Moshe sings a song after the splitting of the sea, which caused the death of the Egyptian army and was the final step in redeeming the Jews from slavery (Ex. 15).
   (2) Moshe sings another song at the conclusion of the forty years in the desert to mark the momentous occasion of the nation's anticipated entry into Israel and the end of the wandering in the desert (Deut. 32).
   (3) King David sings a song to mark the end of his battles as he is victorious over all of his enemies (II Sam. 22).

the rest of their brothers. Both men are hated by their brothers and are thrown out of their fathers' homes. In spite of this, both men become the leaders who save their families.

The tribe of Yosef produces many strong leaders. In addition to Yehoshua and the various judges noted above, Yosef's descendants also serve as kings. Yorovam and Aḥav, who will be discussed later with a focus on their corruption and their leading the Jewish people away from God, are unquestionably powerful leaders who provide a stable and strong kingdom.

Many of the leaders who come from Yosef share other traits and patterns that also reflect back on the stories and traits of Yosef in Genesis.

## SECOND IN COMMAND

Yosef and his descendants serve as leaders to the people. However, similar to Yosef's role in Egypt, the leaders in Yosef's family serve as the deputy leader, never as the ultimate leader. Yosef is second to Potiphar, the officer of the jail, and later to Pharaoh as well. So too, his descendants support the authority of leaders from other tribes. Already in the desert this lower status is evident, as the encampment of Yosef is listed as the third encampment, after those led by Yehuda and Reuven.

### Yehoshua

Yehoshua, member of the tribe of Yosef who leads the Jewish people into the land of Israel, is branded "*mesharet Moshe,*" the helper of Moshe (Ex. 24:13, 33:11; Josh. 1:1).[8] Yehoshua begins his career as a helper to the ultimate leader, Moshe. He follows the command of Moshe, doing only what he is told. Indeed, Yehoshua lives his entire life in Moshe's shadow. He replicates Moshe's actions throughout his leadership: Just like Moshe, Yehoshua sends spies to Canaan (Josh. 2), splits a sea (Josh. 3), circumcises the men, and celebrates Passover (Josh. 5), elevates his hands

8. This might be a unique role, exclusive to Yehoshua, to apprentice with Moshe and attend to all his needs. Alternatively, he might be one of many young men who attended to the countless needs of the leader of the Jewish nation (see Ibn Ezra on Num. 11:28). Either way, Yehoshua clearly excels as he is asked to lead in the battle against Amalek and later to take over the role of leader of the nation.

during the battle as a symbolic act (8:18), sends a plague of hail against his enemies (10:11), and falls on his face in prayer (7:6). Moreover, like Moshe, Yehoshua has an encounter with God: "Remove your shoe(s)… for the place you are standing is holy ground" (Ex. 3:4; Josh. 5:15).

In fact, beyond reproducing Moshe's behaviors, Yehoshua's entire leadership agenda is to fulfill Moshe's commands and ensure his legacy. There are thirteen instances where Yehoshua's action is followed by the phrase "just as Moshe commanded."[9] Even God expects Yehoshua's mission to be a continuation of Moshe's agenda, as evidenced by God mentioning Moshe four times within the opening charge to Yehoshua.[10] The essence of Yehoshua's leadership is captured by the following verse: "As God commanded Moshe His servant, so did Moshe command Yehoshua, and so did Yehoshua; he left nothing undone of all that God commanded Moshe" (11:15).

Therefore, it is obvious to all that Yehoshua's mission is enmeshed with Moshe's legacy. The Jewish people regularly remind Yehoshua that he is to resemble Moshe. For instance, prior to entering the land of Canaan, Yehoshua commands the tribes of Reuven, Gad, and half of the tribe of Menashe to help fight for the land before moving to their portion of land on the eastern bank of the Jordan River. What is their response? "All that you have commanded us we will do, and wherever you send us we will go. Just as we listened to Moshe in all things, so will we listen to you: only if God will be with you, as he was with Moshe" (Josh 1:16–17).[11] Similarly, the tribe of Yehuda

9. Josh. 4:10, 8:31, 33, 35, 11:12, 15, 20, 23, 14:2, 5, 21:8, 22:2, 5.

10. "Moshe My servant is dead; now therefore arise, go over this Jordan, you, and all this people, to the land which I do give to them, even to the children of Israel. Every place that the sole of your foot shall tread on, to you have I given it, as I spoke to Moshe. As I was with Moshe, so I will be with you; I will not fail you, nor forsake you. Only be strong and very courageous, to observe to do according to all the law, which Moshe my servant commanded you: do not turn from it to the right hand or to the left, that you may have good success wherever you go" (1:2–7).

11. *Metzudat David* on Josh. 1:17 explains that this is a condition of agreement that they are presenting to Yehoshua. In effect, they are saying, "Only if you prove that God is with you the way He was with Moshe will we listen to you." Therefore, only after God splits the sea for Yehoshua, thus mimicking the miracle He performed for Moshe, do we learn that the tribes of Reuven, Gad, and half of the tribe of Menashe cross

reminds Yehoshua that Moshe had sworn that Kalev should eventually receive the land of Hebron as a reward for his bravery during the episode of the spies (Josh. 14). After hearing those words, Yehoshua immediately responds affirmatively to the tribe of Yehuda. Also, the daughters of Tzelofḥad remind Yehoshua that "Moshe commanded" they should receive their father's land (17:4). So too, the tribe of Levi reminds Yehoshua about Moshe's command that they should receive cities inside of other tribes' lands (21:2). In each of these episodes, immediately after being told that "Moshe commanded X," Yehoshua complies with the directive.

More than just choosing to focus his leadership on completing Moshe's mission, Yehoshua receives a unique charge from Moshe, as expressed in two events. First, Moshe changes Yehoshua's name from Hoshea to Yehoshua (Num. 13:16).[12] Afterwards, Moshe formally transfers his spirit onto Yehoshua before he dies (Num. 27:22–23). So much of Yehoshua's leadership is a fulfillment of Moshe's unfinished mission. Yehoshua begins his leadership by serving as Moshe's "second in command" and spends the rest of his career adhering to the commands of his mentor and fulfilling his legacy.

---

the Jordan River to fight alongside the Jewish people "as they were told by Moshe" (4:12). It is on that day, when Yehoshua benefits from the same miracles as Moshe, that he earns the respect and loyalty of the people: "On that day God magnified Yehoshua in the eyes of all Israel; and they feared him, as they feared Moshe, all the days of his life" (4:14).

12. There are at least two ways to understand Moshe's motivation in changing the name of his apprentice.
    (1) Strength: Moshe is behaving like a parent who names, or renames, a child (e.g., Yaakov changes his youngest son's name from Ben Oni to Binyamin) to help endow him with additional strength. Hence, Moshe might have changed it immediately before sending Yehoshua to spy in Israel in order to give him extra strength to avoid the evil influences of the ten spies (see Sota 34b; Rashi on Num. 13:16).
    (2) Leadership: In changing Yehoshua's name, Moshe is copying God, who changes the names of people with special potential for the future: God changes Avram to Avraham, Sarai to Sarah, Yaakov to Yisrael. Each of these names reflects the individual's new and greater status or role as founder of the chosen nation. Accordingly, Moshe changes Yehoshua's name when they first meet, to acknowledge Yehoshua's special qualities and potential for the future (see Abarbanel on Num. 13:1).

### Yosef is Second to Yehuda

In many ways, Yehoshua's relationship with Moshe's leadership corresponds to Yosef's relationship with Yehuda (as other interrelationships between descendants of Yosef and Yehuda also do). We can readily see that Yosef is always a step behind the leadership of Yehuda; after all, Yaakov gives the blessing of leadership to Yehuda rather than to Yosef.

Yehuda's progeny is commanded to lead during the time of the judges, but when they don't step up to lead, Yosef takes over. During the period of monarchical leadership, Yehuda is destined to be king, but when Reḥavam (from the tribe of Yehuda) enrages the nation and they revolt against him, Yorovam (from the tribe of Yosef) leads the rebellion and usurps ten tribes from the kingdom of Yehuda. However, Yosef's sovereignty declines much faster than Yehuda's, and his kingdom is exiled years earlier. Similar to Yosef's kingdom being secondary to Yehuda's, in the future, the messiah from Yosef will come first, but will be secondary to the messiah from the tribe of Yehuda.

## EMOTIONAL WEAKNESS

In Genesis, Yosef cries on numerous occasions,[13] displaying an inability to constrain his emotions. Because of this struggle to control his feelings and outbursts, he may have revealed himself to his brothers earlier than he had intended: "Then Yosef could not control himself before all those who stood before him" (Gen. 45:1). So too, members of the tribe of Yosef have a propensity to be overtly emotional, exhibiting extreme bouts of passion and fear. This is in stark contrast to Yehuda and his descendants, who are the epitome of strength, stability, and fearlessness. Of course, Yosef's emotional expressiveness is not necessarily a positive or negative attribute; at times it is a weakness that is overwhelming, while at other times this trait makes the person understanding of others, as well generally easy to relate to.

### Yehoshua

When Yehoshua is selected by God to assume the leadership of the Jewish people, it is an understatement to say that he is nervous. Assuming

13. Gen. 42:24, 43:30, 45:2, 50:17.

the role of Moshe – his mentor and role model, guide and teacher – overwhelms Yehoshua. He is visibly nervous and unsteady. To counter his trepidation, Yehoshua receives words of encouragement and comfort. Moshe instructs Yehoshua to "be strong" ("*chazak ve'ematz*") three times in the book of Deuteronomy.[14] God also repeats this charge to Yehoshua three times.[15] Even the Jewish people say these exact words ("*chazak ve'eamatz*") to Yehoshua in the first chapter of the book of Joshua.[16] What type of individual would require all of these statements of encouragement? Someone who is strong and confident presumably does not need to be instructed to remain strong! Clearly, Yehoshua's repeated charge to be strong demonstrates the universal recognition that he is anxious and panicked, and will benefit from this inspiration directed toward him by his mentor, then by God, and by the nation.

Somewhat paradoxically, Yehoshua's personal sense of trepidation allows him to identify and sympathize with his people when they encounter a frightful situation. For example, early in his leadership, after the Jewish people suffer their first military defeat, Yehoshua acknowledges that the nation will be apprehensive to re-engage in battle against the same city, Ai, or even other cities. Even with assurances from God that they would be successful in the battle, Yehoshua understands that he needs to boost the confidence of his people and alleviate their fears. How so? He utilizes a tricky battle strategy to fight the inhabitants of city of Ai.[17] The nation does not need a cunning strategy in order to succeed – God already promised a victory – so his battle strategy is not intended to facilitate military success; rather, it is designed to inject confidence and remove fear of defeat. In fact, Yehoshua learns to utilize the same charge – "*Chizku ve'imtzu*," "be strong" – to encourage

14. Deut. 1:38, 31:7, 31:23.
15. Josh. 1:6, 7, 9.
16. Josh 1:18.
17. In Josh. 8, Yehoshua sets up an ambush to hide outside of the city of Ai. He sends the majority of the army into the city, instructing them to pretend to suffer defeat and then retreat. As the enemy chases them out of the city, the soldiers who were lying in ambush enter the city and burn it to the ground. Yehoshua raises his hand and stick to signal to the retreating army to turn around and fight. The enemy is sandwiched between the army and the ambush, and is destroyed.

the Jewish people to conquer their territories and fight the remaining nations of Canaan.[18]

**Gidon**

A few generations after Yehoshua, we are introduced to another descendant of Yosef, the judge Gidon, via a series of stories that reveal his fear of leading the Jewish people into war against Midian. When the angel first appears to Gidon to reveal his future role as savior of the Jewish people (see Judges 6:14), Gidon is in denial of his new responsibilities: "Please God, with which shall I save Israel? Behold, my family is the poorest in Menashe, and I am the least in my father's house" (Judges 6:15). Although such an initial reaction of humility is fairly common among Israel's leaders (Moshe,[19] Shaul,[20] and Yirmiyahu[21] all reacted similarly), the new role is typically accepted once God reveals that He will support the new leader. Even after God's promise of support, however, Gidon continues to beseech God for miraculous signs as evidence of His support. Despite an angel's intervention, Gidon's fears remain!

The angel instructs him to put matza, meat, and soup on a rock; the angel then touches the food with a stick and a fire immediately consumes the food, which is followed by the angel's disappearance. In spite of this initial signal, Gidon asks God to soak a wad of cotton located on the threshing floor while keeping the ground beneath it dry. Then he asks for a third sign – for the cotton wad to be dry, but the ground below it to be soaked. But after his request is fulfilled, Gidon is still terrified! God commands him to sneak into the enemy's encampment, where he overhears two soldiers conversing about a strange dream. In the dream, a piece of barley bread roles down a hill and knocks over a tent. The second soldier interprets the dream as foreshadowing the Jewish

18. Josh. 10:25.
19. See Ex. 3:11: "Moshe said to God, 'Who am I, that I should go to Pharaoh, and that I should bring forth the children of Israel out of Egypt?'"
20. See I Sam. 9:21: "Shaul answered, 'Am I not a Binyaminite, of the smallest of the tribes of Israel? And [is not] my family the least of all the families of the tribe of Binyamin? Why then speak you to me after this manner?'"
21. See Jer. 1:6: "Then said I, 'Oh God, behold, I do not know how to speak; for I am a child.'"

people's successful defeat of people of Midian. After hearing this, Gidon is finally prepared to lead. In short, Gidon suffers from an exceptional fear of leading the nation and overseeing the military; he requires four signs from God before accepting his responsibility to lead.

**Yiftaḥ**

Soon after Gidon's leadership, the judge Yiftaḥ is appointed to lead the people. He too suffers from an inner turmoil of emotions as he fears losing the battle against Israel's enemy. In the last moments before the war, his nerves lead him to irrationally make a very costly oath:[22] "Yiftaḥ vowed a vow to God, and said, 'If You will indeed deliver the children of Amon into my hand, then it shall be that whatever comes forth from the doors of my house to meet me when I return in peace from the children of Amon, it shall be God's, and I will offer it up for a burnt offering'" (Judges 11:30–31). Tragically, upon his return from the successful military campaign, his daughter (his only child) emerges from his home! Realizing the impact of his mistaken oath, he screams out, "'Alas, my daughter! You have brought me very low, and you are one of those who trouble me; for I have opened my mouth to God, and I cannot go back.'" (11:35). He clearly deeply regrets the impulsive oath he had previously made because of nervous energy from the burden of leading the military campaign against the enemy.[23]

---

22. A passage in Taanit 4a notes the inappropriateness of Yiftaḥ's oath. How can he know if the first thing to emerge from his home would be fitting for an offering to God? God punishes Yiftaḥ by sending out his daughter to greet him.
23. This oath is similar to other irrational oaths taken in intense situations, which are inevitably regretted at a later point. For example, Yaakov swears to Lavan that no one took his idols, unaware that his wife Raḥel had taken them (Gen. 31:32). Another example: Ḥana swears to commit her son to God's service if she is blessed with a child, but is then saddened by the need to fulfill her oath. She won't even visit Shiloh until Shmuel is weaned and she is forced to fulfill her vow (I Sam. 1:11–25). A third example: Shaul promises to kill anyone who eats during the battle against the Philistines; he then discovers that his own son Yonatan ate some honey to restore his strength during the battle (I Sam. 14:24, 27). In the context of these vows, the leader makes the commitment out of fear or feelings of uncertainty for the future, but later regrets how it affects his loved ones.

In summary, many leaders from the tribe of Yosef express emotional vulnerability. For some, these emotions cause apprehension towards leadership, thus conflicting with their drive to lead (another key characteristic of the tribe). For others, these emotions lead to rash decision-making. This propensity to emotional tumult reminds the reader of the Yosef's own emotional experiences, such as when he sees his brothers for the first time in Egypt.

### CORRUPTIBLE BY POWER

Although Yosef has many constructive leadership qualities that are traceable among his descendants, he also expresses a proclivity to seek and occasionally seize power. During his lifetime, Yosef dreams of his brothers bowing to him, possibly fantasizing about the day he would become the leader of the family. This longing for power may even propel him to engage in otherwise inappropriate behavior. Some examples include: (1) his apparent bragging to his brothers about his visions of leadership rather than keeping them to himself; (2) as viceroy, collecting the wealth and land of the Egyptians when they come begging for food; and (3) frightening his brothers when they come to Egypt to purchase food by making terrible false claims against them. In each of these scenarios, Yosef might be motivated by the grandeur of power. His descendants will similarly struggle with the desire for leadership and may even fall prey to its corrupting influences.

#### Avimelekh

The prototype of a descendant of Yosef that has interest in and is negatively impacted by power is Avimelekh. Like Yosef, Avimelekh is born to a different mother than that of his brothers and he clashes with them over who should lead. However, unlike Yosef, Avimelekh's mother is not the favored wife (she is a concubine). The judge Avimelekh is one of Gidon's seventy sons (born to many wives); since only his mother is a concubine, he is made to feel inferior to the rest of his brothers.

Also, like Yosef, Avimelekh covets a leadership position in the family. In fact, Avimelekh's focus on leadership is evident from his name, Avimelekh – "my father is king." In fact, this may not have been his given name at birth, but rather a name he gave himself: "And he put his name Avimelekh" (Judges 8:31).[24]

In a sort of reversal of Yosef's situation, where his brothers conspire to murder him, but conclude instead to remove him from their father's home, Avimelekh's aspirations lead him to hire mercenaries to murder his brothers, at which point he appoints himself king of Shekhem. In addition to massacring his brothers, he slays anyone who questions his authority. His reign concludes when a woman drops a rock on his head while he is chasing a group of rebels (Judges 9). The Midrash captures Avimelekh's essence in one sentence: "Avimelekh chased after authority, and authority ran away from him" (*Midrash Aggada* on Lev. 1:1).

### Yiftaḥ

A few chapters later in the book of Judges (ch. 11), the elders of Gilad approach the judge Yiftaḥ to lead the battle against Amon and save the Jewish people. Yiftaḥ's negotiations with them reveal his true desires. Initially they offer him to be the general ("*katzin*") of their army. After he refuses, they offer to appoint him as the leader ("*rosh*") of Gilad, contingent on victory against his enemies. Why do the people make this offer? Evidently, they realize that he wants to be their leader. How does Yiftaḥ respond? He agrees, but only if they elect him to lead immediately. Out of desperation, they agree to elect him both as their general, "*katzin*," and their leader, "*rosh*" (Judges 11:6–10). In short, Yiftaḥ agrees to lead the Jewish people in battle principally to fulfill his own selfish yearnings for a leadership position.

### Mikha

Leadership comes in many different forms. For example, one can desire military, political, or spiritual leadership. A short while after Yiftaḥ's story in the book of Judges, beginning in chapter 17, Mikha desires

---

24. This might clarify who is providing him with his name, since it would be a challenge to understand why Gidon – who minimizes his own leadership by rejecting the opportunity to be king only a few verses earlier (8:22) – would name the child of his concubine to celebrate himself as king. Rather, Avimelekh renames himself to act as if his father is king, thus making the case that he deserves to be king as well.

to be a spiritual leader, even if it requires him to step out of the constraints of Jewish law. He builds a house of worship, including a *"pesel umasekha,"* a carved and molten idol, and elects his own son (from the tribe of Ephraim) to be the priest (Judges 18:5). This is a role which is only appropriate for a descendant of Aharon (from the tribe of Levi). Mikha wants his home to be the destination where Jews who hail from all over Israel will come to worship God: a spiritual tourist attraction! (The popularity of his house of worship eventually leads to its downfall, as passersby from the tribe of Dan steal his precious idol.)

**Yorovam**

In I Kings 12, Yorovam is appointed king over the ten tribes of Israel. As ruler, he fears that the Jewish people will return to the kingdom of Yehuda and he will lose his newfound position. He knows that his greatest vulnerability is during the holiday season, when Jews make a pilgrimage to the Temple, which is located in the territory of Yehuda. "Yorovam said in his heart: 'Now will the kingdom return to the house of David: If this people go up to offer sacrifices in the house of God at Jerusalem, then will the heart of this people turn again to their lord, even to Reḥavam, king of Yehuda; and they will kill me, and return to Reḥavam, king of Yehuda'" (I King 12:26–27). To avoid this possibility, he builds alternative places of worship in Beit El, which is in the land of Binyamin, and in the land of Dan.[25] He, like Mikha, assigns the priestly role to non-Levites in his houses of worship since the tribe of Levi is part of the kingdom of Yehuda (v. 31).[26] He even declares the

25. He even places a golden calf in each location (I Kings 12:28). Abarbanel on I Kings 12:25 explains that the calves are not intended for worship, as the Jewish people know the story of the original golden calf and would not repeat the exact same sin. Rather, these calves represent Yorovam's leadership, as they are made of gold and are in the form of the animal that Yaakov uses to describe the tribe of Yosef. Abarbanel explains that Yorovam made two calves to represent Ephraim and Menashe, as a symbol that in his view, "the birthright was given to Yosef, and therefore the monarchy was given to the children of Yosef and not Yehuda."

26. Abarbanel on I Kings 12:25 suggests that he appointed men from other tribes as priests. Symbolically, this highlights Yorovam's view that just as the king does not need to emerge from Yehuda, priests need not come from Aharon. He assembles altars for use in the houses of worship. Therefore, people can bring their own

holiday of Sukkot to be on the fifteenth day in the eighth month instead of the seventh month (v. 32), which, as Abarbanel observes, is another way to separate himself from of Yehuda's kingdom (see Abarbanel on I Kings 12:25). The holiday of Sukkot commemorates the gathering of the harvest that ends by the seventh month in the land of Yehuda. However, Yorovam wants to include the end of the harvest in all of Israel, which isn't until the eighth month. He wants all practices of worship, including dates of the holidays, to be decoupled from the land of Yehuda.[27] In fact, he specifically celebrates the holiday of Sukkot right after building his houses of worship to mimic the celebration of the holiday of Sukkot by Shlomo immediately upon the consecration of the altar which sanctified the newly built Temple (I Kings 8:2).

Yorovam is unwilling to concede anything or anyone to King Reḥavam of Yehuda. The Talmud in Bava Batra 121b even adds that Yorovam assigns guards to prevent anyone in his kingdom from returning to the land of Yehuda for the pilgrimage. In summary, to satisfy his burning desire to remain in power, he builds altars in his houses of worship and introduces idol worship into his kingdom.

### Aḥav

Soon after Yorovam's reign (I Kings 21), we learn about Aḥav, king of Israel, who builds multiple palaces and acquires much wealth. As king, he believes that he can demand land from any of his

---

sacrifices without a priest (as required in the Temple). This may also alleviate the requirement of the Jewish people to give tithes to the priests and Levites – as they no longer serve in the priestly and Levite roles. Yorovam brings the incense (v. 33), the offering that is given by the high priest (Ex. 30:8), to signify that he is the highest authority in the land. When Aharon's sons, Nadav and Avihu, bring an illicit incense offering, they die (Lev. 10:1).

27. Rabbi Alex Israel offers an alternative motivation for Yorovam's change to the calendar. According to this theory, Yorovam intends to convert that year into a leap year; hence, they would believe that the eighth month is the seventh month. In so doing, were someone from his kingdom to travel to the Temple (in Yehuda's territory) on what they perceived as the seventh month (but was actually the eighth), they would find themselves having missed the celebration of Sukkot. This, again, reinforces the message that Yorovam intends to limit connection with the kingdom of Yehuda. See Israel, *I Kings: Torn in Two* (Jerusalem: Maggid Books, 2013), 165.

constituents.[28] He desperately wants to own the vineyard of Navot because of its proximity to his palace. Much to Aḥav's dismay, Navot refuses to relinquish his land to the king. This angers Aḥav, who lies in his bed, faces the wall, and refuses to eat (I Kings 21:4). His wife, Izevel, commits herself to acquiring Navot's vineyard. How so? Izevel organizes a public day of fasting; when the religious elders are gathered, she choreographs the false testimony of witnesses who claim that Navot has cursed God and King Aḥav. The elders condemn Navot to death, thus creating the opportunity for Aḥav to confiscate his land.[29] Years later, Aḥav and Izevel are punished for their roles in this terrible episode (II Kings 9:25–26). The prophet Elisha instructs Yehu to overthrow the kingdom of Aḥav by murdering Aḥav's son Yoram, and usurping the kingdom for himself. There is an ironic justice, as Yoram is murdered in the fields of Navot. His death and the termination of Aḥav's royal line occur in the exact location that is a symbolic reminder of his parents' greediness and corruption.

**Conflict between Ephraim and Menashe**

The impact that results from this intense desire for power divides the tribe of Yosef. The tribes of Ephraim and Menashe, Yosef's sons, who are initially in alliance (Judges 1:22), end up in a civil war. During the time of Yiftaḥ, the tribe of Menashe violently attacks the tribe of Ephraim, resulting in the deaths of 42,000 of Ephraim's descendants. How do Yosef's progeny reach this level of discord?

Very simple: they battle over the opportunity to lead the Jewish people. At first, Ephraim is in power: Yehoshua leads for twenty-eight years, and Devora leads for forty years, during which time there

28. "He [the king] will take your fields and your vineyards and your olive groves, even the best of them, and give them to his servants" (I Sam. 8:14). In this passage, Shmuel affirms the principle of eminent domain. However, he limits it to instances which are only for the sake of "his servants," to help his constituents or for the common good (e.g., for purposes of war). See Radak on I Kings 21:10.
29. There is a rule regarding those who are killed for disobeying or dishonoring the king: their land and possessions are handed over to the king. This law is quoted in Makkot 7a, in *Yalkut Shimoni* 171, in both Radak and Ralbag on I Kings 21:15, and also cited as the law in the *Beit Yosef*, *Ḥoshen Mishpat* 369:14:1.

is peace between the tribes of Ephraim and Menashe. Afterwards Menashe leads for more than seventy years: Gidon for forty years, Avimelekh for three, Yair for twenty-two, and Yiftaḥ for six. During that time, Ephraim's jealousy twice leads to attempted revolts against the leader from Menashe. In response to the first attempt, Gidon is able to calm everyone down (Judges 8:1–3). However, the second time ends much more poorly: The people from Ephraim threaten to burn down Yiftaḥ's home. He responds antagonistically and accuses them of not accepting his invitation to join the war. Yiftaḥ then gathers an army to attack the instigators from Ephraim. This conflict prompts a civil war between the descendants of Menashe and Ephraim.[30] During the conflict, Menashe murders 42,000 men from the tribe of Ephraim. This tragedy is the culmination of generations of jealousy and hatred between the two tribes.[31] The tribe of Ephraim feels that its role is to lead, as predicted by Yaakov in his blessing: how dare Menashe attempt to lead without inviting Ephraim to join in! In response, the tribe of Menashe feels that as the oldest son of Yosef, leadership is their inherent right.[32]

The tragedy of the conflict between Menashe and Ephraim seems embedded in their innate pursuit of power and leadership. They will murder a man for his field, murder their family for a crown, or murder half of a tribe for the chance to lead! The link between power and corruption is sadly evident.

---

30. The hatred between these two tribes is clearly based on issues much larger than the incident with Yiftaḥ. Why else would Yiftaḥ's army attack even those from the tribe of Ephraim who did not join the complainants? Additionally, any man from the tribe of Ephraim who could not pronounce the word "*shibolet*" was killed (Judges 12:6).
31. See Yehoshafat Nevo, *Alei Mikra* (Jerusalem: Mosad HaRav Kook, 2006), 32. He draws a direct link between this story, a battle for power between Ephraim and Menashe, and the original blessing of Yaakov favoring Ephraim.
32. Rabbi Mordechai Breuer writes that Menashe joins Reuven and Gad on the other side of Jordan because he feels that as a rejected firstborn of Yosef, he too deserves to live in the land of the "rejected oldest children." Just as Yishmael and Esav can't live in Israel, so too, the rejected oldest children of Leah, Zilpa, and Yosef decide to live outside the land of Israel. See Breuer, *Pirkei Bereshit* vol. 1 (Alon Shevut: Tevunot, 1999) 250–251.

### LIMITED VISION FOR CONSEQUENCES

The book of Genesis presents numerous stories that illustrate Yosef's limited vision for the consequences of his actions. The prototypical example is that Yosef doesn't anticipate that his behavior might motivate his brothers to feel animosity towards him or cause them to harm him. Another example: he does not appear to realize that being alone with the wife of Potiphar could cause him problems. Ultimately, he doesn't realize that taxing the people of Egypt so heavily and impoverishing the nation could cause blowback against his family. Clearly, Yosef needs to struggle for the forethought to envision possible negative outcomes of his actions. We see this pattern of behavior in his descendants – i.e., not accounting for the negative but plausible results of their actions.

#### Yehoshua

Yehoshua leads the Jewish people in conquering and allocating portions of the land of Israel to each of the tribes. As we know, he leads the people in battle and conquers much of the land; however, he does not conquer all of it. At some point, each tribe is expected to remove the remaining Canaanites from its portion of the land. By chapter 18, Yehoshua rebukes the tribes for being lazy and attempts to motivate them to continue conquering their territories. But Yehoshua does nothing to actually ensure that this occurs. On his deathbed, Yehoshua again warns the people to remove the Canaanites from the land God bequeathed to the Jewish nation, and forewarns them not to serve the Canaanites' gods (Josh. 23:12–13). The remaining Canaanites in the land are a very negative influence on the Jewish nation, leading them to turn towards idolatry, which they do throughout the book of Judges. In two specific instances, the text seems to allocate some responsibility to Yehoshua for not removing all of the Canaanites from the land.[33] Why is Yehoshua being blamed for something that occurred even after his death? As the leader of the people, he is expected to visualize the potentially harmful effects of leaving Canaanites in the land.

33. See Judges 2:21: "The nations that Yehoshua left, and he died," and Judges 2:23: "And God left these nations that they did not inherit quickly, and He did not give them into the hands of Yehoshua."

### Gidon

After Gidon's victory against Midian in Judges 8, he collects the spoils of war, from which he fashions an apron to hang in his city as a reminder of the miraculous triumph against the nation of Midian (Judges 8:27).[34] Mistakenly, instead of acknowledging it as a symbol of God's involvement, the Jewish people worship the apron itself.[35] Gidon lacks the forethought to recognize that building a monument could cause future idol worship, leading the Jewish people to rebel against God.[36]

### Yiftaḥ

As discussed earlier in this chapter, Yiftaḥ makes a rash oath just before battling the nation of Amon: "If you will indeed deliver the children of Amon into my hand, then it shall be that whatever comes forth from the doors of my house to meet me when I return in peace from the children of Amon, it shall be for God, and I will offer it up for a burnt offering" (Judges 11:30–31). His wording lacks any resemblance to forethought; it totally lacks serious consideration for what, or who, may be first to

---

34. See Rabbi Yosef Kara on Judges 8:27. *Daat Mikra* on Judges 8:27 adds that he purposely makes an item resembling the clothing of the high priest; he intends to use the apron to commune with God.
35. Do the people limit their worship of the apron to during Gidon's lifetime? Rashi, *Metzudat David*, Ralbag, and Radak on 8:27 all write that the idol worship begins only after his death, as a later verse states, "And it was when Gidon died and the Jewish people returned and worshiped idols" (8:33). Further support for this approach may be the description of the apron as a "stumbling block" ("*mokesh*"), which could imply that it may cause a future problem. For example, the nations of Canaan are described as a "*mokesh*," "stumbling block," for the Jewish people because in the future they cause the Jewish people to worship idols (see Ex. 23:33, Deut. 7:16, Josh. 23:13, Judges 2:3). However, others argue that the apron is worshipped immediately, even during Gidon's lifetime (see Rabbi Yosef Kara on 8:27). Accordingly, while he is alive, they worship the apron (v. 27), and after his death they worship "*baalim*," the idols of the Canaanites (v. 33).
36. Gidon's actions are reminiscent of Aharon, who collects jewelry in order to fashion a golden calf that is then worshiped by the Jewish people in the sin of the golden calf (Ex. 32). Relatedly, Abarbanel on I Kings 12:25 compares Gidon to Yorovam. Gidon altruistically built the apron, which later ends up serving as an idol; so too, Yorovam fashioned golden calves for the glorification of his temples, but the people eventually serve them.

emerge from his home upon his return. How does Yiftaḥ not show more care in selecting his words? As we know, this episode ends in catastrophe as it is his daughter who runs out of the home to greet her father, singing and dancing upon his victory.[37]

Tragically, members of Yosef's tribe share a negative trait of his – a lack of vision and forethought to perceive the consequences of his actions. This inability leads to a period of idol worship and enslavement to the Canaanites who remain in the land in the time of the judges, as well as idol worship after the time of Gidon, and the death or isolation of the only heir of Yiftaḥ.

## CONCLUSION

Throughout history, members of the tribe of Yosef are strong leaders of the Jewish people, asserting themselves whenever the opportunity presents itself. At times, this is beneficial; when no one else steps up on behalf of the nation, their leadership is valued. At other times, it is detrimental, such as when they try to usurp power that rightfully belongs to a different tribe or individual. This desire leads to many high and low moments in the tribe's history. When other leadership tribes step up, Yosef is forced back into the shadows; however, when a leader with a more emotional approach is needed, a leader from Yosef is best suited. Either way, Yosef never gives up on his aspiration to be a leading force among the Jewish people: not in the stories of Genesis nor throughout the rest of Tanakh.

37. In a passage in Taanit 4a, R. Yonatan rebukes Yiftaḥ for making a foolish and inappropriate oath, for which God punishes him by sending out his daughter.

*Chapter 17*

# Binyamin in Genesis: The Baby of the Family

## BIRTH OF BINYAMIN

> They traveled from Bethel. There was still some distance to come to Efrat, and Raḥel travailed. She had hard labor. It happened when she was in hard labor that the midwife said to her, "Don't be afraid, for now you will have another son." It happened, as her soul was departing (for she died), that she named him Ben Oni, but his father named him Binyamin. Raḥel died, and was buried on the way to Efrat, which is Bethlehem. (Gen. 35:16–19)

In order to understand Binyamin, we begin with his birth. Raḥel's pregnancy must have been a tremendous source of joy and excitement for her and Yaakov because she had experienced so many years of infertility prior to her pregnancies. It seems Binyamin was destined to be the second miracle baby (in addition to his brother, Yosef). Presumably, Yaakov was ecstatic to flee Lavan's home and return to his father's home with the anticipation of the upcoming birth of this new child. But then tragedy strikes: Raḥel dies during Binyamin's birth.

## Death of Raḥel

There are two ways to contextualize Raḥel's death. The straightforward approach assumes that Raḥel's death in childbirth is a tragic but common pre-modern occurrence. During the time when there were no doctors, hospitals, or modern medicine, many women died during childbirth.[1]

Rabbinic tradition offers an additional layer of meaning for understanding her death. When Yaakov and his family run away from Lavan's home, Raḥel takes her father's idols. Lavan chases the family in search of his missing items. When he catches up to the clan and accuses Yaakov of stealing his idols, Yaakov denies it. In fact, he is so confident that no one in his group took the idols that he tells Lavan, "With whomever you find your gods, he shall not live" (31:32). The verse then states that "Yaakov did not know that Raḥel had stolen them" (31:32). The Sages connect this statement to Raḥel's death.[2] Many commentators disagree with the literal nature of this interpretation. For example, Ibn Ezra on 31:32 writes that Yaakov meant something much more limited – specifically, that if Yaakov became aware that someone stole the idols, he (Yaakov) would want to kill them. He argues that there is no evidence to assume that Yaakov's proclamation is the basis for Raḥel's death, as there are numerous other instances in Tanakh of women dying in childbirth with no similar proclamation.[3] In other words, Ibn Ezra is observing the empirical reality that death in childbirth was a common enough event to preclude assigning a specific spiritual cause. In a similar fashion, Rashbam on 31:32 writes that Yaakov's statement is just his assertion that he himself would take revenge on whoever took the idols. Why would Yaakov react so strongly? Sforno on 31:32 explains that Yaakov presumes that if anyone in his clan is guilty, it was likely one of his servants who would have stolen the idol in order to worship it, thereby becoming deserving of death.

---

1. *Tosafot* on Ketubot 83b (s.v. *mita shekhiḥa*) suggest that the talmudic reference to the commonness of death is an allusion to the regularity of women dying in childbirth. Relatedly, *Meshekh Ḥokhma* on Gen. 9:7 explains why women are not commanded in the mitzva of "*peru urevu*," procreation: The Torah does not command an act that can often result in the person's own death.
2. Genesis Rabba 74:9, cited in Rashi on Genesis 31:32.
3. For example, the wife of Eli's son Pinḥas, who dies in childbirth (I Sam. 4:19).

One of the implications of how to understand this question and why the debate surrounding Raḥel's death is so critical is its role in the early stages of the Yaakov-Binyamin relationship. In short, does Yaakov view Binyamin (i.e., the physical reality of his birth) as the cause of Raḥel's death, or rather as a reminder of his guilt for his own mistake (i.e., cursing the thief)?

There is a related question, central to understanding Binyamin's role, which does not appear directly in the text of the Torah: Does Binyamin share Yosef's favored-child status in Yaakov's eyes? More specifically, is Binyamin promoted to this status only after Yaakov thinks that Yosef is dead? In summary, does Yaakov view both sons of Raḥel equally, or does he initially place Binyamin in Yosef's shadow?

Whatever the exact basis for Raḥel's death, Binyamin's birth clearly imbues Yaakov with complex emotions. This is in stark contrast to the undiluted joy associated with Yosef's birth, when he was able to enjoy his new child along with his wife. What about their childhoods? Genesis 37:3 refers to Yosef as the "*ben zekunim*," "son of [Yaakov's] old age." Why does Binyamin not receive a similar title? Ramban ad loc. suggests that this title is unique to the child placed in a designated position within the home: it is descriptive of the singular child selected to stay home and care for Yaakov's needs. This prestigious job suggests that Yosef is originally the favorite child, more so than Binyamin. Similarly, Yosef receives the special coat, and we never learn that Binyamin receives a similar one. Therefore, one can conclude that Binyamin was never supposed to be a favored child. This is the conclusion of *Ḥizkuni* on 37:3, who writes: "The love that Yaakov had for Binyamin was not like the love that he had for Yosef because when he was born, Raḥel died."

What was the Yaakov-Binyamin relationship lacking when compared to the Yaakov-Yosef relationship? Binyamin's birth was simply devoid of the excitement and newness of being the first child. In other words, although the Yaakov-Binyamin relationship may still reflect the unique love associated with being a child born from Yaakov and Raḥel, it lacks the excitement of being the first.

Unfortunately, the evidence noted above may fall short of justifying one of these explanations if one considers Binyamin's age in these stories. For example, perhaps he was already a favorite of Yaakov's, but too young to earn the title of "*ben zekunim*" or receive a special coat. As in Yosef's case, Binyamin would need to be older to attain these status symbols. In fact, when Binyamin is older, Yehuda calls him the "*yeled zekunim*," "child of [his father's] old age" (Gen. 44:20). Further, in another episode, Yaakov refuses to send Binyamin to Egypt with the rest of his brothers, perhaps because he intends to keep Binyamin home. This may imply that once Binyamin is old enough to have the special job of serving his father, he too receives the same status as Yosef. However, one could counter that this title and special role may have been transferred to him only after Yaakov believes that Yosef is dead. In the end, the evidence is inconclusive and we are left wondering about the nature of their relationship before the sale of Yosef.

These two perspectives on the early years of the relationship between Yaakov and Binyamin will help us understand their dynamic throughout the story.

### NAMING OF BINYAMIN

Binyamin is the only one of the brothers to receive two names – one from his mother, "Ben Oni," "the son of my affliction," and one from his father, "Binyamin." For the first and only time, Yaakov renames one of his children. Evidently, Yaakov doesn't want his son to carry the baggage associated with "Ben Oni" that connects Binyamin's birth to Raḥel's pain and eventual death. To walk around with that name would be a constant reminder of his mother's death in childbirth.

What does "Binyamin" mean? Ramban on Gen. 35:18 translates it as "the son of one's right hand," meaning, "the son of my strength." The right hand is considered the stronger and more dominant hand. Hence, he is blessing Binyamin with strength and dominance. Radak on 35:18 suggests that it means "the son that is beloved to me," i.e., the son born when I was old and who will be loved and cherished by me.

In other words, avoiding the name Raḥel chose is not Yaakov's only motivation in selecting "Binyamin." Rather, he feels an immediate bond with Raḥel's second son and wants him to bear a name with a positive association. Recall, Yaakov does not change Reuven's or Shimon's negatively charged names, which refer to their mother's feelings about the effect of their births on her relationship with Yaakov. (Leah chooses

Reuven's name because "maybe my husband will love me" [Gen. 29:32], and Shimon's because she has despaired of that love: "My husband hates me" [Gen. 29:33].) Evidently, at an early stage in their relationship, Yaakov has high hopes for his bond with Binyamin, unlike his weak bond with Leah's first two sons.

From the very beginning, Yaakov shows a special love and bond with his youngest son. While this is clearly true, as noted above, Yaakov may just be renaming his son to dissociate the boy from his mother's death.

**AFTER THE SALE OF YOSEF**

Yaakov is especially protective of Binyamin, whom he believes to be his only remaining child from Raḥel. For example, he does not send Binyamin to Egypt with his brothers in search of food. Yaakov might have considered Egypt a dangerous foreign land. Hence, he would rather not expose Binyamin to the risks of going there. In fact, when the brothers return from Egypt and explain Yosef's insistence that they bring Binyamin there, Yaakov refuses. He is so determined to shelter Binyamin that he risks his family's wellbeing. Eventually, Yehuda is able to convince Yaakov of the illogic of his position – why spare Binyamin when that risks the wellbeing of the whole family, including Binyamin! Yaakov concedes, but only when his strongest and most reliable son, Yehuda, takes responsibility for Binyamin's welfare.

In Yaakov's refusal to allow Reuven to be responsible for Binyamin, his words give us insight into his feelings for his youngest son. He says, "'My son shall not go down with you; for his brother is dead, and he only is left. If harm happens to him by the way in which you go, then you will bring down my gray hairs with sorrow to my grave'" (Gen. 42:38). Yaakov is acknowledging what we already sense: at this point, Binyamin's unique role is linked to Raḥel and Yosef. As this verse illustrates, Binyamin lives in the shadow of Yosef, specifically as a consequence of Yosef's disappearance. This is summarized in Yaakov's statement regarding his potential sadness if anything were to happen to Binyamin.

Even more striking than this citation, Yehuda's oration to Yosef in Egypt portrays the relationship between Yaakov and Binyamin since the sale of Yosef: "We said to my lord, 'We have a father, an old man, and a child of his old age, a little one; and his brother is dead, and he alone is left of his mother; and his father loves him.' You said to your servants, 'Bring him down to me, that I may set my eyes on him.' We said to my lord, 'The boy cannot leave his father: for if he should leave his father, his father would die'" (Gen. 44:20–22).

Yehuda is describing the deep love Yaakov has for Binyamin. In fact, this is the language of love that Yaakov uses to express his affection for Raḥel and Yosef: "Yaakov loved Raḥel" (29:18) and "Now Yisrael loved Yosef more than all his children" (37:3). This straightforward assertion of love is never utilized to describe Yaakov's relationship with his other wives or children.[4] Yaakov's love for these two sons connects to his singular love for their mother. Then, when Yaakov experiences the sudden tragic death of Raḥel in childbirth followed by Yosef's supposed death, he pours the collective love for them into Binyamin. Their bond is so strong that without Binyamin, Yaakov sees no purpose to go on living; he would die from the sorrow of his loss.

What happens to that love and to that relationship once Yaakov is reunited with Yosef? How does Yosef's return impact Yaakov's bond with Binyamin? Unfortunately, the Torah provides us with no interactions between Yaakov and Binyamin from this point forth. We are left wondering, with no clear resolution.

### BINYAMIN'S PERSONALITY

When reviewing Binyamin's appearances in the book of Genesis, we are struck by his passivity. What do we know about his life? Binyamin's birth is impactful (his mother dies), but he is passive in the process. Later, when his brothers want to take him down to Egypt, Binyamin utters not a word (Yaakov does the talking on his behalf). He plays no active role in that episode. Even later, when the situation is desperate and their father permits Yehuda to take him, Binyamin is silent. When he is eventually brought down to Egypt, he is listed among the objects

4. The only other time that the root *alef, heh, beit* is used with regard to Yaakov's family is in comparing the superior love of Yaakov towards Raḥel in comparison to Leah: "He loved also Raḥel more than Leah" (29:30). In effect, the depiction of a loving relationship is between Yaakov and Raḥel; his affection for Leah is less intense.

and items (not the people): "The men took that present, and they took double money in their hand, and Binyamin" (43:15). When they arrive in Egypt, Binyamin's mere presence transforms Yosef's emotional state, compelling him to leave the room and cry (43:29–30). Binyamin does nothing in particular to elicit this response. He stands there, evidently clueless about Yosef's emotional response. What happens next? Yosef presents Binyamin with five times as many gifts as he does to the other brothers (43:34). This generosity elicits no reaction from Binyamin. Throughout these episodes, Binyamin is part of the narrative only in a passive manner.

Amazingly, even when his own life is at stake, Binyamin does nothing. When Yosef's goblet is discovered in Binyamin's bag and he is consequently sentenced to a severe punishment (a lifetime of slavery), Binyamin is silent! Presumably, he does do the same begging and falling on his face, pleading with Yosef, as do the other brothers. However, at no point does Binyamin attempt to defend himself or beseech Yosef's compassion.

This all seems baffling! How can he not say a word? Why would he not try to defend himself? It seems that Binyamin completely relies on his brothers for his rescue. Perhaps, he is so confident in them (particularly Yehuda) that he feels no need to interject, or perhaps he never developed the life skills required to stand up for himself. Either way, Binyamin is passive.

Binyamin's only act in the book of Genesis is to hug Yosef when Yosef attempts to embrace him. Even this could be perceived as merely yielding since he does not initiate the hug (45:14). In short, Binyamin is compliant, behaving submissively to his father and to his brothers.

### RELATIONSHIP OF BINYAMIN AND YOSEF

It is natural that the two orphaned sons of Raḥel would share a special bond. They suffer the traumatic loss of their mother. As the children of their father's favorite wife, Yosef and Binyamin are favored by their father. Yaakov attempts to compensate for their loss by showering them with excessive affection, but his feelings for them and treatment of them isolate them from the other brothers (and in Yosef's case, it's clear that this paternal favoritism makes them resent him). Until the moment that

Yosef is sold, their relationship must be especially close; perhaps Yosef even stepped up as a parental figure for Binyamin during those early years.

This might explain why Yosef insists that the brothers bring Binyamin. He wants to see him and make sure that he is well in spite of being in the care of the other brothers, who had orchestrated Yosef's expulsion from the family largely because of his status as the favorite son. Yosef conditions their survival on seeing Binyamin, and he gets his way.

As noted above, Binyamin's reaction to the meeting is muted. What is Yosef's reaction? In two instances, the Torah notes that Yosef "sees" Binyamin: "When Yosef saw Binyamin with them" (43:16) and "He lifted up his eyes, and saw Binyamin, his brother, his mother's son" (43:29). Yosef connects to his brother and associates their bond back to their mother, Raḥel. "Yosef made haste; for his heart yearned over his brother: and he sought a place to weep; and he entered into his room and wept there. He washed his face and came out." (43:30–31). Yosef's reaction is passionate and intense. As noted earlier, Yosef then gives Binyamin more gifts than he gives to the other brothers. He hides his goblet in Binyamin's bag, potentially to ensure Binyamin remains with him forever. We don't know if Yosef plans to send everyone else back to Canaan, but he seems intent on keeping Binyamin with him. Later, after revealing his true identity, Yosef's first hug is with Binyamin (45:14). Lastly, when Yosef introduces some of his brothers to Pharaoh, rabbinic tradition[5] assumes that Binyamin must be among that group of brothers. Evidently, Yosef wants to introduce his beloved younger brother to Pharaoh.

The genuine love that Yosef feels for Binyamin is unmistakable. However, because of Binyamin's passive responses, it is hard to ascertain whether Binyamin feels the same way. Of course, there is certainly potential for Binyamin to love Yosef because of the circumstances that made Yosef an almost parental figure in Binyamin's life.[6]

With that as context, let's consider what role, if any Binyamin might have played in the sale of Yosef. Was Binyamin present with the other brothers when it happened? Did he witness the whole ordeal? Did he participate?

---

5. Genesis Rabba 95.
6. See Rashi on Gen. 43:30, according to which Binyamin named his ten sons in remembrance of Yosef.

Theoretically, if Binyamin were present with the other brothers on that fateful day, it would still be difficult to assume that he approved of their treatment of Yosef. Recall that Binyamin is a passive figure who defers to his older brothers in every other life event, including those where his own life is at risk; therefore, even if he had been present, his mere presence would not have been an indication of his personal feelings.

There is a rabbinic tradition[7] that firmly asserts Binyamin was not there when the brothers sold Yosef. What motivates, or at least supports, this tradition?

The first support for this theory is Yosef's treatment of Binyamin in later stories. In all of the later stories, he shows no ill will towards Binyamin. In fact, he embraces him in a way that suggests that he views Binyamin as a victim, much like himself. Regarding the other brothers, Yosef throws them in jail, calls them spies, and plays mind games with them. In contrast, Yosef simply shows Binyamin love and care.

The second support for this theory is viewing the story from Binyamin's perspective. After Yosef's disappearance, Binyamin stays home with Yaakov. How could Binyamin live with his father, observing his constant sadness at the loss of Yosef, and keep that secret? Presumably, he is unaware that Yosef is still alive. Further, a close reading of Yehuda's oration implies that the brothers need to keep the secret about Yosef from Binyamin. Specifically, Yehuda initially tells Yosef: "One of our brothers is missing," circumventing the truthful situation that Yosef is gone because they sold him (Gen. 42:13). However, when Yehuda later repeats this story to Yosef, he claims that they had told him, "Our brother is dead" (44:20). Why would Yehuda insist on keeping the truth hidden in the second instance? Perhaps it is because Binyamin is present for the second iteration. Yehuda needs to maintain the lie that Yosef is dead when in front of Binyamin. Perhaps this is because Binyamin was not present on that fateful day when Yosef was sold; Binyamin believes that a wild animal devoured Yosef on his journey to check on his brothers in the field.

Let us now turn to Binyamin's age, which is another key factor in considering Binyamin's role in the sale of Yosef.

---

7. See Megilla 16b and Genesis Rabba 99:1, quoted in Rashi on Gen. 45:12.

## AGE OF BINYAMIN

There is a large gap of time between the births of the other brothers and Binyamin. All of the others are born while Yaakov and his family live with Lavan in Ḥaran. After the birth of Yosef, Yaakov decides to return home to his father. Binyamin is the only child who is born during their travel to Israel. How many years younger is Binyamin than the other brothers? Throughout all the stories, they refer to him as the "*katan*," "small one," or "*naar*," "young boy," implying that he is still a child.[8] However, many years pass between these various stories, making it difficult to believe that he is really a child in all of them. Rabbinic tradition offers two ways of calculating the age of Binyamin.

One approach, presented in Numbers Rabba 14:8, is that Binyamin's name is the source for calculating his age. Yaakov named him "Binyamin," "*ben*" meaning "son of" and "*yamin*" meaning "right" (i.e., my right hand). The Hebrew letters of "*yamin*," *yud, mem, nun,* numerically total one hundred (*yud*=10, *mem*=40, and *nun*=50), which could imply that Yaakov was one hundred years old when Binyamin was born. Accordingly, since we know that Yaakov was one hundred and thirty when the family moved to Egypt (Gen. 47:9), Binyamin would be thirty years old at that point.

*Seder Olam Rabba* (chapter 2) presents a second way to determine Binyamin's age. There, it is noted that Binyamin is eight years younger than Yosef. How might we know this? Yaakov works for Lavan for seven years for the right to marry Leah and seven more years for the right to Raḥel (Gen. 29:18, 27). After completing these fourteen years of servitude, he works for six more years, as evidenced by Yaakov's remarks to Lavan: "These twenty years have I been with you" (31:38). According to the Sages, Yosef's birth is the event that demarcates the transition from

---

8. The word "*naar*" is used to refer to Yishmael when he is sent away soon after he receives his circumcision at the age of thirteen (Gen. 21:18). Yitzḥak is called a "*naar*" at the story of *akeidat Yitzḥak,* when his father almost sacrifices him to God (22:5, 12). So too, Yeter, Gidon's son, is called a "*naar*" in the context of him being too scared to kill the enemy (Judges 8:20). Shmuel is referred to as a "*naar*" when his mother makes him a "small coat" and brings him one each year (I Sam 2:18–19). He is obviously still in his growth phase, requiring his mother to make him a larger coat each year. David is teased by Goliat because he is a "*naar*," and it is clear that he is too young to be a soldier and too young to battle Goliat (I Sam. 17:42).

the required fourteen years to the additional six years, as it is assumed that Raḥel marries Yaakov immediately after the deal is made to work for the second unit of seven years. After Yosef's birth, Yaakov works for Lavan, but from a distance (i.e., not under the same conditions as prior to his birth).[9] After these six years, they leave Lavan altogether to journey back to Israel. Their travels include eighteen months in Sukkot (33:17)[10] and six months in Beit El (chapter 35), for a total of eight years. Then Binyamin is born.

If this is true, then at the sale of Yosef, Binyamin is a nine-year-old child.[11] This approach aligns with the understanding that he is a child during this ordeal (and perhaps not even present). However, what about his age during the later stories, when he is still passive and childlike? We know that Yosef is thirty years old during his ascent to Egyptian leadership (41:46). This is followed by seven years of plenty (41:53) and two years of famine (47:18). Accordingly, at the time of their meeting, Yosef is thirty-nine and Binyamin is thirty or thirty-one years old. Obviously, he is no longer a child when he is being "given over" by his father, "taken" by Yehuda, and silent when accused of stealing. However, they all treat him this way and refer to him as one.[12]

It is obvious that the brothers view Binyamin as the kid. Even when he is over thirty years old, with a large family of his own, he is still the baby of the family. Around his family, he acts childish, allowing everyone else to dictate his every move. He takes no responsibility for anything, just like a young child.

While it is true that Binyamin is the baby in the family, when he's away from his older brothers, he likely expresses a personality of his own. Unfortunately, because of this dynamic, his true personality is hidden from us in the stories in the Torah. However, he is often alone with his father, away from the impact of his brothers, where his true personality

9. "It happened, when Raḥel had borne Yosef, that Yaakov said to Lavan, 'Send me away, that I may go to my own place, and to my country'" (30:25).
10. See Rashi on Gen. 33:17.
11. See Gen. 37:2, where the text states that Yosef is seventeen years old at the time of his sale.
12. In Gen. 42:13 they go down to Egypt the first time when Binyamin is thirty years old, and they call him the "small" (i.e., young) one. When the brothers return to try taking him to Egypt, Yehuda refers to him as "the boy" (43:8). Yehuda refers to Binyamin as "young, small boy," or "young one" and in similar terms in his oration to Yosef when begging for Binyamin's life.

could emerge. Thus, we might still glean hints about his attributes from the deathbed blessings of his father. Furthermore, we may not really be able to understand the full meaning of the blessing or the depth of Binyamin's personality until we study his descendants.

### YAAKOV'S BLESSING

> Binyamin is a ravenous wolf. In the morning, he will devour the prey. At evening, he will divide the spoil. (Gen. 49:27)

From everything we know so far about Binyamin, this description is striking and unexpected. Why compare him to the aggressive wolf when his behavior much more closely resembles a passive, peaceful animal? Evidently, there must be another side to Binyamin's personality that Yaakov sees. However, there is one facet of the wolf that does resonate with the version of Binyamin that we are already familiar with: The wolf acts quietly when sneaking up on its prey. This silent, seemingly passive feature does resemble Binyamin. In the future, his descendants will be individuals who are quiet and operate alone, like the lone wolf.

### MOSHE'S BLESSING

> Of Binyamin he said: "The beloved of God shall dwell in safety by him; He covers him all the day long, He dwells between his shoulders." (Deut. 33:12)

Fascinatingly, Moshe's description of the tribe of Binyamin is the beautiful blessing that we would have expected from Yaakov. Binyamin is so beloved that even God wants to dwell with him. This fits Binyamin's place in the family as the baby whom everyone circles around.

Combining the two blessings presents a dual nature to Binyamin. There is a side of him that sneaks up and attacks, as described by Yaakov, and there is the peaceful and beloved component, as described by Moshe. We will encounter both sets of characteristics among Binyamin's progeny. The pinnacle of Binyamin's trajectory is when his tribe is chosen to house the Temple. We will have to explore why this tribe's land is the best fit for the central station of religious life among the nation.

## *Chapter 18*

# Binyamin in Tanakh

Apart from the slight glimmers of Binyamin's personality that shine through the stories in Genesis and the blessings bestowed on him, where Yaakov describes his tribe as sneaky and clever, like a ravenous wolf who hunts his prey, we are left relying heavily on other stories in Tanakh to piece together a more nuanced understanding of Binyamin.

In fact, a pattern emerges among Binyamin's descendants. His children are sly and devious leaders, as Yaakov's blessing predicts. However, many of them are passive, like Binyamin in Genesis, and rely heavily on others or need coaxing into action. When they do act, they choose to operate on their own, resembling Binyamin's own isolationism in Genesis.

## BINYAMIN'S PROGENY

### Ehud

Binyamin's prototypical descendant is Ehud son of Gera, the second leader during the period of the book of Judges (Judges 3:15–30). During this time, the Jewish people are under the control of King Eglon of Moab, who has succeeded in penetrating Israel's defenses and capturing Ir HaTemarim, a city inside the territory of the tribe of Binyamin.

Sadly, nobody comes to Binyamin's aid to remove the enemy, so Ehud must rescue his tribe.

In response to Moab's control over Israel, Ehud is a member of the delegation representing the Jewish people, offering peace gestures and gifts to King Eglon. Ehud is not the primary leader, but rather is part of a select representation of the people.

During his encounter with Eglon, Ehud distinguishes himself from the rest of his group. After presenting the king with a gift, Ehud separates himself from the others and requests a private meeting with the king. Pretending to have an important message from God, he tricks the king into sending away all of his soldiers. The two of them are alone in a secluded room.

Why would a king allow himself to be alone in a room with a man from a rival nation? This is plausible only if Ehud had already succeeded in creating a bond of trust with the king. Eglon forgets that Ehud is the enemy. Ehud takes advantage of this bond and sneaks a knife into the palace for their encounter. How was he able to hide this knife? Typically, people are right-handed and carry their swords on the left side their bodies. Therefore, Ehud knew that the guards would check the left side of his body for weapons. The text informs us that Ehud was left-handed (Judges 3:15) and therefore could hide a knife on his right side, confident that the guards would not search there.[1]

Once alone with Eglon, Ehud waits for the optimal opportunity to attack. When King Eglon rises to hear Ehud's alleged message from God, Ehud takes advantage of the opportunity to stab him in the stomach. Knowing that Eglon is obese, Ehud stabs him in the abdomen in such way that the knife is swallowed inside Eglon's stomach. He leaves the knife inside of Eglon's body to minimize the unavoidable splatter of blood. Having successfully avoided suspicion, Ehud leaves the room, locks the door and escapes.

1. Ehud, who was so meticulous in all the details of the plan, would risk going into the palace with a knife only if he knew that they would not check the right side of his garments for it. This assumes that Ehud had previously been in the palace to visit the king and bring him presents.

The wolf-like qualities of Binyamin are exposed in this story. The first component of this is the loner element of his tactics. Every part of Ehud's plan is self-coordinated without the knowledge of his peers. As the text emphasizes, "He sent away the people who bore the tribute. But he himself turned back" (Judges 3:18–19). He doesn't tell anyone about his plan before he attacks the enemy's king, though his compatriots could have benefited from the extra time to gather an army while he was in the palace. Why does he carry out the assassination of King Eglon single-handedly? This was done either to protect the others in case the plan failed, or to facilitate a more efficient escape path. Or, perhaps, he didn't really trust the other delegates. After he escapes, there is no partner awaiting the success of his attack. Rather, he gathers the army to lead them into battle only after killing the king.

The second component of the tribe's qualities is wolf-like cunning. Ehud's detailed plan perfectly considers how best to take the enemy by complete surprise. Each aspect, including how to hide his knife and build Eglon's trust, is planned meticulously to ensure maximum success while minimizing any evidence of his crime.

This component is equally exhibited in the escape plan, a vital process for him to save the Jewish nation. He has to return home quickly, notify the Jewish people of the king's death, gather an army, and attack Moab – all while the enemy is unprepared and disorganized by the shocking discovery of the murder of its leader. If Ehud's exit takes too long or if he is captured, Moab will reorient itself and appoint new leadership that will facilitate a prolonged subjugation of the Jewish nation. His plot would then offer no help to the Jewish people! How does he escape successfully?

After assassinating Eglon, Ehud walks out of the room and simply locks the door behind him. He knows that the guards would assume that a locked door means the king is relieving himself in the restroom (Judges 3:24).[2] This waiting period allows Ehud the necessary time to walk right out of the palace gates without raising any suspicion. He knows that the servants and guards will not attempt to open the door – for walking in

2. This detail is another proof that Ehud has been to the palace many times and knows how the guards act when the king's door is locked.

on Eglon in a compromised situation would lead to severe personal punishment. And so, "They waited until they were ashamed" (3:25): They wait as long as possible, until it would be embarrassing for the king to still be relieving himself. When there is finally no choice other than to unlock and open the door to enquire about his wellbeing, they discover his dead body on the floor. "Behold, their lord was fallen down dead on the earth" (3:25). The verse describes Eglon as "dead" and not "killed" to reveal that a major part of Ehud's plan was to make it look like the king died of natural causes. They likely called the royal physician to examine him, thus providing Ehud with even more time to escape. By the time they confirm that the king has indeed been murdered, Ehud is a far distance away from the palace, well on his way to gather the Jewish people for battle.

Binyamin's quiet and passive elements are also displayed in Ehud's character. He is quiet and unassuming until the moment he slays Eglon. The other members of the delegation think nothing of his departure from the group to return to the palace. When there, he does not raise the guards' suspicions, and he is so trustworthy that the king easily orders all his servants to leave the room. He blends in as a passive figure who is comfortable in the background. In fact, after this episode and his subsequent successful leadership in a war against Moab, he does not lead the Jewish people. Unlike other judges who lead the nation in battle and then retain their leadership, the text never says that Ehud judges the Jewish people for the rest of his life. Rather, the story concludes with the words, "The land had rest for eighty years" (3:30), implying that he is not the designated leader; he returns home and resumes the life he led before this episode.[3]

Ehud embodies so much of what we know about Binyamin. He alone eliminates the enemy's king through his wily, wolf-like skills. He pretends to be an ally until the last moment, when he pounces and attacks. Although Ehud's personality generally reflects Binyamin's amicable one in Genesis, his actions verify Yaakov's description of his tribe as a "ravenous wolf who attacks his prey" (Gen. 49:27).

---

3. The phrase "*vayishpot et Yisrael*," "and he judged the Jewish people," is absent from the description of Ehud. This phrase is found in the stories of Otniel (Judges 3:10), Devora (4:4), Tola (10:2), Yair (10:3), Yiftaḥ (12:7), Ivtzan (12:8,9), Eilon (12:11), Avdon (12:13, 14), Shimshon (15:20, 16:31), Eli (I Sam. 4:18), and Shmuel (I Sam. 7:15).

## The Concubine at Giva

After receiving no aid from their neighboring tribes either in conquering their land (Judges 1:21) or in removing King Eglon from their land (thus requiring Ehud's heroic act, described above), the tribe of Binyamin grows detached from the rest of the Jewish people.

These feelings of loneliness and abandonment from the other tribes reach a crescendo in Judges 19 and 20. These chapters begin with the story of a Levite living in the land of Ephraim with a concubine from the tribe of Yehuda. The concubine flees from the Levite, returning to her father's home in the land of Yehuda. The Levite travels from the land of Ephraim through the land of Binyamin to the land of Yehuda in an effort to bring her back home. He is successful, and on their way back to return to the Levite's home in the land of Ephraim, night falls while they are stranded in the land of Binyamin. No one from the tribe extends an invitation! An old man, originally from the land of Ephraim, allows them to eat and sleep in his home. That evening, shortly after they finish eating, there is a knock at the door. A group of men from the tribe of Binyamin, acting like a pack of wolves, demand access to the guests in order to rape the concubine and kill the Levite. How does the Levite react? He forces his concubine out the door, to a night of rape and torture from these men of Binyamin.[4]

This appalling behavior from a small group of Binyaminite men probably does not fully display the values of the entire tribe. However, the episode does expose another, broader issue: members of the tribe of Binyamin view people from other tribes as outsiders.[5] In fact, when the nation's representatives approach the tribe of Binyamin asking them to hand over the perpetrators, the tribal leaders refuse. "But Binyamin would not listen to the voice of their brothers, the children of Israel" (Judges 20:13). The language of "brothers" highlights the Binyaminites'

---

4. The behavior of these men from Binyamin resembles the characteristics of the men of Sodom, as described by the Sages. "Now the men of Sodom were exceedingly wicked and sinners against God" (Gen. 13:13). A gang of men from Sodom knock on Lot's door demanding that he give them his guests, thus paralleling this story. However, in our story, the evil men are Jewish people, as opposed to the people of Sodom, who are not and are wiped out by God as a result of their immoral ways.
5. This is reflected in the story when no one from the tribe would invite the Levite into their home.

lack of brotherly feelings towards the greater nation. Their priority is to stand up for the transgressors, whom they view as their "brothers."

This event precipitates a devastating civil war between the tribe of Binyamin and the rest of the Jewish people. When the battle is over, only six hundred men from Binyamin are still alive.

The nation, which had sworn not to allow their daughters to marry into Binyamin, eventually relents, allowing the remaining six hundred Binyaminite men to marry women from other tribes.[6] Although the tribe is saved from annihilation, the damage is done. In retrospect, only a tribe that is so isolated from the rest of the nation could become the target of such violent retribution.

## Shaul

King Shaul, the first king of the Jewish people and a Binyaminite, embodies many of his tribe's traits. His leadership is passive; he does not originally want to lead and is happy to rely on others to do his job.

Shaul's public career begins when the prophet Shmuel informs him of his selection as king of Israel. Does this news excite him? He insists it must be a mistake, especially because he is from the tribe of Binyamin. "Shaul answered, Am I not a Binyaminite, of the smallest of the tribes of Israel? And [is not] my family the least of all the families of the tribe of Binyamin? Why do you speak to me about this matter?" (I Sam 9:21). To convince Shaul that he is God's true choice, Shmuel offers a series of predictions.[7] While initially rejecting a prophet's message and insisting

---

6. The book of Judges concludes with details of how they resolve the issue of finding wives for the six hundred unmarried men from Binyamin after they had sworn never to let any of their daughters marry the survivors of the tribe. At first, they allow the men from Binyamin to marry the surviving women of Jabesh-Gilead, a city that didn't join the war. This solution applies to four hundred of the six hundred men. The remaining unmarried men are then permitted to select wives from the other tribes (Judges 21).
7. The three predictions are:
   (1) Shaul will meet two men who are able to tell him that his father's donkeys have been found.
   (2) Shaul will meet three men carrying food and wine, who will greet him and offer him food (bread).
   (3) Shaul will encounter a group of prophets who are actively prophesying; he will start to prophesy as well.

on signs is fairly common in Tanakh,[8] Shaul's approach is atypical in the severity of his refusal. Even after he is privately anointed and all three predictions are actualized, he hides the news of his ascension, not even telling his uncle, whom he meets on his way home: "But concerning the matter of the kingdom, whereof Shmuel spoke, he did not tell him" (I Sam. 10:16). Subsequently, when the prophet is supposed to formalize the coronation by picking his name from the lottery in front of the entire Jewish people, the unexpected occurs: "But when they sought him, he could not be found" (10:21). Knowing that he is about to be pronounced king of Israel, Shaul hides in a closet.[9] They only find him through divine intervention: "He has hidden himself among the baggage" (10:22). Shaul is so petrified of his new role that he attempts to evade his own coronation.

Shaul's reign is plagued by lack of centralized monarchical control and his lack of ownership over his actions on behalf of the nation and himself. At the very beginning of his reign, Shmuel orders Shaul to wait seven days and then offer a joint offering to God (on behalf of Shmuel and Shaul) before fighting the Philistines. However, when Shmuel is late, Shaul brings the offering on his own. Shmuel admonishes Shaul for not waiting for him. What is Shaul's reaction? He blames everyone but himself: "Shaul said, 'Because I saw that the people were scattered from me, and that you didn't come within the days appointed, and that the Philistines assembled themselves together at Mikhmash'" (13:11).

Not long after this, Shaul disobeys God's command to fully destroy Amalek, showing mercy to the king and some animals. Again,

---

8. For example, Moshe and Gidon each say that they are undeserving and unable to lead, and both receive three signs as well. Moshe says, "Who am I, that I should go to Pharaoh, and that I should bring forth the children of Israel out of Egypt?" (Ex. 3:11). God answers by giving him three signs: (1) his stick turns into a snake, (2) his hand becomes leprous, and (3) water turns to blood. Gidon also claims, "Oh, Lord, with which shall I save Israel? Behold, my family is the poorest in Menashe, and I am the least in my father's house" (Judges 6:15). Similarly, God provides three signs: (1) a fire comes down from the sky to burn his food offering, (2) water fills the cotton but the threshing floor remains dry, and (3) the next day, the cotton is dry and the threshing floor is wet.
9. When he is found in the closet, a group of men show him disrespect: "But certain worthless fellows said, 'How shall this man save us?' They despised him and brought him no present" (10:27).

Shaul blames his transgression on others when he argues, "I have transgressed the commandment of God, and your words, because I feared the people and obeyed their voice" (15:24).

This tribal characteristic to fear positions of leadership is depicted in two more episodes. Shaul is scared to lead the Jewish people in battle. At each battle, someone else leads in his stead.

The first episode is in I Sam. 13, where Shmuel rebukes Shaul. Sadly, without Shmuel, Shaul is so petrified to lead the battle against Philistines that he freezes, unable to lead the nation into battle. In the end, Yonatan, Shaul's son, leads the military in battle, putting his father at ease and thus enabling him to join the battle.[10]

By the conclusion of this episode – where Yonatan steps into the role of his father – Shaul has lost an element of his hierarchical leadership. For example, Shaul commands his men not to eat. If anyone eats, asserts Shaul, they will be punished by death. Yonatan doesn't hear his father's ruling. During the battle, he eats some honey to renew his strength and thereby enable himself to continue fighting. When God notifies Shaul of Yonatan's crime, Shaul declares that Yonatan must die. He is unable to take back his words, too scared that it will undermine his authority. But the nation interferes and threatens Shaul: "The people said to Shaul, 'Shall Yonatan die, who has performed this great salvation in Israel? Far from it: as God lives, one hair of his head shall not fall to the ground for he has worked with God this day.' So, the people rescued Yonatan; he did not die" (14:45). The people argue with the king, showing they are not afraid of him. They are able to intimidate him into allowing Yonatan to live. Shaul is a king without the authority of a king.

The second episode revealing Shaul's reluctance to act as a leader is in I Sam. 17. Goliat challenges a Jewish warrior to fight him to the death. Shaul, who is described as tall ("From his shoulders and upward he was

10. The story of Yonatan and how he too has the personality traits of Binyamin will be discussed later in this chapter. Although in this story he actively gets up to fight, he fits the role of a Binyamin figure as he only steps up when needed, when everyone is in hiding, too terrified to act. Somewhat reminiscent of Ehud, Yonatan approaches the enemy and engages them in battle, accompanied only by his weapon carrier. Only after his small victory does the rest of the nation, including Shaul, join in to fight.

taller than any of the people" [I Sam. 9:2]), refuses to step up. Instead, he offers to reward the soldier who is willing to fight Goliat in his stead. David offers to battle the giant and is eventually selected. Shaul dresses David in his own armor, including his royal sword (17:38–39). David is both symbolically and literally stepping into King Shaul's role. Alternatively, Shaul wants the people to believe that he – Shaul – is the valiant warrior, consistent with his royal position.

At this point, Shaul loses even more respect from his people. After the war ends, "The women sang one to another as they played, and said, 'Shaul has slain thousands, David has slain tens of thousands!'" (I Sam. 18:7).

Shaul is plagued by the passivity endemic to Binyamin's family. He fears being a leader. He prefers to rely on subordinates such as Yonatan and David to perform his roles. Ironically, once introduced to the power of being king, he struggles not to relinquish it. Instead of shying away from leadership, he becomes obsessed with it.

**Yonatan**

The best elements of Binyamin's personality are manifest in the inspiring stories of Shaul's son, Yonatan. He has every reason to harbor animosity towards David, his principal contender for Shaul's attention and, eventually, his throne. But instead of envy or rage, Yonatan extends only love and friendship to David. This is reminiscent of Binyamin, who never seems to be envious or irritated by the favoritism showered upon Yosef. Even though Yosef and Binyamin are both children of Raḥel, Yosef is clearly the favorite.[11] In spite of this imbalance, Binyamin never shows any resentment towards Yosef. Upon Yosef's reuniting with their father, Binyamin steps out of the limelight, respecting Yosef's place in the family.

Relatedly, Yonatan's care for David is extraordinary. They first meet when David uses his music to calm the king's sour moods. Over time, the relationship between David and King Shaul develops, and the text states that "he loved him greatly." Shaul promotes David to be

11. "Now Yisrael loved Yosef more than all his children" (Gen. 37:3), including Binyamin. Yosef receives a special colored coat, symbolizing his preferred status. Never does the text imply that Binyamin has a similar coat.

his personal arms bearer (I Sam. 16:21). For a typical prince and heir apparent, this would be a source of envy and anger. But Yonatan, son of Shaul and heir to the throne, expresses none of those emotions. Furthermore, after David kills Goliat and is praised by the entire nation as the savior of the Jewish people, Yonatan could react defensively out of fear for losing his right to the throne, but he instead reacts lovingly towards David: "The soul of Yonatan was connected with the soul of David, and Yonatan loved him as his own soul" (18:1).

Shortly after David's successful battle against Goliat, Shaul brings him to live in the palace permanently: "Shaul took him that day, and would no more let him go home to his father's house" (18:2). Yonatan certainly could have interpreted this as a literal encroachment on his territory. Yet, their relationship as best friends does not waver. The next verse states, "Then Yonatan and David made a covenant, because he loved him as his own soul" (18:3). Yonatan acts beneficently, well beyond any reasonable expectation: "Yonatan stripped himself of the robe that was on him, and gave it to David, and his clothing, even to his sword, and to his bow, and to his sash" (18:4). Yonatan ceremonially acknowledges that David is the future king of Israel. He graciously hands over the role that was destined for him.[12] Yonatan is content to step aside, allowing David to rule as king.

An even deeper commitment to David is evident when Yonatan asks Shaul why he wants to kill David. Shaul yells back at his son, "For as long as the son of Yishai lives on the earth, you shall not be established, nor your kingdom. Therefore, now send and bring him to me, for he shall surely die" (I Sam. 20:31). Yonatan refuses to hand over David. Instead, he runs to warn David to escape from Shaul. Clearly, Yonatan is happy to facilitate David's rise to leadership, even at his own expense.

Yonatan lacks any jealousy towards David. He is a man of peace who risks his own life to ensure that David is safe, and provides the

12. This might remind us of when Moshe removes Aharon's special ceremonial garb and presents it to his son Elazar, symbolizing his transition in role to high priest after his father (Num. 20:28). Similar language is utilized in both contexts, including the root *peh, shin, tet,* "to remove," when the text speaks of Aharon's clothes being removed and of Yonatan removing his clothes.

opportunity for David to become the appropriate leader of the Jewish nation. Yonatan's experiences remind us of Binyamin's ability to step aside when Yosef takes his rightful place as favorite son of Raḥel and becomes the firstborn of the Jewish people.

**Ishboshet**

Tragically, at the conclusion of the book of I Samuel, Shaul and his three oldest sons, including Yonatan, are killed (I Sam. 31:2). Ishboshet, Yonatan's youngest brother and Shaul's youngest son, is the only prince to survive the war against the Philistines. Therefore, Ishboshet becomes the heir to his father's throne. Sadly, he is weak and easily controlled by his father's chief military officer, the general Avner. In fact, Ishboshet attains the monarchy only because of Avner: "Now Avner the son of Ner, captain of Shaul's host, had taken Ishboshet the son of Shaul and brought him over to Mahanaim; and he made him king over Gilead, and over the Ashurites, and over Jezreel, and over Ephraim, and over Binyamin, and over all Israel" (II Sam. 2:8–9). Ishboshet follows Avner's leadership, listening to his every command.

Just as Avner establishes Ishboshet's leadership, he is the one to undermine it, too. When Ishboshet recognizes Avner's manipulations, he makes bold accusations about Avner – namely that he is lying with King Shaul's concubine (II Sam. 3). In effect, he claims that Avner is trying to act like the king by being intimate with the former king's concubine. How does Avner react? Immediately, he deserts Ishboshet. Avner switches his allegiance to David, and the entire Jewish nation changes allegiance along with him. Without Avner or his leadership, Ishboshet has no one left in his kingdom (II Sam. 3). Evidently, the nation follows and trusts the leadership of Avner, not Ishboshet. As befitting Shaul's son and a member of the tribe of Binyamin, Ishboshet is passive and powerless.

**Mefiboshet**

Mefiboshet is also a peaceful and passive character, thus resembling his grandfather, Yonatan, and his ancestor, Binyamin. He prefers to ignore and forgive injustices rather than confront a villain. Consider what he does when David flees from his rebellious son Avshalom, who wants to depose his father, in II Sam. 16. Everyone chooses an allegiance with one side, and Mefiboshet wants to align himself with David. Unfortunately, because of Mefiboshet's leg impediment, he cannot reach David to pledge his loyalty. Instead, he sends food and drink to David and his army via Tziva, his assistant. But Tziva betrays his master and lies to David. He claims the food is his own and that Mefiboshet's absence is because of his siding with Avshalom. David is enraged and punishes Mefiboshet for his betrayal by decreeing that all of his property be transferred to Tziva. After a short while, David defeats his son and returns to his palace (ch. 19). When Mefiboshet greets him, David questions Mefiboshet about his betrayal. Mefiboshet attempts to correct the situation, assuring David that he received incorrect information and that in fact, he has always been his supporter. Uncertain about the truth, David declares that Mefiboshet and Tziva should divide the land in half.

What is most striking about this story is its conclusion. Mefiboshet does not get angry at David for taking away his land; instead, he complacently accepts the situation. Rather than berating David for believing Tziva, he states, "But my lord the king is as an angel of God: do therefore what is good in your eyes" (II Sam. 19:28). He is composed about David's resolution, even though it mandates that he hand over half of his land to his deceitful servant.

**Mordekhai and Esther**

Two heroes from Binyamin, Mordekhai and Esther, share the same quiet and passive temperament.

Virtually every description of Esther in the first half of the book of Esther focuses on her obedience to those around her. In two instances, she is taken away (Esther 2:8, 16), once to the king's palace to prepare for her encounter with him, and then later to the king's private chambers, all the while never saying a word. She never reveals her identity, as Mordekhai has told her not to (2:10, 20). She asks for nothing (2:15). When she informs the king about an intended coup, she speaks in the name of Mordekhai (2:22). She begins to fight her natural tendencies only after Mordekhai rebukes her. At that point, she mobilizes herself in a grand effort to save the Jewish people (4:13–16).

Interestingly, when her active qualities are manifest, her behavior resembles the wolf-like qualities of Binyamin. How so? By inviting

Haman to a private party, she knowingly manipulates Aḥashverosh's jealousy. She tricks Haman by pretending to be his friend, and then forgoes their bond when he least expects it. Her entire strategy is to turn the king against his most trusted advisor.

Mordekhai is similarly passive. While he insists on sitting by the gates of the palace every day to find out about Esther's welfare, he is powerless to do anything to help her (2:11). When he becomes aware of the plot against Aḥashverosh, Mordekhai instructs Esther to inform the king instead of telling him personally (2:22). Soon after, he angers Haman by refusing to bow to him (3:2) but never actually confronts him. Haman is angered – not by any direct confrontation, but by Mordekhai's lack of sufficient respect for him. Haman doesn't even know who Mordekhai is. When Haman resolves to take revenge on Mordekhai and his people, Mordekhai implores Esther to act, but does nothing to help her. Esther is expected to devise and carry out a plan on her own.[13]

Both Esther and Mordekhai are heroes who save the Jewish people from the evil plot of Haman. However, they do it within the framework of the characteristics of Binyamin, exhibiting a seemingly unlikely combination of passivity, manipulation, and staying in the background until the final moment, when they surprisingly become active.

## THE TEMPLE IN BINYAMIN'S TERRITORY

> Of Binyamin he said: "The beloved of God shall dwell in safety by him; He covers him all the day long, He dwells between his shoulders." (Deut. 33:12)

---

13. In the second half of the story, Mordekhai also learns to become more active. He is promoted into a formal role in the monarchy, wearing the king's ring, and is entrusted with sufficient authority to document his story for posterity. The Talmud in Megilla 12b–13a writes that Mordekhai's father is from the tribe of Binyamin but his mother is from the tribe of Yehuda. This duality helps explain Mordekhai's ability to transition from a passive leader (characteristic of Binyamin) to a stronger, more active leader (characteristic of Yehuda). A possible basis for the Talmud's association with Yehuda might be that Mordekhai is described as "*ish Yehudi*" (Esther 2:5). Likely this means that he is a man with lineage from Yehuda.

God will rest among this tribe – that is Moshe's blessing for Binyamin. True to the blessing, the Holy Temple is built primarily within the territory of Binyamin (with a portion of the Temple in the territory of Yehuda). Even prior to the construction of the Temple, God's presence rests in the territory of Binyamin. Specifically, during the time of Shmuel's leadership, the Ark containing the holy tablets causes a period of unsettled movement. Initially, it is located in the land of Binyamin in Shiloh, but is taken by the Philistines during battle with the Jewish people, after which members of the Philistines start dying. In fact, as they move the Ark from one location to another, local Philistines die at the respective locations. Even when it is returned to the Jewish people, the Ark's presence leads to death until it is returned to a home in the land of Binyamin (I Sam. 7:1). Avinadav, from the tribe of Binyamin, hosts the Ark until King David is ready to move it to the City of David. The Ark remains among the tribe of Binyamin for all those years and is then placed permanently in this tribe's territory in the Temple.

Why is the tribe of Binyamin selected for the special role of housing the physical manifestation of God's presence on this earth? One might have instinctively placed the Temple in the territory of Yehuda or Yosef. Why do the descendants of the quiet loner, the youngest, next-to-favorite son of Yaakov, receive this honor?

### The Peace-Keepers

King Shlomo, the monarch who builds the Temple, is selected by God to do so. Presumably, the location of the Temple is also intentionally selected by God. Perhaps the selection of King Shlomo can offer insight into the selection of Binyamin's territory to house the Temple.

King David explains to his son Shlomo that because of David's involvement in war, God told him he is not entitled to build the Temple:

> It was in my heart to build a house to the name of the Lord my God. But the word of God came to me, saying, "You have shed blood abundantly, and have made great wars: you shall not build a house to My name, because you have shed much blood on the earth in My sight. Behold, a son shall be born to you, who shall be a man of rest; and I will give him rest from all his enemies

> round about; for his name shall be Shlomo, and I will give peace and quietness to Israel in his days: he shall build a house for My name; and he shall be My son, and I will be his father; and I will establish the throne of his kingdom over Israel forever." Now, my son, God be with you; and you will prosper, and build the house of the Lord your God, as He has spoken concerning you. (I Chr. 22:7–11)

Later, King Shlomo repeats his father's words to explain to his ally King Ḥiram, the Phoenician king of Tyre, why David did not build the Temple. "You know that David my father could not build a house for the name of his God for the wars which were about him on every side, until God put them under the soles of his feet. But now God has given me rest on every side; there is neither adversary nor evil occurrence" (I Kings 5:17–18).

Evidently, the Temple must be built during a period of peace by a leader who represents harmony. Therefore, one can extrapolate that the location of the Temple would be selected with a similar message of peace and harmony. It is abundantly logical that the tribe of Binyamin is selected since it is the consummate peacekeeping tribe.[14]

From the beginning, this tribe avoids confrontation, stepping back from opportunities that would create dissension. In Genesis, Binyamin is the next-to-favorite son. Even so, he never mentions this favoritism to his brothers. Unlike Yosef, he never motivates them to rage or envy.[15] Rather, it is possible that as the baby of the family, he is universally loved by his brothers. His brothers divide into factions (according to their mothers and their ages), but as the motherless youngest, Binyamin appears to be outside of these divisions. Older siblings commonly love and cherish the baby of the family; in Yaakov's family, the brothers fuss over Binyamin even when he is grown. They view him as the baby who requires the protection of older brothers.

---

14. There is a small group of men from Binyamin who act violently in the story of the concubine at Giva; however, the majority of the tribe tries to avoid confrontation by refusing to hand over the perpetrators.
15. Regarding Yosef, see Gen. 37:4, 5, 8, 11.

Binyamin is the only child of Yaakov not contaminated by the tensions with, and eventually the sale of, Yosef. The Sages infer that Binyamin is rewarded with hosting the Temple because of his non-involvement in selling Yosef.[16] What is the evidence of this connection? In Psalms, King David says, "Why do you look in envy, you peaked mountains, at the mountain where God chooses to reign? Yes, God will dwell there forever" (Psalms 68:17). The Hebrew word for "peaked," "*gavnunim,*" has two meanings – to peak or to steal. The former is the literal usage in Psalms but the latter evokes the imagery of Yosef's accusation of his brothers, "*Ganov ganavti,*" "I was stolen" (Gen. 40:15). Stealing and selling their brother signifies that the other brothers are inappropriate hosts for the Temple. By dint of not being present at the sale of Yosef, Binyamin is still worthy of this honor. Binyamin is the peaceful brother. He would not sell Yosef, both because of his internal goodness and because he lacks jealousy towards him. His attributes therefore make him a worthy host of the Temple.

When his two central characteristics – passivity and harmony – are in tension, rabbinic tradition presumes that Binyamin opts out of his usual passive role to ensure harmony in the home of Yaakov. In other words, in spite of his passivity, Binyamin steps outside of his comfort zone to ensure a peaceful home. How so? According to tradition, Binyamin is responsible for actively facilitating harmony between Yaakov and his sons. As per this tradition, Binyamin discovers the truth about the brothers selling Yosef yet he remains quiet because he does not want his father to curse or excommunicate his brothers.[17] Binyamin refrains from sharing this information to keep the peace in his family.

This may also explain why Binyamin remains silent during periods of tension. For example, he is mute when the brothers fight with Yaakov regarding the need to take Binyamin to Egypt. Next, he is voiceless when the brothers argue with Yosef to free him. If he doesn't have a way to increase harmony, Binyamin avoids confrontation even when he is the center of the fight.

Binyamin's descendants are the keepers of the peace. Recall that Ehud is a member of the delegation sent to deliver gifts to King Eglon

16. Genesis Rabba 99:1 quoted in Rashi on Gen. 45:12.

17. Genesis Rabba 72:8 quoted in Rabbenu Baḥya on Gen. 37:33.

as a peace gesture with Moab. Later, unlike most competitors for leadership positions, Yonatan never clashes with David over being the next in line for the monarchy, even when it is clear that David may supersede him. He goes out of his way to attempt to make peace between David and King Shaul.

**Yehuda and Yosef**

A second element that makes Binyamin's territory a perfect home for God's Temple is hinted to in the words of Moshe, "He dwells between his shoulders" (Deut. 33:12). Binyamin's land is sandwiched between the tribes of Yehuda and Yosef. The relevance of this placement is reinforced later when the tribe of Binyamin is allocated its land: "The lot of the tribe of the children of Binyamin came up according to their families: and the border of their lot went out between the children of Yehuda and the children of Yosef" (Josh. 18:11). God purposely situates Binyamin between the two leadership tribes.[18]

These relationships were formed much earlier. In Genesis, we observe that Binyamin has a close relationship with both Yosef and Yehuda. As we noted previously, Binyamin and Yosef are born to the same mother, both favored by their father and both suffer the same loss of their mother when she dies. Yosef may have helped raise Binyamin in their mother's stead. Later, Yosef creates a ploy to force the brothers to bring Binyamin to Egypt and then tries to keep him there forever. Yosef cries when he sees Binyamin and embraces him first after finally revealing his true identity. Yosef and Binyamin's relationship is distinct and deep.

Additionally, we find Binyamin forging a special relationship with Yehuda. Recall that Yehuda is responsible to care for his youngest brother in Egypt. Yehuda risks his own life when begging for Binyamin's safe return.

Throughout history, the tribe of Binyamin maintains strong connections with both of these tribes. Binyamin is included within the encampment of Yosef (Num. 2:22), traveling through the desert

18. Interestingly, the book of Judges presents the first three judges in this specific order: Otniel from Yehuda, Ehud from Binyamin, and then Devora from Ephraim (son of Yosef).

together with the descendants of his older brother. Later in history, however, Binyamin joins the kingdom of Yehuda to fight the kingdom of Yorovam, who is from the tribe of Ephraim, thereby fighting against Yosef (I Kings 12:21).

Because of his having developed deep relationships with both Yehuda and Yosef, Binyamin can be a bridge between these two strong tribes. The Temple in his territory is thus in a neutral location, where both Yosef and Yehuda can feel comfortable serving God. Even though there are many instances of fighting between these two brothers' tribes, Binyamin's territory is purposely placed right between them to be the neutral zone where both sides would be welcome.

**Unifier of the Nation**

Not only can Binyamin serve as a safe location for the two leadership tribes, it is the only tribe with the capacity to unite all twelve tribes. From his early beginnings in Genesis, Binyamin is the only brother loved and cherished by all of the others. While the children of Leah resent Yosef and mock the maidservants' children, Binyamin, as baby of the family, is everyone's favorite. All of the brothers return to the house of Yosef to plead on his behalf. When that proves unsuccessful, they fall on their faces in despair. They are devastated at the idea that he may not return home with them and the effect this would have on their father.

Throughout history, Binyamin is the tribe that brings the nation together. One instance occurs under the rule of Shaul (from the tribe of Binyamin). The people of Jabesh-Gilead are under attack by Naḥash, king of Amon. Shaul responds by organizing an army, requiring everyone to participate. He threatens to eradicate the flock of anyone who does not join him in saving the people of Jabesh-Gilead. How does the nation react? "They came out as one man" (I Sam. 11:7). After their victory, the Jewish people unite again to celebrate the crowning of Shaul as their king: "All the people went to Gilgal; and there they made Shaul king before God in Gilgal; and there they offered sacrifices of peace-offerings before God; and there Shaul and all the men of Israel rejoiced greatly" (11:15).

A second occasion of national unity occurs during the epoch of the judges. The central challenge of that period is the disunity amongst the tribes. Ironically, to fight against the atrocity committed by the gang from Binyamin, the other tribes gather "as one man" (Judges 20:1). These words are repeated only a few verses later: "All the people arose as one man, saying, we will not any of us go to his tent, neither will we any of us turn to his house" (v. 8). It is repeated one more time: "So all the men of Israel were gathered against the city, together as one man, friends" (v. 11). After the war ends, they all gather to find a solution to save the tribe of Binyamin from extinction.

In both of these instances, the key phrase – "as one man" – is repeated to highlight the unity of the people.[19]

The third instance of national unity occurs during the lives of Mordekhai and Esther (from the tribe of Binyamin). The Talmud (Shabbat 88a) explains that the words "*Kiyemu vekibbelu,*" "[The Jews] ordained and took upon themselves" (Esther 9:27), suggest that this generation of Jews was united in re-accepting the Torah upon themselves, i.e., that they are again accepting now what had already been accepted at the time of the revelation at Sinai. In short, it is under the leadership of Binyamin that the Jewish people unite to retake upon themselves all the laws of the Torah.

The Temple is the one place where the entire Jewish nation is enjoined to unite together "as one man, friends." Three times a year – on Sukkot, Pesaḥ, and Shavuot – the people are commanded to leave their homes to celebrate with God in His home. In fact, beyond the unity of the Jewish people, God's Temple is a place of unity for all of humanity.[20] The tribe of Binyamin, the source of national unity throughout history, is the perfect location for the House of God.

---

19. Not surprisingly, Rashi on Ex. 19:2 borrows this phrase to describe the unique unity of the Jewish people at the revelation at Sinai, when he states: "They stood together as one man, all friends."

20. Verses that support this idea include the following: "For My house shall be called a house of prayer for all nations" (Is. 56:7); "It will happen that the mountain of God's temple will be established on the top of the mountains, and it will be exalted above the hills, and peoples will stream to it. Many nations will go and say, 'Come, and let us go up to the mountain of God and to the house of the God of Yaakov, and He will teach us of His ways, and we will walk in His paths'" (Mikha 4:1–2); "All nations You have made will come and worship before You, Lord…" (Psalms 86:9).

## CONCLUSION

Binyamin, the youngest son of Yaakov, plays a passive role among his brothers in Genesis. Out of all twelve tribes, it is his territory that becomes the religious and spiritual center of the Jewish people. Why is Binyamin, of all of the tribes, given this great honor? We suggested various explanations; however, in truth, there is not just one reason. Rather, it is the collective weight of these explanations that warrants Binyamin's housing the holy Ark in the time of Avinadav, the Tabernacle of Shiloh, and ultimately the Temple. First, Binyamin is the peacemaker in the family, just as his descendants ensure peace and harmony among the Jewish people. The Temple of God must dwell in a peaceful environment, making all nations of the world feel comfortable worshiping there. In addition, Binyamin is the bridge between the two great leadership tribes of Yosef and Yehuda. To ensure that both tribes can join together, the Temple ought to be located in a tribal land that both tribes can appreciate. Moreover, Binyamin, the youngest child who is beloved by all, is the only tribe who can unify all of the Jewish people. For all of these reasons, Binyamin is blessed to have the House of God permanently in its territory.

# *Conclusion*

This book was born out of a desire to share the texture of life in the patriarch Yaakov's family and the impact of each family member's natural proclivities, experiences, and choices on the family and the family's descendants. Each person is complicated and multifaceted. This is true for each of Yaakov's wives as much as for his children. As unique individuals, they each develop their own behaviors and patterns. In this book I sought to convey the vitality of the tribes, which I've been blessed to observe while studying and teaching about their lives and impact.

As we expanded beyond the patriarch Yaakov's nuclear family, I intended for this book to share the ways that each tribe's unique traits are reflected in his descendants. The tribes are not just a random amalgam of blood relatives. Rather, they all display distinctive manifestations of their ancestral heritage. These traits follow them throughout history and the patterns are remarkably clear in the stories of their descendants.

Reuven tragically loses his firstborn privileges to Yosef, and his leadership potential to Yehuda, though his tribe always maintains a lower-level leadership position. Levi and Shimon struggle to contain their anger and animosity against injustice and corruption, but their paths diverge because of their variant expressions of these qualities.

Yehuda proves to be a strong, fearless leader destined to be the king of Israel. Yissakhar and Zevulun, too young to lead their older brothers, form a beautiful partnership in which they are able to sanctify God's name throughout history. Dan and Gad bear a grudge for not being able to exercise their status as their mothers' (Bilha and Zilpa's, respectively) firstborns. Naftali and Asher, the younger children of Bilha and Zilpa, contentedly follow the lead of the children of Leah and Raḥel. Yosef struggles to establish his leadership in the shadow of Yehuda. Throughout history, the two powerful tribes of Yehuda and Yosef trade off instances of leadership. Binyamin, the youngest of Yaakov's children, provides the one safe space that all the tribes can coalesce around. His territory is the natural home for God's house of worship, His Temple. Each tribe has a particular role. Each one is a vital part of our nation and our history.

The message of the twelve tribes is relevant in every family, community, or nation. Variety is necessary and provides life with its color, balance, and beauty. Each tribe is essential to create the Jewish nation. Each one adds an inimitable and special quality to the whole. Similarly, we must each find our role, the colors that we can add, and the contributions we have to offer to the world around us.

Other books in the *Maggid Tanakh Companions* series

*To This Very Day: Fundamental Questions in Bible Study*
Amnon Bazak

*Textual Tapestries: Explorations of the Five Megillot*
Gabriel H. Cohn

*Creation: The Story of Beginnings*
Jonathan Grossman

*Abraham: The Story of a Journey* (forthcoming)
Jonathan Grossman

*Subversive Sequels in the Bible: How Biblical Stories Mine and Undermine Each Other*
Judy Klitsner

*Elijah* (forthcoming)
Elhanan Samet

*The fonts used in this book are from the Arno family*

*Maggid Books*
*The best of contemporary Jewish thought from*
*Koren Publishers Jerusalem Ltd.*